Get Back Up

Get Back Up

From the
Streets to
Microsoft Suites

GEORGE A. SANTINO
with M.J. Beaufrand

GREENLEAF
BOOK GROUP PRESS

Some of the names and identifying characteristics of persons referenced in this book have been changed to protect their privacy.

Published by Greenleaf Book Group Press
Austin, Texas
www.gbgpress.com

Distributed by Greenleaf Book Group

For ordering information or special discounts for bulk purchases, please contact Greenleaf Book Group at PO Box 91869, Austin, TX 78709, 512.891.6100.

Design and composition by Greenleaf Book Group
Cover design by Greenleaf Book Group
Cover images: ©iStock/loops7; ©Shutterstock/Evgeny Karandaev

Cataloging-in-Publication data is available.

Print ISBN: 978-1-62634-276-7

eBook ISBN: 978-1-62634-277-4

TreeNeutral®

Part of the Tree Neutral® program, which offsets the number of trees consumed in the production and printing of this book by taking proactive steps, such as planting trees in direct proportion to the number of trees used: www.treeneutral.com

Printed in the United States of America on acid-free paper

16 17 18 19 20 21   10 9 8 7 6 5 4 3 2 1

First Edition

When Suzie said the words "for richer or poorer, in sickness and in health," I'm sure she had no idea that the early years of our marriage would be nothing but poor and sick. Through it all Suzie supported me and took care of me. No matter what hair-brained get-rich-quick scheme I wanted to try, she was always ready to tell me to go for it. And when I hurt my back and was laid up for years, she was there. Even when I was told I would never work again, she never wavered. She always believed in me, supported me, and had confidence in me. I will never find the words or deeds to thank her or repay her for all she has done for me. But I will never stop trying.

CONTENTS

PROLOGUE

The first time I see a baseball bat used on a human face is in 1967. My brother Dennis and I are in Lanier Park, close to the Tasker Street Projects in South Philly. Dennis is twelve; I am eleven. We're supposed to be playing baseball.

There's a possible double play, with a player on first. The man at bat hits a ground ball to the shortstop. The shortstop fields it and throws it to the second baseman, who tags the base. One out.

The second baseman gets ready to throw the ball to first base to complete the double play. We all know the guy running to second should try to take him out by sliding low and hard. But instead of sliding at the second baseman's legs to knock him down, he jumps into the air and drives his shoes, cleats and all, into his legs. He tears the second baseman's calf open.

The second baseman's scream is loud, and blood pours from the gash.

Dennis and I are standing near third base, so we see exactly what happens next.

The benches are suddenly empty. Punches are thrown, and soon baseball bats are being used on something other than baseballs.

I still remember the sounds of the bats hitting bodies. It's like a fighter hitting a heavy punching bag.

One bat hits a guy right in the face. It looks like his skin has been ripped off. You can see the face's *shape*, but where the skin should be, there's only blood and bone.

At first, I just stand there watching. I know I should be worried, but somehow I'm not. But Dennis knows this isn't a time to stand out in the open. He grabs me and forces us both under the bleachers. My brother has a baseball bat of his own, and I know he won't hesitate to use it if someone comes looking for us.

Nobody bothers. We keep hiding there, while over on the baseball diamond, kids are still using bats on each other, hitting skulls and backs and bodies. It seems to go on forever.

Then the cops show up and start swinging their batons, and we escape.

I don't think we went to another game at the park.

I'm not sure if Lanier Park even *had* another game.

Nobody ever handed me anything.

My family was on welfare, and then we weren't, and then, when my father's business closed, we were again. I can tell you, firsthand, about the taste of government cheese, or the ends of bologna when bologna itself is too expensive to feed a family of nine.

I never finished college. I joined the army, but I left without finishing basic training because of a "Service Connected Disability."

After a debilitating back injury, I was told that I would never work again.

With a partner, I opened a business that thrived and expanded before failing completely.

I interviewed with the Microsoft Corporation *four times* before getting a job.

And yet, after all of that, I retired at fifty-five from a position at Microsoft with the title of Partner Engineering Manager and enough of a nest egg to ensure that neither my wife nor any of my four children will ever have to know what the ends of bologna taste like, or have to cower under bleachers for fear that they'll get hit in the face with a baseball bat.

I've lost count of the times when life has knocked me down, or when I was told that there was something I couldn't have, or that I wasn't good enough, or that my body was too damaged for me to hold any kind of job. But every time life tried to beat me down, I learned something.

And each time, I got back up.

One

TASKER STREET PROJECTS

Whenever someone says "South Philly Projects," one word almost always comes to mind: *rough*. But if you grew up in the country or the suburbs, your idea of rough might be different from mine.

My last name, Santino, means *Little Saint* in Italian. It definitely didn't describe any of us.

My father, John Santino, was a salesman, and from what I heard, he was a good one. He fashioned himself after Frank Sinatra, with the fedora and the smooth voice and everything. He certainly sold one of the most difficult products anyone ever had to move: himself.

When he was twenty-eight years old he met my mother, Florence, a sweet girl of eighteen who worked at the West Philly Five and Dime. The lunch counter was close to where he sold shoes, so Dad would stop by. He stopped by more and more often as time went on. He sold himself as a charming bachelor, and my mom bought him.

By the time I was born in 1956, the fourth of what would be seven kids, Dad was not a salesman anymore. He may have been charming outside the home, but he wasn't to us.

As I first remember him, I was four years old and he was forty. He was already a beaten-down old man.

At first, my sisters and brothers and I thought that our lives were no different from anyone else's. My parents always put food on the table and presents under the tree at Christmas. It didn't matter that our Thanksgiving turkey came from the church or that our presents came from the Salvation Army. The fact that my father didn't go off to work didn't seem strange. We knew he was disabled because he'd filed for Social Security disability—a check we didn't see until years later. But we didn't know what was wrong with him.

Everyone explained away the fact that he didn't work. Mom said that he had been the victim of a root canal that went too deep, causing him constant facial pain. He had also slipped on ice while waiting for a bus, shattering his knee. He'd had a major operation to fix it, but this was before arthroscopic surgery, so he had a scar so long it looked like the surgeon had "fixed" him with a butcher knife. He had to walk with a cane for the rest of his life.

Whatever the reason, he was in pain and couldn't work.

In my memory, he's either coming after one of us, or he's sitting on an easy chair, surrounded by the smoke of unfiltered Pall Malls, watching baseball over and over on TV. With a beer in his hand, of course. There was always another beer.

His drinking, when we were in the projects, was a case-a-day habit. Unlike the cigarettes he smoked, he didn't care which label of beer he had as long as there was another within reach. He also took painkillers, something called Paregoric, which was a kind of opiate, even though we didn't know that at the time.

His only real goal in life was trying to get his disability check. He never talked to anyone about anything, but we always heard him yell whenever rejection letters arrived at the house. He'd tear them up and shout that he was going to get a lawyer and sue the sons of bitches. It seemed impossible to believe he'd ever get it.

Without going into a lot of detail out of respect for my family, suffice it to say that he was an abusive alcoholic, and we stayed out of his way when we could.

Mom always says that without *him*, she wouldn't have had *us*. We never thought that she was blind to his faults. We just think she loved us more. And she thought children should have a father—even one like my dad.

The Tasker Homes in South Philly were two-story row houses with three bedrooms and one bath. The four boys (my oldest brother, Johnny; then Dennis; then me; then my younger brother, Anthony) had one room, the three girls (Joanne, Florence, and Madelyn) had another, and my parents had the third.

From the very beginning, we all had jobs to do. Dad might have been around physically, but he had clocked out mentally. Mom could've gotten a job outside the home to supplement the welfare money, but she had her hands full with feeding, washing, and dressing seven kids. We were her full-time job. So we all had to contribute, whether it was sweeping the kitchen with a broom, helping to hang the clothes on the line, or making our beds—or should I say, *bed*. All four boys slept in the same one.

One of my jobs was making the milk. We drank powdered milk because that was what we got from the Surplus Food Warehouse. The Surplus Food Warehouse wasn't like a normal grocery store. They had no fresh fruit or vegetables or meat, just rows of metal shelves that held cans with black and white labels. The cans were all filled with things like string beans and spinach, and there were also boxes filled with powdered milk and eggs. This was in the early sixties, before food stamps existed. At the Surplus Food Warehouse, you showed them a card from the welfare office, and they gave you the food for free.

I can tell you firsthand that Surplus Food Warehouse powdered milk, mixed with water, made liquid that tasted like chalk. But we got other things from the Surplus Food Warehouse that made it fixable: cans of evaporated milk and tins of chocolate powder. When you added them to the mixing pot, you wound up with something that was okay to pour over cereal or Cream of Wheat.

Other kids we went to school with, the ones who lived outside of the projects, shopped at places like the Acme Market or Food Fair. They actually got milk that was in liquid form and eggs still in their shells. They also had nicer houses and more toys to play with.

My brothers and I used to walk around those other neighborhoods. We would see the houses and the cars. We saw kids with bikes, kids who talked about going to the movies. We knew a life like that cost money, which we weren't going to get from our dad.

I don't know what my brothers dreamed of, but me? I dreamed of this better life.

My brother Dennis and I decided to try to earn money. Glass soda bottles were worth two cents, and you could return them to any supermarket or corner store for the money. So we would look all over for them, including other people's trash.

Collecting bottles worked for a while. And then came the guy that you usually hear about in stories like these. The one with the turnip truck.

Only this guy had tomatoes.

The guy would pull up in the neighborhood in a truck with wood paneling. The bed of the truck was loaded with bushel baskets filled with Jersey tomatoes that he'd bought at the docks. People came up to the truck and bought a bag of tomatoes for a quarter. When people stopped coming, he would drive off and come back a few days later to start all over.

I was only eight years old at the time, but I realized that rather than just selling his tomatoes from a parked truck and then leaving, he could do more business if he went door to door. So I told him my idea.

He said, "Who would watch the truck while I was going door to door?"

"I would. For a quarter."

He didn't like it. But he asked, "Would you be willing to do the footwork?"

"Yeah."

"I'll give you a nickel for every bag you sell."

The first time, I sold ten bags and made fifty cents. That was more money than I'd ever had, and I was eager to spend it. I bought candy and movie-theater matinee tickets. Practically as soon as I had the money, it was gone.

Soon, though, my father found out that I was earning money. He started taking half.

"The house always gets its cut," he said. There wasn't anything I could do about it. Trying to argue with him wouldn't have been worth the pain.

Between my father and the candy and movies, the pennies I made just weren't adding up.

That's when I first thought about using money to make money.

I decided that instead of going to the store and buying something just for me, I would buy something to sell to someone else.

So I bought a box of ice cream bars. The box cost a dollar. It came with three bars, and I sold them for fifty cents each. Then I bought more boxes of ice cream and sold them the same way until I had enough to buy a small snow-cone-making kit. I'd put an ice cube into it and then turn a crank to make the snow, and then I'd cover it with the syrup. We sold these snow cones to the neighborhood kids out of our back window.

My brother Dennis and I decided to pool our money and buy a fake alien from the back of a comic book. We were going to use it to put on a neighborhood show. Sadly, what turned up in the mail was nothing more than a balloon with cardboard feet that popped when we inflated it. So the money was gone, but we learned some valuable lessons: Save your money, make your money work for more money, and don't buy crap from the back of a comic book.

There are a couple of things you should know about growing up in the projects in the 1960s. The first was that it wasn't a miserable childhood. All the kids from the projects got along with each other, and at first, everyone got along with the people who lived outside the projects too. There were always friends around to play with. Kick the can. Stick ball. Rat fishing.

Yeah, that's right. Rat fishing.

The projects themselves were kept fairly clean, but in any big city neighborhood, you had to deal with rats. We never saw them in the row houses, but we knew they lived under the streets. One day, we saw one run into a hole where the sidewalk met the dirt. The neighborhood kids found sticks and started to poke at the hole, but nothing came out.

Then one kid brought a fishing pole. We baited it with government cheese from the Surplus Food Warehouse. We took the baited hook and line to the hole and slowly lowered it in.

After just a few seconds, something bit on the cheese, and we pulled out the line. There was a rat attached to the cheese—not to the hook, but to the cheese itself—and when he came out of the hole, he ran right at us. None of us had really expected we'd catch one. We started running in all directions, but it seemed like the rat knew which way we were going, because he always seemed to be at our feet.

We finally got away, breathless and scared—but not so scared we didn't try again. This time, we would be armed.

We all had either a bat or a stick. We went back to the hole and, after playing a quick game of odds or evens, the loser put in the line. The rest of us waited, and when the rat came out, we started swinging. The rat was faster than us, so we missed a lot, but when the first blow landed, the rat exploded like someone had attached a bomb to him. He was big and fat, and when the bat hit him in the body his guts flew everywhere. Something sticky even hit one of the kids.

The kid yelled, "Get this off of me!"

But we could only laugh.

Gradually, the fun started getting out of hand. The bashing wasn't limited to rats anymore.

Across the street was Lanier Park—the one where I saw a kid take a baseball bat to the face. Long before that, it had been a nice park with two baseball diamonds, a basketball court, a slide, and lots of swings. The little league teams played there. So did all the neighborhood kids—the ones both from in the projects and the ones outside. It was run by the city, and they even had an office where you could check out basketballs and footballs to play with.

As we got older, though, that park seemed to be the center of all the trouble. There were older kids drinking and doing drugs. It was the sixties, after all.

But the tension ratcheted up from there. *Who* could hang out in Lanier? People started saying that those of us *from* the projects should *stay* in the projects. The lines were starting to be drawn.

Fights broke out. First with sticks and bottles, then with knives, and eventually with guns.

Even the younger kids got caught up in it. If you didn't want to get jumped, it made sense to join up with a group: safety in numbers. Gangs formed.

When I was eleven, those of us who lived in the projects had a gang called Mountain Drive, since that was the name of the street in the middle of the projects. We had our own tag, and we spray painted it on places we considered our territory.

We didn't even consider ourselves a real gang—just a bunch

of guys looking out for our own. But since there were other gangs tagging what they thought was their territory, and since their territory sometimes overlapped with ours, you didn't want to be caught alone in the wrong place.

I got caught—but it wasn't while I was tagging.

I had earned a quarter collecting bottles, and I decided to go to the movies. The theater down the street from us was playing the horror classic, *Creature from the Black Lagoon*. The theater was less than a mile from my house, but it was outside the projects. This had never been a problem before, but times were changing.

As I walked down the street, I saw three kids walking on the other side. At first I didn't think much about it—I was too excited about seeing that monster climb out of the swamp on the big screen.

The three kids watching me were from the rival gang outside the projects, the kind who shopped at Acme Market and could go to the movies whenever they wanted. I had seen these guys before in church, and they knew where I was from, but they would never mess with me in church. There were always nuns around, and everyone knew nuns could be scary.

They saw me first. Before I knew what was going on, one of them yelled, "Go back to the projects where you belong!"

I knew these guys were trouble. I should have just shut up and kept walking. But even at eleven years old, I never backed down. I replied with a standard tough-guy comeback: "Make me."

That was a mistake.

They came running across the street, and before I could react, I was punched in the gut. The air left my body so fast that I thought I would pass out. I doubled over on the ground.

As I looked up, I saw one of the kids had a straight razor in his hand—the kind you see in the old movies when guys get a shave at the barber shop. I was trying to catch a breath when I felt the razor graze my face. It wasn't a bad cut, only about an inch long, but there was enough blood that the guys decided to take off.

Later, after remembering the size of the razor, I realized the damage could've been much worse.

I went home, hoping the whole time that my father wouldn't be there. But he was, and he saw me. After slapping me on the other side of the face for "starting trouble," he put a bandage on the cut. I still have a faint scar.

When my brothers found out I'd been jumped, we went looking for the guys who cut me. We took our friends Tommy, Frankie, David, and others. Dennis explained it: We couldn't let them start to think they could go after any one of us without having to deal with all of us.

We knew the kids who jumped me hung out on the other side of Lanier Park near the Acme Market. So I walked there, apparently on my own, the bandage on my cheek. The kids came walking over.

"Didn't you learn your lesson the first time, punk?"

They were so fixed on me, they didn't see the rest of my guys coming up fast from behind. When they finally did, it was too late, and the punches started flying.

Dennis was a much better fighter than I was. While I started fights by throwing wild and wide, swinging lefts and rights, Dennis would always start by throwing a few well-placed left jabs. When his opponent raised his hands to try and block them, Dennis would move his attack to the body.

At first, the guys who jumped me were holding their own pretty well. But when I spotted the guy who cut me, I headed straight for him. This time I didn't swing wildly. Instead I threw a single punch that landed on his jaw, and he went down. I stood there looking down at him. The feeling of his face collapsing under my fist had felt good.

As I stood, I shouted, "You ever touch me again, I'll fucking kill you!"

One of the shop owners who saw this happening must have called the cops, because soon we heard sirens, and we were off to the projects. The cops didn't go in there. There were just too many of us.

The Tasker Street Projects were too dangerous even for the police.

It wasn't over.

Just as we'd gone looking for them after they jumped me, they came looking for us. For the next few nights, we couldn't go anywhere without stones being thrown and bottles being tossed.

The projects were never the same. Fights broke out all the time.

I saw a man die in front of me.

I was wandering around the edge of the projects near 30th and Tasker Street one winter night, looking at the burning trash cans. The big kids usually lit them so they could warm cans of beer. To Dad, there wasn't any reason in the world to drink a warm beer.

But to the big kids it was simple: It was cold out, so they wanted
to drink something warm. It wasn't the stupidest thing they did.

It certainly wasn't stupid enough to warrant what came next.

The homeowners across the street from the projects didn't like the
idea of teenagers hanging around trash cans and drinking beer, and
lit trash cans also meant that fighting would soon begin. As always,
within a few minutes, teenagers from the nonproject houses started
to yell. "Put out those fires!" "Get out of the park!" Then the curse
words got tossed around, and the bottles and rocks started flying.
Within a few minutes, sirens started up and the gangs scattered.

But this time, a few guys stayed in the park.

I was watching from across the street when the cops showed
up. Two or three cars. One cop got out of the car and yelled to the
guys who were left, "Please leave the area."

One guy replied, "Fuck you!"

So the cop started to walk toward the kid. The kid, instead of
running away, picked up one of the trash cans and threw it at the
cop. The can landed right at the cop's feet. The cop backed up and
got in the car.

He yelled from the car, "I order you to disperse!"

The guy who'd thrown the can walked up to where it had
landed, picked it up, and threw it directly into the windshield of
the cop car. The glass shattered.

This could have ended right there, I knew at the time. The cop
had already returned to his car. He could've decided there was nothing more to do and pulled out. Instead, he got out of his car in what
seemed like a very calm way, pulled out his gun, and fired twice.

He hit the kid who threw the trash can right in the chest.

That kid's death wasn't like it was in the movies. Anytime you
see someone shot on TV, they fly backward, sometimes even in

the air. But this kid just crumpled to the ground as if someone had thrown his "off" switch. There was dead silence. The snow on the ground started to turn a dark red. When the ambulances arrived, there was no frantic work by the paramedics.

This was the first time I saw someone shot. But it wouldn't be the last.

A few weeks later, there was a domestic disturbance a couple of buildings down from us. A husband and wife were fighting, and the cops were called to break it up.

While the cops generally wouldn't follow teenage gangs into the projects, they did have to respond to domestic disputes. Especially if they were taking place on someone's front lawn, with a woman waving a knife around, which is what had happened when the police arrived.

The couple, not content to stay inside, had moved to the yard in front of their building. The woman had a knife and lunged at the cop, who pulled out his gun and shot her. The bullet went right through her side, continued down the yard, and hit our house.

My sister Florence, who was seven years old, was there. She picked it up. What should she do with a bullet? Should she give it to the cops? They might arrest her. But after watching the police looking all over for the thing, Florence finally handed it over.

All the while we were living, and playing, and fighting in the projects, my father was trying to collect Social Security disability. In the end, he did have to hire a lawyer, and it took about eight years. But the Social Security Administration finally decided to grant my father full disability status. In the fifties and sixties, when you got Social Security disability, you got it retroactively from the day you first applied. So he got an eight-year payoff all at once, minus whatever he had to give to the lawyer.

It was now March 1969, and we finally had enough money to move out of the projects. My mother's brother, Joe, lived in Tampa, and he liked to talk about how crime-free and warm the place was. There was no discussion or deliberation, just a declaration. My father didn't care whether we wanted to go or not; we were going. He hired a truck and a driver and drove off separately with all our furniture. My mother and the rest of us kids would fly down a few days later.

Until then, we stayed at a friend's house. That night, as I was walking in the front door of their house, I heard a loud bang—a shot. The next day, we went outside and saw where the bullet had hit. It hit the cross beam of the cover over the door. If that beam weren't there, the bullet would have hit me right in the head. I never knew if my friend was the target or I was, but it didn't matter. I'd dodged a bullet. So had the rest of my family.

When I think about growing up on Tasker Street, I remember all my friends and how many of them there were. But then I remember what happened when we got older and our playing started to turn ugly. Some of my old friends from Philly are dead or were violently injured. Stabbed. Clubbed. Shot. One even fell (was pushed?) off a roof.

On the one hand, I'm grateful my dad got us out of there when he did. But there's still a voice at the back of my head that says maybe if my dad had gotten up and worked, we wouldn't have been there at all.

Two

OUT OF THE PROJECTS

I don't know how much money my father got from the Social Security Administration, but I can't imagine it was much. I'm sure he thought it was a fortune.

He found a house for us to rent in Tampa while he looked for something to buy. Size-wise, the place wasn't much bigger than Tasker Street. It also had three bedrooms and one bath, but at least this one had a second bath in the garage.

The rental house may have been small on the inside, but it had a big backyard with fruit trees. We had never seen those before. We could go outside and pick oranges, lemons, and grapefruit that were all ours.

Dennis and I explored our new neighborhood. The street was clean and all the houses had cars in the driveways. Most of them were new. As we walked, we saw a lady working in her yard, and she said, "Hi," as if she knew us.

Were all the people here so nice? I felt safe already.

My oldest brother, Johnny, was at Penn State. He'd been accepted to the ROTC program, which he'd applied for because it was the only way he could afford the tuition. My father was so proud he hugged him. That was the first and only time I saw my father hug anyone—including my mother. Johnny didn't seem to enjoy it.

I was jealous he was getting out: The rest of us still had to live with Mom and Dad and go to school.

It was March 1969. If we'd stayed in the projects, I would've finished seventh grade at Audenreid Junior High in South Philly, and Dennis would've finished his final year, ninth grade, at Audenreid as well before moving on to high school.

But now we couldn't. This was a big deal to us. Where we grew up, you stayed with the same kids from the time you started school until you graduated. I had a big desire to get out of the projects, but no desire to leave my friends. We were also at the end of the school year with only three months to go. Why couldn't we wait until the end of the school year and move in the summer? It made no sense to Dennis and me.

We also had to take a bus to get to our new school in Tampa, Wilson Junior High. In South Philly, we could just walk down the street.

The bus didn't go right to our school. It dropped us off near Bayshore Boulevard. Even though I didn't know it then, that's where my world first started to open up.

Bayshore Boulevard was a street that ran alongside Tampa Bay. From where the bus dropped us off, Dennis and I could walk to the sidewalk that ran along the seawall and look out over the water. I'd never been near a big body of water other than a river or a small pond. The bay was so huge it might as well have been the ocean, and it smelled like raw fish. The only thing I could compare it to was the smell from the fishmongers on Market Street. If we looked down we saw blue crabs, something else I'd never seen and certainly had never eaten.

And Bayshore Boulevard had houses. *Large* houses. They were two stories tall with big yards. I could only imagine how much I could make mowing those lawns. These houses not only had more than one bathroom, but they also had things, like sports cars in the driveway, red tiles on their roofs, and probably a pool in the backyard. Dennis and I thought about how much money you'd need to live in such a house.

But we could only stand there staring for so long. Eventually we had to go to school.

Our new school, Wilson Junior High, was old and had no AC in hot, humid Florida. They had these horizontal glass windows you could open with a hand crank. Most of the time there wasn't a breeze, but when there was, it was hot and wet and it made you feel sticky. I didn't know how we would survive the weather in the coming summer. We also didn't know anyone at the school, and we had already learned the subjects they were teaching.

Dennis and I were bored and alone. We'd always been close, but this experience made us closer. We knew we would have to form new friendships at our new school, but until we did, we had each other. For now, that was plenty.

While we were exploring our new world and approaching the end of our first school year in our new town, my father decided to buy a business with his social security settlement. I found this interesting, since he'd never had a job in my entire life, and I didn't know what he knew about running a business—if anything.

He wanted to buy a restaurant. He looked at a McDonald's franchise, but he didn't like the idea of someone else telling him what to do. The fact that McDonald's *knew* what to do and had a history of success didn't matter to him. To this day I think about how our lives would have been different if he'd bought that McDonald's. It turned out to be one of the busiest sites in the state.

Instead, he bought a restaurant called The Little Inn, a tiny hole-in-the-wall that sold sandwiches and Hungarian goulash. The Little Inn wasn't in the best part of town. There were always a few men walking up and down the street, usually with a brown paper bag in their hands containing a bottle of beer. People called this area rough. That might have been true by Tampa standards, but Dennis and I didn't think it was so bad. We had no problem walking around the neighborhood. Other people would tell us we were crazy, that it was a dangerous place, but we weren't worried about a bunch of winos.

Dennis and I worked at the restaurant after school, waiting tables, washing dishes, and busing tables, but we weren't paid anything except tips. At the end of the week, my brother and I turned out our pockets and deposited our money on the kitchen table. We watched while Dad counted our change and took half. He'd done it since our tomato-selling days. Now, especially since we worked with him, we knew it wasn't worth trying to keep anything back. The house still always got its cut.

At first, the restaurant seemed to do fine. The lunch crowd was good, but the dinner business was slow, and usually at around six or seven in the evening the crowd would change from business-men and secretaries to mostly men who smoked and drank beer, in no hurry to leave.

I don't think my father charged the drinking crowd most of the time. In fact, he joined them. He was happy to have people to drink with.

My father still drank a case of beer and smoked two packs of unfiltered cigarettes a day. Now, his habits had started to tell on him. He was short—only five feet six inches tall—and as he got older, he put on weight. Though his hair started to recede, he never really went bald, and over the years his hair turned gray and his mustache turned white.

He was only forty-eight years old, but he looked a lot older. He always used a cane, which helped him when he walked, and which was a nice tool to pull an out-of-reach bottle of beer across the bar.

Just before the end of the school year, he bought us a house. Our new place was in a suburb of Tampa called Town 'n' Country.

It was yet another three-bedroom house. This had only one full bath and what was called a half bath—a toilet and a sink—in the master bedroom. I don't think my father understood that a family our size with seven kids (technically six, since Johnny was in college) needed a bigger house. For him it was simple math: a bedroom for the boys, a bedroom for the girls, and a bedroom for the parents.

The house didn't have any fruit trees, but it had a nice backyard that had what looked like a creek behind it. It was really a drainage ditch, but it was cool to mess with the frogs that lived there.

Since we were in a new neighborhood, I once again had to go to a new school. I'd finish the school year at Wilson Junior High, and in the fall I'd go to a different school.

I didn't really like changing schools again. I went to two different junior high schools that year: the first, where I'd left my lifelong friends, and the second, where I made no new ones. In the fall, I would go to a third: Webb Junior High.

That summer between seventh and eighth grade was a big one for me.

As my father's drinking and smoking escalated, so did his temper. We all had different ways of dealing with that, since everyone in the house was affected by it. Until that summer, I'd responded to his demons by caving in and crying. I was no different than the rest of the family who had to suffer this existence with him. And like the rest of the family, I was growing tired of it.

At one point, my father had brought home a pool table he won in a card game. It wasn't there long. He either sold it or lost it in another card game. That's the way things appeared and disappeared in our house. One time he brought home a motorcycle that Dennis thought was for him, but it was gone the next day.

In any case, we were playing pool. My father was pretty good, and he would certainly never let you win. I don't think self-esteem was invented yet, so he didn't worry about building you up with a false victory. That was okay with me, because I practiced all the time for no other reason than to beat him. I don't mean the way he beat *me*—but in the only way I could.

One day it happened. We were playing eight ball, and we both had only the eight ball left. It was my shot. I looked over the table and took my time to pick the perfect pocket. I called my shot. I was so confident that I would make it that I asked my father if he wanted to make a bet. My father knew it was a shot I could make, so he didn't make the bet. Instead he just said, "Take your shot, Smart Ass! And try not to choke."

I lowered my stick, pulled it back, and hit the cue ball just hard enough to move the eight ball toward the pocket. I sank the ball.

I shouted, "He shoots! He scores!" I was thrilled, but he was pissed.

"You were lucky."

"You're just a sore loser," I said.

Dennis was also in the room, but you would never know it based on how quiet he became. No one had challenged my father like this before, and I'm sure he was waiting to see what would happen next. I know I was.

"How'd you like a smack in the mouth?" my father asked.

"You can't hurt me. I'm the pool champion of the house."

I remember the look in his eye even today—not when he came toward me, but when he realized that I wasn't going to back up. It was the rage I'd seen before. No one talked back to my father. That wasn't something you did. It just wasn't worth it. But for some reason I was emboldened. Maybe it was because I'd just beaten him at pool, or maybe it was because—looking at him standing there in his wife-beater shirt, all 5 feet 6 of him—I really thought I could take the punch. Whatever the reason, I talked back.

I pushed out my stomach and said, "Take your best shot."

He hauled off and punched me in the gut. I bounced back a step, and the only sound you heard was me passing gas because I'd clenched my stomach so hard. Dennis couldn't help laughing, but I waited for what my Dad would do next.

And then: nothing. He stormed out of the room.

I looked at Dennis, pride all over my face, until he said, "You know you're fucked now, right?" I didn't feel quite so good then.

I wish I could say my father found a new respect for me after that, but instead I think he found a challenge. From that point forward, I was the first person he'd come after. But I wouldn't back down. I wouldn't strike back, either. He was my father, after all.

But I resolved that he would no longer see me afraid or hear me cry, not ever again.

Three

JOURNEY'S END

At the beginning of eighth grade, I had new confidence. I was now at Webb Junior High, my third school in less than six months.

Dennis was in high school, and we would not be at the same school again. I wouldn't have him to shove me under the bleachers when the next fight broke out. I wouldn't have him to walk with me along Bayshore Boulevard and look out over the open water and wonder what kind of lives people had with these cars in the driveway and those big yards.

He'd always been more than a brother to me—he'd been a friend. At our last school, he'd been my only friend. Now that I was on my own, I'd have to make new friends. And now that things had gotten worse at home, I needed good friends more than ever.

While I was busy with new beginnings at school, my father's restaurant, The Little Inn, had come to an end. There was a homeless shelter down the street, and my father had a soft spot for people worse off than him. (From what I could tell, there weren't a lot of those.) To him, the people in the shelter he hung out with were just down on their luck, but basically decent and hard-working. Though that may have been true for a few of them, when I looked at the rest, I saw people who had given up. In my father, they saw an easy mark.

The people who hung out with my dad at night started to hang out during the day. They drank for free, they ate for free. He seemed to like them, and the more free drinks he gave them, the more they hung around.

I remember making myself a sandwich once in the restaurant kitchen. As soon as I'd set it on a plate to carry to the table and enjoy, one of my dad's friends grabbed it.

"This is for me, right?" he asked, the sandwich halfway to his mouth.

"No, it's for me," I said, taking it away from him and setting it back on the plate.

"I hope you like it, then," he said, smiling. "I just went to the bathroom and didn't wash my hands."

I slid the plate over to him. "Enjoy it," I said.

What my father was doing with these guys reminded me of the speech I'd heard on our plane trip to Florida. The flight attendant had said, "In case of emergency, the oxygen masks will deploy. Always put your mask on before helping others." That made sense to me. After all, how could you help everyone around you if you couldn't breathe?

My father wasn't with us on the plane, but even if he were, he certainly wouldn't have understood the logic. By helping the guys from the homeless shelter, he was putting his business at risk.

By all accounts, my father's new friends were just as charming to the lunch crowd he was starting to develop as they had been to me, and soon the lunch crowd quit coming around. In the end, it didn't take long for The Little Inn to fold. Without the restaurant, he couldn't help his friends, and he couldn't provide for us. Once again, we were back on welfare.

Even then I understood that the best way to help the poor was not to *become* one of them—like we'd just become. Again.

Welfare in Florida felt different than it did in South Philly. There was no Surplus Food Warehouse in Florida. At least everyone in the Surplus Food Warehouse was poor, so there was no shame in going there.

In Florida, we were given food stamps, which was much worse. You used food stamps at a regular grocery store, and everyone who shopped there wasn't poor. With food stamps, your money didn't even look the same. Instead of green dollar bills, you handed the cashier multicolored bills that really stood out. Everyone in Town 'n' Country judged us.

When I was younger, it never bothered me that we lived in the projects and that we were poor. There was always powdered milk to be made and rats in sewers to be caught.

But now, in Florida, I knew there was something better. We had lived like normal people for six months, and I wanted to keep being normal, even though I now knew that my dad would never be normal again.

I didn't want my new friends to know how poor I was. Without the tips I had been getting waiting tables at The Little Inn, I didn't have any money of my own. If I wanted to go to the movies or hang out at McDonald's, I had to do something. The only thing I knew to do was to work.

I was still only thirteen years old, so no one would give me a real job. I cut lawns and helped neighbors home with their groceries. It helped that I had my own cart that I happened to "find," if you know what I mean.

There were two grocery stores in two competing strip centers across the street from each other. Grocery carts usually had the store name engraved on the handle and again on a metal label on the side. When I'd finished with the cart I *found*, it had the name of one grocery store on the handle and the name of the competing store on the side, so neither store could claim it was theirs. I would stand outside whichever store looked busier that day, and when a woman would come out (I learned pretty quick that men always said no), I'd ask if she'd like help home. I never said I would charge. I never asked for money at the end. All I did was say, "Have a nice day," and I was almost always paid. After a while, some of these ladies would expect me to be there and would come over and put their groceries in my cart automatically.

My father still took half the money I made, but I saved enough that I could go out from time to time.

In the summer between eighth grade and ninth, the school district formed a new boundary, which meant that I would not be attending Webb Junior High in ninth grade. I would be going to Pierce Junior High. This would be my fourth junior high school. I had made a few friends at Webb, but all but one of them would be staying there. Once again, I'd have to make new ones.

Webb was a new school in a middle-class neighborhood. Pierce Junior High was different, an older school in an older neighborhood. It looked a lot like my first Tampa school, with its wood-framed buildings and slatted glass windows, but at least it had air conditioning. It also seemed to have a tougher crowd. A lot of the kids wore torn jeans and tattered shirts. We dressed that way too, but that was because that's all we could afford. Here it seemed to be a fashion statement.

Also, Pierce had a smoking area in the back of the school near the Dumpsters. It didn't smell great, but I guess the school thought that if you didn't mind smelling like cigarettes, you shouldn't mind the smell of the Dumpsters.

There were no gangs in Florida like there were in South Philly, which was a good and a bad thing. There were fewer bullets, but without the gang, I didn't have "built-in" friends anymore. The closest thing I could find to the people I'd known before were the smoking area kids. They were mostly guys, and they looked like my crowd.

Not only that, but I had an in—cigarettes.

When The Little Inn closed, my father had started drinking and smoking at a dive called The Journey's End. I guess he was spending most of his days there—or in the hospital. Normally he didn't have the money to pay fifty cents a pack for cigarettes, so he bought a kit that allowed you to use loose tobacco and roll your own. It was my job to roll them for him, just as it was my job to cook his dinner and to get him his beers.

I would set up the machine on the kitchen table and make my own assembly line. The machine was in front of me with the paper to my left and the can of tobacco on my right. I would fill the machine with the tobacco and place the paper in the front of the machine. I would then turn a roller, which would pull the paper in and fill it with the tobacco. After wetting the end of the paper with a sponge, I'd turn the roller one more time, which would adhere the ends to make one cigarette about twelve inches long. Finally, I'd cut the long cigarette into regular-size cigarettes.

To make friends, I took one of the full-size cigarettes to school. I didn't smoke it, but it was my "in" with the cool kids. I walked up with this long cigarette in my mouth, and when they realized it was real, they wanted to smoke it. Of course I let them.

My father kept a tight inventory on his tobacco and his papers, but I still thought I could get away with taking some to school, so I did. Luckily for me this wasn't the best-tasting tobacco, and the cigarette wasn't filtered, so the novelty wore off pretty quickly, and I stopped bringing them to the smoking area before my dad caught me. But they'd done their job. I was in with the smokers.

Looking back, I sometimes think, *There. I could've gotten side-tracked there.* These guys were enough like my friends in South Philly that I could've settled for being part of the smoking crowd and gone on that way for the rest of my life.

But while the smokers were the first new friends I made, they weren't the only ones.

I began to realize I could live in multiple worlds. I always got As in my classes because anything less in my house wasn't worth the pain, which meant I could be friends with the honor students. In PE class, the coach saw that I was a pretty good runner (I had to be, running *away* from stuff in the projects) and asked me join the track team, which meant I was friends with the jocks. And I cursed all the time and wasn't afraid to get into a fight, so the kids in the smoking area still liked me, even though I didn't smoke.

I liked being able to be with multiple crowds. I liked being in a track meet one day, acing a test the next, and still hanging out in the smoking area. Anything was better than being at home.

Dad's health was failing. He drank and smoked too much. And he was still taking Paregoric like he did in Philly. I'm sure he was addicted to that on top of everything else.

He'd get up in the morning and leave for The Journey's End. He would come back around three and nap until seven, when it was my job to wake him and fix him something to eat. The rest of us always ate the dinner my mother made at five, but my father didn't want to be disturbed for that. Even the few times when he was up at the same time as us, he would eat his dinner in front of the TV while we sat at the table. He ate better than us, and he really liked the way I made his pork chops. I asked him once if I could have one too, but he said no. Of course, since it was my dad, there was a put-down with it. "You know what a pork chop costs?" he would say. "Do you think I'd waste that money on you?"

Hey—it was worth asking. You can't get anything without asking.

After dinner, he was off to the bar again. He drank a lot at home, too. His behavior was getting more erratic day by day. One day he came home drunk and gave *me* the change from his pocket. At the time, I couldn't believe it, although a few days later he accused me of stealing his change while he napped.

It was almost as if he were two different people. He was always mean, but now he seemed tired and old, too. That didn't stop him from throwing punches when he felt the need, but even that was becoming less frequent. He was just too tired.

Over the years, my father spent a lot of time in the hospital. As far as I knew, these visits started the year he stepped off an icy curb in South Philly and destroyed his knee.

Every time he went to the hospital, I took the bus to see him. One summer, while I was staying at my aunt's house, he went into the hospital without anyone telling me. As soon as I heard about it, I demanded that they take me home so that I could visit him, but by the time we got there, he'd already been released. If I wanted to see him, the nurses told me, I could just go home. Seeing him in the hospital was one thing, seeing him at home was another situation altogether, so I went back to my aunt's.

I worried about him, but I didn't seriously expect anything to happen. He'd go to the hospital; he'd be back. Same as always.

We didn't know that he'd begun to spit up blood.

We didn't know he had a severely compromised esophagus.
We didn't know his liver was shot.

He was a difficult guy to live with, but sometimes he'd reach out.
It used to be easier for me to think he was an altogether bad guy.
But like a lot of people, he was a mix of good and bad.

Take singing, for example. My father was a pretty good singer.
He actually sounded a little like Sinatra. He often talked about
how he could have been big if he followed his dream of going to
New York to become a professional singer.

I had a pretty good voice as well, and my father wanted me to
develop it. He had no idea how, so he told me to sing everywhere,
because I never know who might hear me. I might be discovered.
That sounded great to me. Maybe being discovered would get me
out of the house for good.

I also sang at school assemblies from elementary school until
high school, but Dad never came to a single school concert, no
matter how much my mother tried to make him. At one point, I
decided I wanted to be a professional singer. At Pierce, my chorus
teacher told me I could be the next Sinatra if I applied myself. So,
following my dad's advice, I sang all the time.

In March of 1972, just before my sixteenth birthday, my dad went
into the hospital again. This time, he didn't return.

A friend of his drove him. He didn't take any of us with him,
which was no different than usual. I remember running out of

the house saying, "Hey, Dad, when you go to the hospital this time, can you bring us home a thermometer? Ours is broken." I remember him yelling something about us kids not taking care of his stuff, but he didn't start swinging.

I remember the phone ringing at three in the morning. It sounded louder than normal (I don't know why), and it woke me up. My mother took the call. I heard her talking but couldn't really hear what she was saying. And then she yelled "No!" and started to scream and cry. My mother's brother, our uncle Joe, came over a few minutes later to calm things down.

Though I hadn't been told yet, I knew Dad was gone. He was only fifty-one years old.

I didn't understand my mother's tears and shrieks, because all I felt was relief. The nightmare was over for all of us.

But my mother wasn't ready for what came next. Before he died, my father had treated all of us like children, including his wife. She was expected to follow the same rules as the rest of us, and she was disciplined in the same way when she didn't. My father wanted people to remain dependent on him. If my mother needed to go somewhere beyond walking distance, he had to drive her, which meant she had to accommodate his changing standards or she wouldn't be able to go anywhere. In spite of everything, she needed him.

Now he was dead, and he had left no will or insurance. My mother didn't know where anything was, how to pay the bills, or even how to drive a car. She was eighteen when they met, and she was forty-one when he died. She knew how to take care of us, but she didn't know how to take care of herself or the house.

Since there was no insurance, my uncle Joe arranged for a military funeral. The service would be held at the funeral home, but he would be buried in a military cemetery in Pensacola for free.

I remember seeing my dad in the casket when we first arrived at the funeral home. He looked like he did every night when I woke him up from his nap. For a second, I thought he was just pulling a joke. Then I got closer and saw the makeup on his face.

I bent over to give him a goodbye kiss on the cheek. When I felt his cold skin hit my lips, I knew I wouldn't be waking him from this sleep.

There weren't many people at the service. He must have made friends at The Journey's End, but none of them were there. He also had eleven brothers and sisters, but only one brother came for the service. And where were all of those people he fed for free? The ones that contributed to the closing of his restaurant? They were nowhere to be found. It didn't make sense.

After the service at the funeral home, my uncle Joe, my brothers Johnny and Dennis, and I flew to Pensacola with my father's remains crammed in the hold with the other baggage. My mother didn't hold up well at the service, so she didn't come with us.

There were more soldiers than family at the gravesite. They were there to give Dad a final sendoff by playing taps on the bugle and firing a few shots from their rifles. These strangers would give him the proper farewell that his friends couldn't provide.

The soldiers lifted their rifles and prepared to fire. The sound was so loud and the percussion so deep that I felt it in my chest.

Dad did try to help people when he could, but he treated the people closest to him—his family—the absolute worst. He was a smart man, but he used his intelligence to manipulate the government for a handout whenever he felt he needed it. And yes, he finally did get us out of the projects, but he was the one who had put us there in the first place.

I decided, that moment at the funeral with the rifles firing, that I would have a different life. Even at sixteen years old, I knew that long-term dependency was no way to live. I started to believe in a hand *up* instead of a hand*out*.

And soon enough, the soldiers stopped firing, and John, Dennis, Uncle Joe, and I went back to the car to go home to Tampa to clean up the mess left behind. My dad was dead.

Four

THE WAY THINGS WORK

first met Mark Johnson when we were in the eighth grade at Webb Junior High in Tampa, Florida.

Johnson and I were the same height, but he was thinner. He had brown curly hair and was always moving and talking. I had never seen so much energy in one person. He seemed to know something about everything.

As far as anyone could tell, he didn't pay attention in class. Our teachers would wait until it was obvious that he wasn't paying attention and then call on him with a question. I think they hoped to embarrass him, but it never worked because he always knew the answer.

In South Philly people called each other by their last names. If people knew what family you were from, they knew if you were a friend or a foe. In the projects, you'd often hear people say, "Leave him alone. He's a Santino." (Or more often, "Get him! He's a Santino.")

So I never called him "Mark." It was always "Johnson."

Johnson noticed it, and he tried to correct me a few times, but I never got into the habit.

Johnson and I had a certain lack of enthusiasm for school in common. Even though I got good grades in school, I always wanted to be somewhere else. School was so boring, and there wasn't any money in it. Further, there was no reason I could see to learn what they were teaching me. When I asked my math teacher why I needed to know this stuff, she couldn't think of a comeback.

"You might want to be an astronaut or a teacher," was all she could offer. That wasn't enough for me.

At one point, I even looked into dropping out and taking the GED test. But it was a rule of our school district that no one could take the GED test until six months *after* we were scheduled to graduate, supposedly to stop kids like me from doing what we wanted to do.

My reasoning was simple: If I got my GED, I wouldn't have to waste my time in school, and I could get a full-time job instead. With a full-time job, I could move into my own apartment and have the life I wanted.

I can't believe how naïve I was. Thank God the school didn't allow it.

Johnson didn't have patience for people who weren't smart. I didn't know as much as he did, but I was smart enough that we got along, and soon he saw that I caught on fast.

Johnson and I had all the same classes, including PE. Johnson was what some people would consider a nerd, although in the seventies in Tampa, Florida, we didn't call them that. A few of my friends made some nasty cracks about his briefcase, but that was the extent of the trouble he had.

He never dressed out for PE. While he was a straight-A student in academic classes, he would fail PE every semester. I used to tell him, "All you have to do is put on a pair of shorts. You don't really have to do anything." But he wouldn't have it. The rest of us ran and exercised, and he would just sit off to the side and read.

One day after school he invited me over to his house.

I knew by now that we were poor and didn't have what other kids had. Johnson's family wasn't rich, but his father was retired military and his mother had a job. So they had good food, and Johnson had *stuff*. I didn't have any stuff.

When we got to his house, he offered me a soda to drink. Luxury. Then we went to his room, and on his desk—he had a desk!—was something that looked like a board with holes in it and wires. I didn't know what it was, so I asked. Johnson told me it was a circuit board. He was playing around with resistors and capacitors to see if he could wire a light and a motor. I asked why. He said, "Because it's fun."

He showed me how to do it, and he was right—it *was* fun.

He also had one of those invisible man models, the one where you can see the heart and lungs inside the body of a plastic model. It was about a foot tall, but you could see a lot of detail, down to all the veins and intestines. It was a balance of gross and cool. Again,

I asked him why he had it. He asked, "Aren't you ever curious about how the circulatory, nervous, or digestive systems work?"

The only thing I knew about the digestive system was that my stomach made noise when I was hungry.

Johnson was curious about everything. He never accepted statements like, "that's just the way it works." The subject didn't matter. He always wanted to know how a thing worked and why.

He had to understand the practical application of this knowledge. I would sit in class and listen, and I would learn, but I'd dismiss what I'd learned later as worthless. Why should I remember everything about algebra when even our teachers had trouble explaining when we'd use it?

But Johnson could explain it. He showed me how he used algebra-based physics to create the equations that told him how much resistance his circuit boards would need. There was a reason we were being taught all this "useless" stuff.

After hanging out with Johnson for a while, I started to want to know everything too.

Over the next year Johnson and I developed a friendly competition. I hope it helped him; I'm sure it helped me. We always worked hard to get a good grade in the class, but now that we knew each other, that was no longer good enough. Each of us had to get a better grade than the other. This motivated us to do better, and it's the main reason we both graduated with honors from high school.

When Johnson and I were in the ninth grade, we had to go to different schools, but that didn't stop us from getting together in the afternoons. We both had money. I got a job as a clean-up boy at the local Burger Chef, and Johnson got an allowance. That was another concept that was foreign to me. Parents giving their kids money? Any time I had money, my parents wanted to know where their half was. Here was a kid getting money from his parents.

We would spend our money going to the movies and buying electronic kits. We were just starting to hear about computers, and sometimes we daydreamed about what it might be like to work with them for a living. Soon, the first computer kits started to become available; whenever we could, we bought them and built them.

Once, we were planning on going to the movies, but we had some time to kill. Johnson suggested we get something to eat. We usually went to fast food restaurants together, but Johnson said he had money. "Let's go to a real restaurant," he said.

As soon as we were seated, I noticed that we each had two forks. I said, "Hey Johnson, they screwed up and gave us two forks instead of one."

Johnson said, "No, that's right. One is for the salad."

One was for the *salad*? I'd had salad before, but I never got a separate fork for it.

It was the first time Johnson had to set me straight about "normal" living, but it wasn't the last. Johnson didn't judge me. He didn't laugh when I didn't know about the salad fork or any of the other things I would learn from him over the years. He knew I was from a different place, and he didn't care.

After ninth grade, we both went to Leto High School in Tampa, where we were in all the same classes. At first I thought these classes were going to be difficult, especially Advanced English, Advanced Biology, and Advanced Algebra. But our "friendly competition" continued, and we spent plenty of time screwing around in class as well.

Johnson and I were different in that respect. I was the tough kid who wouldn't take shit from anyone. Johnson was the skinny kid who could talk his way out of anything.

In English class, we had an elderly female teacher who was very passionate about English. She really knew her stuff, and she didn't have patience with students who didn't take the subject seriously. Students like me, for example.

One day while she was writing on the board, Johnson and I were telling jokes and laughing. The teacher turned around and told us to knock it off.

"Yes, ma'am," said Johnson.

"Yeah," I said.

The teacher turned to me. "Is that all you have to say?"

Johnson tried to prompt me, but I just said "Yeah" again.

The teacher said, "Get out! Get out!" And out to the hall I went.

After class, Johnson asked me, "Why didn't you just say 'Yes, ma'am?'"

"Why should I?" I asked angrily.

Johnson said, "So you don't get kicked out of class, for one."

Another time, Johnson and I were in science class together. He was sitting in the front of the class and I was in the back row.

While the teacher, a large and ominous man, was talking, Johnson and the kid next to him were hitting a BB back and forth across the table with a pen. The teacher asked Johnson, "What do you think the Dean of Boys will think of that behavior?"

The Dean of Boys (or Girls, for that matter) wasn't someone you wanted to see. In junior high, he could hit you with a paddle. I didn't think they did that anymore in high school, but he could still give you detention or suspend you. I honestly don't know why the teacher felt he had to make that threat. He was scary enough on his own.

Johnson said, "I don't think he'd be too thrilled."

In the end, the teacher decided to separate them by moving me to the front next to Johnson. Johnson turned to me and said, "He has no idea what he just did."

It didn't take long for Johnson and I to get caught screwing around. The teacher told us to knock it off.

Johnson, of course, said, "Yes, sir."

I replied with my standard "Yeah." I never did get that *yes sir, yes ma'am* thing down.

"Either you'll also say 'yes sir,'" the teacher told us, "or you can both get out."

While Johnson and I were standing in the hall, Johnson said, "I could have talked him out of this if you didn't jump up to head out of the room so quickly." But that was my habit. The second I heard the words, "Get out," or more specifically, "Get out of my sight," I moved fast.

"He told us to get out," I told Johnson.

And Johnson said something I'd never forget. "You know the first words *begin* the negotiation—they don't *end* it."

I don't think I got thrown out of another class after that, and it's not because I became a model student.

Johnson got a car when we turned sixteen, and he started driving me and some of his other friends to school. Because he could drive us, we were able to get better jobs, which meant we had more money to do other things.

I'll never forget the first time we went to Disney World. It was only a ninety-minute drive, but I'd never been. Johnson had gone a couple of times. We found a cheap hotel outside the park. When we got off work that night, we drove straight from Tampa to our hotel in Orlando.

The hotel had a standard cheap room with two beds, a TV, and a bathroom. Johnson walked over to his bed and removed the bedspread. Under it was a flat sheet.

Then he did something that surprised me. He started to pull down the sheet as well.

"What the hell are you doing?" I asked. "Are you going to sleep on the mattress?"

He had no idea what I was talking about. "I'll sleep on the bottom sheet," he said.

I thought, *What the hell is a bottom sheet?* My bed at home and every bed I had ever slept in had covers and a fitted sheet, but that was all. This bed had a top sheet and a bottom sheet, and you apparently slept between the two. Again, Johnson didn't laugh at me for not knowing.

We had a great time at Disney World. I had never seen anything like it. I was very childlike there, and I'm sure I embarrassed Johnson a couple of times, but I was having fun. I was a kid for those two days—a kid with money.

I liked having a top sheet. I liked having fun. I was done being poor.

That Sunday, as we drove back to Tampa, Johnson asked how much money I had left. I had a few dollars, and so did he. Johnson suggested we stop by the grocery store, get a couple of steaks, and take them to my house.

My mother had to get a job outside the home after my father died, and she was working as a waitress. By the time we got back to Tampa, she would be at work, and we could use the kitchen.

I thought that was a great idea. We didn't eat that well at home. Dad hoarded his pork chops. I'd only had steak a couple of times in my life, and that was in the form of a Philly cheesesteak. I thought this would be a great way to end the weekend.

In the meat section of the grocery store, I immediately honed in on the biggest steak I could find. It was a ten inch round steak, and it was only a couple of dollars. Johnson grabbed a tiny steak called a filet mignon that was three times the price of the big steak I had picked. He told me I was making a mistake picking the round steak. I told him he was nuts. My steak was way bigger than his, and it was cheaper. He made some comment about how much higher quality his steak was and that it was worth the money, but I didn't care.

We went to my house and cooked our steaks. We both sat

down and took our first bites. Johnson asked me how mine tasted. I told him it was good, because it was.

Then he ruined it for me by giving me a taste of his. My God! It was so juicy and tender that it made the hunk of meat I'd picked taste like shoe leather in comparison.

I knew it would be a long time before I could afford to eat filet mignon, but from that day forward, the only time I ate round steak was when it was ground into hamburger.

Five

THE BUDDY SYSTEM

Johnson and I were never big fans of school. I still had trouble figuring out why I needed to know algebra, and Johnson was just bored. And we couldn't afford college anyway. At some point, we started talking seriously about what we might want to do instead.

The army at the time offered something called the "Delayed Entry Program." This meant three years in the army and then three years after that in inactive reserve. We worked it out together: If we enlisted in May (Johnson's birthday; he was younger than me by two months), we wouldn't report for duty until the end of August. Plus, if we did decide to go to college at some point, by going into the army first we'd have the GI Bill to help us pay for it.

Our minds made up, in May 1974 we visited the recruiter and enlisted in the army. We should have been thinking about Vietnam, but Nixon was pulling the troops out. There was a chance that the war could still escalate, but we didn't worry about it. We left that for Nixon.

Before we could pick what we wanted to do in the army, we had to take a test at the recruitment center in Tampa. The office was in a warehouse district, and it looked just like any other warehouse. You wouldn't know it was filled with military people unless you went inside.

It was a long but easy test. The higher the score you got on the test, the more options you had when it came to picking a specialty. If you scored low enough, the only choice was the infantry.

At the end of the test, Johnson and I went into the recruiter's office. Our goal was to join under the "buddy system," which would guarantee that friends who joined the army together would spend their entire service at the same bases. We would go to basic training, advanced training, and then be assigned to the same duty on the same base, be it in the United States, Germany, or Vietnam. Vietnam in 1974 was unlikely, but still a possibility. We had been through a lot together, and we knew the army wouldn't be easy, but going through the buddy system might make it easier.

First, however, we had to score about the same or we wouldn't be able to pick the same specialty. The recruiter, a short, stocky man with glasses and a large mustache, went over my scores first. Both Johnson and I also had mustaches at the time.

"Can you have a mustache in the army?" I asked.

He said yes, which was good, because I'd had a mustache since I hit puberty, and I hoped that I wouldn't have to shave. I would learn later that it didn't matter much what the recruiter told you.

I remember the recruiter's face when he opened up my test

results, looked at me, and said, "These are the highest scores I've ever seen!"

Johnson, without missing a beat, said, "You haven't seen mine yet."

I wasn't surprised when the recruiter opened up Johnson's results and we learned that my friend had bested me.

The recruiter told us we could pick any job we wanted. Of course, since we were kids, our first choice was "spies." They didn't have that job, but they did have something called "Communication Security Specialist." This sounded cool, and we would get to bug phones.

The only person in my family that I told was my mother. She wasn't happy to hear that I was going into the army, but there wasn't really anything she could do. While I think she was worried about me going to Vietnam, she was probably just as scared about my not being around for the other kids. My older siblings had all moved out, so I was the man of the house. My younger brother, Anthony, and my two younger sisters, Florence and Madelyn, were still living at home, and my mother was working nights. She needed my help, but I wouldn't be around to give it to her. I was ready to move on.

I tried to enjoy my last few months of high school, but my real concern was getting in the best shape I could so that I could get through basic training. Johnson and I started lifting weights and doing a lot of running. I was a pretty good runner, and I could do the mile in under five minutes. I thought being able to run fast and far would come in very handy in the army.

That would come back to haunt me.

The end of the school year came pretty fast. Our friends all talked about their plans after graduation: college, jobs, the usual. When Johnson and I told them that we'd enlisted in the army, they told us we were nuts.

Johnson and I had no intention of attending the graduation ceremony, which we figured would be boring. The Dean of Boys told us that unless we had a note from our mothers, we had to walk across the stage to get our diplomas.

"We're eighteen," I told him. "We don't need a note from anybody."

The dean looked as though he wanted to say something, but he kept it to himself. He was never going to have to see us again anyway.

A few weeks later, we went to the school office to pick up our diplomas. Both of us had graduated with honors. Gee, I wonder what we could have done if we had applied ourselves.

Over the summer, we spent plenty of time at Clearwater Beach, which was a short drive from Tampa. We also spent plenty of time working out. We knew basic training would be hell, especially in the heat and humidity of South Carolina, but we were training in Florida, so we thought that wouldn't be a problem.

When August came, Johnson and I went together to the

Greyhound bus station and headed north to Fort Jackson. I don't remember any of our families coming with us, but we expected that. Basic training hadn't even started, and already we were on the buddy system.

We got off the bus in South Carolina at what seemed like a very nice facility. New brick buildings, great cafeteria where we ate breakfast, lunch, and dinner, and nice rooms with great beds. We spent the first day getting our buzz cuts and uniforms, and then we got in line for our clothes. There were tables filled with socks, underwear, pants, shirts, belts, and hats: everything you would need. As we moved down the line, I saw that the man handing out the underwear was just alternating between handing out jockeys and boxers. I had never worn boxers in my life, but as I moved down the line and saw the order and the number of people ahead of me, I quickly used some of that math I didn't think I would ever need and realized that I was about to get boxers.

When he handed me the boxers, I said, "Excuse me, but I prefer jockeys."

The man replied, "I'd prefer not to be handing a bunch of kids their new underwear."

It seemed that every time we turned around, it was time to eat. An hour for breakfast, then an hour for lunch, then an hour for dinner, and then we had the nights to ourselves to explore. I said to Johnson, "This eight weeks of basic training is going to go by fast."

But we were in for a big surprise.

Three days later, a bunch of trucks showed up. Actually, they were more like cattle cars. We were loaded into them, and we drove for about twenty minutes. We were all standing shoulder to shoulder and couldn't really see out. Finally, we came to a stop. There was marching band music.

And then the yelling started.

"Get out of those trucks, you maggots! Get into line, you worthless pieces of shit! Get your fat asses in line!"

Some idiot said, "Yes, sir!"

The drill sergeant went off on him. "Who the fuck are you calling sir? I'm not an officer! I work for *my* money!"

He didn't stop yelling at the rest of us, though. "Dump out those fucking duffel bags!"

One kid's mouthwash bottle smashed on the ground. Another kid passed out. It could have been the heat, but more likely it was the stress. I looked around for Johnson and didn't see him. Was the buddy system over already?

And then the sergeant spoke up again. "Any of you stupid idiots who signed up for two years, go over to the first building on the left. You guys are in the fucking infantry."

A lot of people were upset. One guy had the nerve to speak out. "My recruiter told me I wasn't going to be in the infantry," he said.

The drill sergeant said, "I don't care what anyone's douchebag recruiter told them. You're in the fucking infantry!"

Luckily, Johnson and I had signed up for three years.

Once the new infantry recruits were gone, I could see Johnson just a couple of people down in line from me. We were marched into a building. Rather than the new brick buildings with air conditioning, nice beds, and well-manicured lawns we had been in at the reception center, we were now staying in very old wooden buildings sitting on sandlots. We were still in Fort Jackson, South Carolina, but it looked like another planet.

And it was hot as hell.

The bathroom was a single room with toilets on one wall and what looked like one big sink on the other. As we soon learned, it was one big urinal. The shower was basically an empty space where cold water fell from the ceiling.

Once we were inside, the drill sergeant yelled at us until three in the morning, when we were finally allowed to go to bed. This sucked, but at least we had those three meals a day to look forward to—or so I thought.

At 5:30 a.m., after just two and a half hours of sleep, the yelling started again.

"Get out of bed, you worthless pieces of shit! You have five minutes to line up for chow!"

We all rushed downstairs and across the street to the mess hall. Before we could go in, we had to swing across monkey bars and yell out our names.

Boy, did "mess hall" have the right name. Unlike the wonderful cafeteria at the reception center, this was a single room with a group of cooks—and I use that word lightly—ready with spoons to throw slop on your tray. Cold half-cooked eggs with shells still in them, lumpy oatmeal, toast with no butter, and a cup of milk. And as if that wasn't bad enough, instead of an hour, you had five minutes to eat it.

Then we had five minutes to go back to our barracks and change into our dress uniforms. They were going to take our pictures so that we could send them home to our families.

The army really liked five minutes.

I was changed and back down in five. But I was one of the only ones who made it under the deadline. So once everyone was downstairs, the sergeant yelled at us all. He yelled something about our mothers, and something else about his wife being on the rag and using him as the tampon. I didn't understand that one.

The barracks were two stories tall, and we were on the second floor. You got there by going through a door and up a flight of stairs. The door was wood, and its top half was made up of nine square window panes. In the end, we had go back up these stairs so that we could run downstairs again—only faster this time.

As I mentioned, I was pretty fast, and I was determined to be the first one down. I waited at the top of the stairs, just waiting for the yelling to start, which meant that I could start running outside. The yelling started, and I ran. But just before I got through the doorway, the sergeant closed the door, and I was going too fast to stop. The glass window shattered as my arm went right through it.

"What the fuck are you doing to my door?" yelled the sergeant. "You worthless piece of scum!"

There was a sharp pain in my right arm. Blood was squirting out of my wrist like a geyser.

"Get your ass back in line," yelled the drill sergeant.

I tried to keep my blood in by squeezing my hand. "Why did you close the fucking door?" I yelled back.

"Don't you ever talk to me like that!" he yelled. "Get in line!"

With that, he grabbed my arm, which moved my hand off of

my wrist. The blood shot up so high it almost hit him in the face. I was in pain, but I laughed. He covered my wrist faster than he had closed the door that broke it.

He yelled, "Stay here. I'll get my car." There wasn't even a curse word in that sentence.

He came back a few minutes later and picked me up. I knew I was hurt bad, but I didn't know how bad until I saw how fast he was driving. *At least he'll be nice to me on the way to the hospital,* I thought, but soon he started yelling at me for bleeding in his car.

"It's your fault," I yelled back, and my drill sergeant got quiet.

Within a few minutes, we were in the emergency room. He left me there, either to go back and terrorize more recruits or to get the blood off his upholstery. I never knew. All I knew was that the doctors started working on my wrist right away.

The pain was intense. My entire arm was throbbing like it had its own heartbeat. At first, I thought they would stitch me up and send me right back, but soon I realized that they were prepping me for surgery.

The damage turned out to be much worse than I had thought. The tendon of my thumb had been severed, and the radial nerve was destroyed and had to be removed.

I spent the next couple of months in the hospital. They spent a great deal of time working on my right hand in daily physical therapy, but they had very little hope that I would ever use that thumb again. And if I didn't have a right thumb, I didn't really have a right hand, and if I didn't have a right hand, I couldn't hold a rifle correctly, or throw a hand grenade, or make a fist.

If I couldn't do those things, I wasn't going to make it through basic training. And no one stayed in the army without making it through basic training.

Soon, I began to realize that I would be discharged. At the time, it seemed as if it might be worth the nerve damage never to have to see that drill sergeant again.

One day, four weeks into basic training, Johnson was allowed to venture outside the barracks to visit me in the hospital. His clothes and face were covered with dirt. I think he was so anxious to get out of basic that he didn't have time to shower. Either that, or they wouldn't let him.

"You've got dirt under your nose," I said.

"I just came back from a five mile hike," he said. "And it's not dirt under my nose; it's dirt *from* my nose. I can't get rid of it no matter how many times I blow. When are you coming back?"

I looked at Johnson and his dirty fatigues, his nose that wouldn't stop bleeding mud.

"I'm probably not coming back at all," I finally said.

I was about to get discharged, but I wasn't thinking about that right now. The two of us had joined on the buddy system. We'd known each other since eighth grade. But now he would be spending the next three years in the army, and I would be going home.

Six

QUALITY OVER SPEED

Eventually, Johnson did get the communications job we'd signed up for, and he was stationed in Germany. He did his three years, and we hung out whenever he was on leave, exchanging letters and audio tapes whenever he wasn't. We've remained friends, and later he would come back into my life in a way neither of us might have expected back in the eighth grade.

But before all of that happened, I was discharged from the army with a medical disability. I'd only served a few months. My first plan had failed, and now I had to decide what I was going to do with my life.

My right thumb still wasn't working fully: I could move it a little bit, but not as much as I'd been used to. I had to use my left hand to write. But despite the inconvenience, I was glad to be home. My mother was thrilled: Not only had I never gone to Vietnam, but now she'd have an adult around again to help with the three younger children.

Johnson and I hadn't wanted to go to college, but at least we knew that through the army, we could pay for it if we ever decided to go. But because I'd left the army suddenly, I didn't get the GI Bill. Instead, I had to apply for the Disabled Veterans Bill. The funds would still be there, but I'd have to wait for it, and then wait. And wait.

I also had to wait for a new term to start in Hillsborough Community College, where I wanted to study business management. I planned to learn how to avoid the things that had driven my father's restaurant to extinction. I knew that I could do better than he had, and I was sure that college could help me.

Because of the timing of my discharge, however, I couldn't start studying for months. I've never liked waiting. So instead of spinning my wheels until the new term, I did what I always did: I went to work.

One of the odd jobs I'd had when I was younger was as a cleanup boy at the local Burger Chef, so I applied for a job there. They had an assistant manager position open. I had no experience, but in my interview, I talked a lot about my great attitude and my ability to learn.

Since Burger Chef was a franchise, once I was hired, they handed me a binder full of rules and protocols. It was called an Operations Manual, and it was *huge*. But I was a hard worker, I wanted to move up the ladder to manager as quickly as I could, and I didn't mind studying.

It wasn't until years later when I realized what the purpose of those binders was: to keep me straightjacketed when I tried to make any kind of change.

At first being an assistant manager was a fun job, and I loved having money in my pocket. My family sometimes complained about the grease smell, but I was around it all day, and I didn't even notice it.

The kids who worked there with me were teens aged from fifteen to seventeen. At eighteen, I was the old guy, except for the manager, who was over thirty. That seemed ancient.

I had no real management experience, so I tried to lead by example. If I wanted someone to do something, I told them what needed to get done and why. I always thought that if you gave an employee a reason for doing their task, they'd give you a lot more support, and the end result would be better.

I thought my team was working well. They weren't just my employees, they were my friends. We were all from the same neighborhood, and sometimes—once I'd been working long enough to be able to afford my own place—they'd come to my apartment after work to hang out or go out to bars together. I even dated one or two of the girls.

It might've gone on that way forever if I hadn't decided to improve on one of the systems in the three-ring binder.

Burger Chef didn't have a good system for tracking controllables. According to the binder, you were only supposed to use a certain number of napkins per customer to keep costs down, but the binder didn't have any good procedures for controlling food costs. So on my own, I decided to count buns and compare them to the number of sandwiches we sold.

According the register, we'd sold 100 burgers, but 110 buns were gone. Ten burgers hadn't been paid for.

This was in the back of my mind one day when I watched one of my "friends" chatting with five of his friends, who were placing an order at the counter. Something about it bothered me. Normally when an employee took an order, they'd call it back to the kitchen, and whoever was working back there would prepare it. This employee took the order, but then he walked back to prepare it himself.

Suspicious, I watched him take the food to his five friends in the dining room. They looked like the rest of us, regular teenagers, but I started to think of the deadbeats my father used to feed for free.

I checked the register to see how many burgers had been sold, and I checked how many buns were missing. Today, the numbers were off by five.

After double-checking everything, I confronted him. "Did your friends pay for their food?"

"Of course," he said.

I explained to him that I was counting buns. To my surprise, he looked at me as if *I* had done something wrong. How dare I accuse him of doing something he did? He started to walk away from me, and then he turned back. "What do you care? It's not your money."

For a moment, I wondered how my father might have handled this situation, but I wasn't allowed to beat up my employees. Any idiot could swing, and I wanted him to understand that what he was doing was wrong. So I tried to explain to him about how controllables worked, and how the store couldn't function if he was stealing. I told him that I was the assistant manager and had to be responsible.

He still didn't get it, so finally I had to tell him that if it happened again, I would fire him.

I was eighteen years old. Lots of adults, when they have to fire someone, get nervous. How will they take it? Will they sue me? Will they cry? Will they come after me when I'm not looking?

None of those things crossed my mind. Maybe that made me an ignorant teenager, but I don't think so. At eighteen, I'd already had a lifetime of experience. I'd been shot at in the projects. I'd had a father who wasn't afraid to keep us in line the old-fashioned way. And now, even though I was an assistant manager, I was still that kid from the projects, and what my employee was doing was wrong.

I wound up not having to fire that particular kid, but I caught more people doing the same thing. The atmosphere changed at work. My friends—or rather, my employees—started to say that I wasn't as much fun as I used to be. But that was their problem, not mine. I had a business to run. I had seen what my father had done to his family by not managing The Little Inn. I was never going to let that happen to myself. I would have loved to maintain some of these friendships, but not at *that* cost.

Ever since then in my working life, I've separated friends and employees. As far as I'm concerned, you can be friends with your coworkers and direct reports outside the office, but once you're in the office, I'm the manager. If you screw up, I'm going to tell you, and I'm going to mean it.

Years later, when I worked at Microsoft, I would have heated arguments with my direct reports (who were also my friends) one day, and the next we'd be eating lunch together and talking about Sunday's football game.

It's my experience that good people, even when they screw up, know the value of responsibility, and they know how to separate their home lives from their work. And true friends will always have each other's back, no matter what the context— work, sports, barbecues.

I spent five years in the fast food industry, and it wasn't all arguments all the time.

Lots of people dismiss the fast food industry. The employees smell like grease. They're the paper hat guys your teacher always warns you about: "If you don't pass this test, you'll spend a lifetime asking people, 'Do you want fries with that?'"

But I think there's merit in managing fast food. You have to multitask like no other job, and that means you need to have great awareness of your surroundings. Is the dining room dirty? Are the employees in the back room washing the dishes or screwing around? How many cars are pulling into the parking lot?

And you have to know the answer to one of the most important business questions I've ever learned to ask: Are the fries fresh?

Fries stay hot and fresh for six or seven minutes, tops, after they're cooked. After more time than that under the heat lamp, they start to get limp and cold. Many counter people in fast food restaurants face this dilemma every day. There's a big line of customers asking for fries, but the fries that are available are cold and soggy.

It's a customer service dilemma, and one that I've learned goes beyond fast food. I've worked for companies that thought they needed to get a product out on a date, thinking that the release date was driving the product—not the quality.

I say, pick quality over speed. Take your time and do the job right. If anyone complains, tell the customer that you're going to make them fresh fries and bring them right to their table. Nobody cares how fast they get *cold* fries. They'll appreciate the effort, and you'll see them again.

At the beginning, I was supplementing the lessons I was learning on the job with college. Initially I went to Hillsborough Community College, where the classes were small and I had access to professors. Later, I transferred to the University of South Florida, where I took classes in an auditorium.

I remember one management class I took. We were doing a roleplaying exercise, and I was playing the manager. The situation was similar to the one I'd recently faced: An employee was doing something wrong, and my job as manager was to get them to do the right thing.

The professor gave me some advice. "Remember, you need to get the employee to see things from your perspective," he said.

"That's wrong," I told him. "The employee doesn't care about my perspective. They just care about how whatever they're doing will impact them."

We debated the point for a little while. In the end, he told me that he believed that given the choice, employees would always choose to do the right thing.

"If I'm the manager, am I supposed to believe that stealing food to feed your friends is the right thing?" I asked him.

He got defensive. "I'm not talking about fast food management," he told me. "I'm talking about *real* management."

I didn't see the distinction. All the time, lately, I found myself thinking, *What a big fat waste of time*.

The truth was that I didn't have a mentor. My father was dead, and I wouldn't have taken his advice anyway. My mother only finished the eighth grade, so anything more than that was outside her experience. Johnson was still in the army. I had to go my own way. And honestly? I don't think my own way was that bad.

I still remember the day I decided to drop out. I had just finished a double shift at Burger Chef, and I had tests the next day. This wouldn't be the first time I'd stayed up all night and studied. But that night I asked myself, what was the point? The concepts they were teaching me didn't seem to apply to the world I was working in. So I decided, right in the middle of the quarter, that I wasn't going back.

The decision felt like the right one at the time. But a few months of not going to class later, my report card came. Three Fs.

I didn't feel right leaving school on such a down note. So I took the report card the way I always did—as a challenge. One more quarter. I would give this juggling act—working and studying and not sleeping—one more quarter, and then I'd leave school at the top of my game.

But though I worked as hard as I could, it wasn't any use, and my next report card wasn't much different. Something had to give, and I was learning more on the job than in the classroom. I had a decision to make, and I made it.

This time, I left college for good.

Over the years, I would face the same question many times. "Why didn't you get a degree? Why didn't you finish college?" I sometimes remind people that Bill Gates didn't get his degree either. Sometimes I don't defend myself at all. Why does it matter?

The reality is this: I didn't finish college because I was learning more working at Burger Chef. *Burger Chef.*

Over the next year, I went from being an assistant manager at Burger Chef to being the unit manager. The unit manager is the person in charge of the entire store. Everything is his responsibility, and everyone looks to him for direction.

I worked there in this role for another year, but in the end, a Wendy's opened next door. The Burger Chef owner couldn't compete, so he decided to close. He had two other restaurants, and he offered me a job at one of his other locations, but I decided it was time to move on. My thumb had finally healed, everything seemed to be going well, and I was anxious to take on a new challenge.

Soon, I learned that there was a manager trainee opening at the Arby's a few miles away. They were a much bigger operation, and I thought I could learn a lot more there. So I applied for the job and got it.

Arby's had more systems to track costs and sales than Burger Chef did. If someone was giving away free food, the manager would know right away. Arby's also had ways of tracking how much money they were making per pound of meat. That was the key to their business: How much could you make from one roast?

I liked my manager at that Arby's. His name was Carl. He was a short, stocky man with a loud voice. He could be sarcastic, but he ran a great restaurant.

Like Burger Chef, Arby's also had an Operations Manual. Theirs dictated that no matter the hour, even if it was closing time, there should always be a roast beef sitting on a slicer behind the counter so that the customer could see the meat being sliced for their sandwich. It was a good policy in theory, but it was a waste to keep a full roast beef on display in the slicer until the end of the day. It meant that we couldn't break down and clean the slicer until after we'd closed, which added time and cost. Also, the more roast beef you had at the end of the day, the more you had to reheat in the morning, which would lead to shrinkage and less money per roast. It was such a waste, and I had no idea how Carl dealt with it while keeping the restaurant as profitable as the company wanted it to be.

After a few months, the corporate office offered me a restaurant of my own to manage. But Carl, who'd mentored me so well, told me not to take the job. "You're not ready," he said.

Since I'd stood up to my father that summer when I was twelve years old, I never backed down from verbally taking on anyone I disagreed with, whether it was a nun or a drill sergeant—*a drill sergeant*. I disagreed with Carl now.

"I understand how to run the place," I told him. "Come on, you know me—I run everything completely by the book."

"Sure, you know how to run things by the book," Carl said.

"But do you know when *not* to?" At the time, I didn't understand him.

But no matter what I tried at my new Arby's, our profits were never high. I tried to tell upper management that what they wanted couldn't be done—I couldn't follow all the directives in the Operations Manual and still make as much money per roast as they needed me to make. But they thought the lack of profit was *my* fault. According to them, because Carl's restaurant was making a steady profit, mine should be too. In the end, I accepted a demotion and went back to being assistant manager again, reporting to Carl.

Carl, loud and sarcastic, wasted no time. "Told ya you weren't ready."

Shortly after, I finally figured out how his business was working: He was cutting corners. He didn't have a full roast beef on display at the end of the shift. Instead, he estimated how many customers we might get in that last half hour before closing, and then he estimated how much roast beef we'd need the rest of the night, sliced it, and put the rest away.

This wasn't quite like the betrayal I felt when my employees were stealing from me, but it still didn't feel right. I'd been demoted, and upper management thought it was my fault. I was pissed enough to accuse Carl of faking protocol to make his profit margin look good.

He didn't care. It was my second big business eye-opener.

I stayed at Arby's as an assistant manager for a few months, but it wasn't what it used to be. Now that I knew Carl was cheating, I didn't feel the same way about learning from him.

I decided I'd give fast food one more try by accepting a job at Wendy's as an assistant manager. I hoped that at least in a different franchise, I might be able to run things more efficiently.

I was wrong. They also had an Operations Manual. And upper management still wanted the impossible: everything out, everything fresh, right up until closing.

It would've been doable, if it hadn't been for the salad bar.

At Arby's, you had to have that roast beef sitting on the slicer until you closed. At Wendy's, you had to have the crocks in the salad bar heaping with vegetables until you closed. This not only made it take longer to close the store, increasing your labor costs, but it also meant that more perishable items would spoil, increasing your food costs.

I hated the waste of food. I'd watched my father hoard his pork chop while we ate government cheese. I hated it so much that this time, *I* cut corners. I placed smaller containers inside larger ones and placed the food on the top. That way the containers looked full and heaping, but there wasn't actually a lot of food out.

While other Wendy's managers complained about how it was impossible to control costs with the new salad bar, my profit margin didn't suffer, nor did the late-night customers.

I would've been ready to clock out of fast food entirely, if it hadn't been for two things: disco, and Suzie.

I liked my coworkers at Wendy's. Lots of times when our shift was over, we'd take off our hats, put on our colorful polyester shirts and bell-bottom pants, head straight to the discos, and stay there. Often, we'd head to our morning shifts without sleeping at all.

We thought discos were cool. Our favorite place was the ABC Liquors in New Port Richey, Florida. They would play loud music, and they even had one of those big disco balls. Dancing to the beat was easy. Anyone could do it: even me.

Finding someone to dance with was also easy.

The seventies were almost over, but it was still the seventies. Every night the "Last Dance" came too soon. Suzie's impact has lasted a lot longer.

I had been at Wendy's for only a few days when I became quick friends with Olivet, one of the counter girls. She was a very fun-loving girl, seventeen years old and almost six feet tall. She could be intimidating, but she loved to joke around. One day I was working the front drink station and Olivet was making sand-wiches when Suzie walked through the door to clock in. She had long auburn hair, hazel eyes, and a smile that cut right into me. I couldn't take my eyes off of her. I asked Olivet, "Who is that?"

I'll never forget what Olivet replied. "You leave her alone. She has a boyfriend."

I said, "I don't care."

Olivet said, "You hurt her and I'll hurt you."

That didn't bother me. Later in the day, while we were both working, I introduced myself. We got along well, but I was older than her by four years. It doesn't seem like a huge difference now, but when I first met her, she was eighteen and I was twenty-two. In spite of that age difference, we became friends. I wanted to take her out. It took a few months to work up the nerve, despite Olivet's warning, but when I did ask her out, she said yes.

A couple of years later, we would be married. I didn't hurt her, and Olivet didn't have to hurt me.

I was still tired of the fast food industry, even with Suzie and the friends I'd made. I was tired of the cost-cutting, the cheating, and the smell of grease. But it wasn't any of that that finally severed my connection with the fast food industry—it was something much more dramatic.

Looking back, I should've known that drinking for all hours and staying at discos wasn't a good idea. I'd nearly wrapped my car around a telephone pole once, but that didn't stop the party. I would show up at the clubs declaring that I was on my last drink, but then I had another, and another.

Then one night, at three in the morning, I got behind the wheel and headed home. I remembered my last near miss, so I turned the radio up to keep me awake. I thought the best thing to play was Elton John. I could crank up "Goodbye, Yellow Brick Road" and sing to it. That should keep me awake.

It didn't work. When I opened my eyes, my car was heading right for a tree. I only had time to say, "Shit!"

The next thing I remember, I was walking down the street and saying "Help me!" over and over again.

Then I was in the back seat of a car filled with newspapers. A couple who were delivering papers that morning had put me in their car and taken me to their house. Later, I learned that they had called an ambulance. At the time, all I knew was that I was in pain.

When I woke up, the first person I saw at St. Joseph's Hospital was a priest. He was standing next to my mother and Suzie. They looked worried, and I struggled to remember why.

The priest told me it was a miracle I was alive. I'd hit a tree going at least seventy miles an hour. He also said the doors were locked and the windows were up in my car. The steering wheel had been embedded into the front seat.

Yet I not only got out of that wreck, but I walked away.

I looked at my car's damage for myself once I was out of the hospital. It was a complete wreck. It didn't seem possible that I could have survived. But I did.

I had a slash across my chin that took twelve stitches. I had cuts on both my legs, and my right eye was swollen shut. My right knee was bruised and swollen, and my back was so wrenched I couldn't stand or walk.

I spent weeks in the hospital, and the doctors told me it would be some time before I would walk again. I wasn't ready to hear that, so after a few weeks of intensely painful physical therapy, I did manage to walk out of that hospital. It would be months before I returned to work at Wendy's, but my days of hitting the discos were done.

Working at Wendy's wasn't as easy for me as it had been before. Every day, I was learning the hard way that having a job where you stand on your feet for hours and hours might not be the best choice for someone who'd been through months of intense physical therapy. Although I could walk again, my legs hurt constantly, and I no longer had the physical stamina that a fast food career required.

So I started looking into other options. I also started to think about my own mortality. I had almost died, and I realized I'd have left nothing behind if I did.

I decided that I needed to buy life insurance, and I found a salesman who was more than happy to accommodate me. His name was Reggie. He was a tall, confident man with an outgoing personality who seemed very happy with the career he had chosen. As he saw it, he was selling security.

His pitch was compelling. He talked to me about different policies. As he tried to sell me, I asked questions. Term or whole life? Which was better? I'd never stopped challenging authority figures. I had a brain, and I wasn't afraid to use it, even when the results were as disastrous as my wrist spurting blood while I yelled at a drill sergeant.

Looking back, I realize that our conversation could've gone very differently. Reggie could've said okay to whatever I wanted, just to make the sale and get me out of his hair. Instead, he said something that would change my life: "You really catch on to this stuff fast. Have you ever thought about being in sales?"

He explained more about what was involved in selling insurance. Of course I'd have to study and pass a test to get a license, he told me. But in his opinion, I might have a good future at it.

I didn't have to think for long. I could keep working in a uniform and a paper hat, smelling like french fries every day, or I could work from an office wearing a suit. I was sold.

It took a few weeks, but soon I had my life insurance license. Then I told Tom, my boss at Wendy's, that I'd be leaving. Tom tried to talk me out of it, but my mind was made up. It was a hard conversation because we were friends, and both of us thought that we wouldn't be seeing any more of each other. Neither of us realized that he and his father would resurface in my life, and soon.

The priest in the hospital had told me it was a miracle that I walked away from a car wreck. Leaving fast food felt like a miracle as well, only one of my own making.

I'd worked at Burger Chef, Arby's, and Wendy's. With each job I learned more about how to run a business and how to manage people and resources. I danced all night, met the girl I would marry, and almost died. But I also learned that fast food was no way to get where I wanted to be in life. All the things I hated about the industry were never going to change: The hours were long, the grease smell never left you; and most importantly to me, no matter how hard you worked, there was always some thick Operations Manual filled with rules that wouldn't let you do the right thing.

I was still only in my early twenties, but I wore my experience like the new scars on my skin. *Next time,* I thought. *Next time I'll be able to make a difference.*

Seven

CARVING OUT A DEATH

E ver since my car crash, I'd thought a lot about mortality. What if I died? What would happen to the people I left behind? If my father ever had these thoughts, he never acted on them. I'd seen the toll his lack of foresight took on my mother when he died, leaving her with nothing.

I didn't want to be like him. I wanted to plan ahead, so that if in the future, I succeeded in accidentally killing myself as I nearly had on that Florida highway, at least my mom would get something. So now I had life insurance, and I had my new life insurance sales career to take me out of fast food.

Reggie was my boss and my mentor. He worked with me through the one-month training period. It seemed like it would be easy stuff. Other than learning the different products, there wasn't much to know.

Then I started cold calling.

Reggie and the senior salesmen all had their own offices, but the other new salesmen and I worked out of a giant bullpen, a huge space with desks and phones along the wall. After a day of working my way through the phone book, listening to everyone else in this huge room doing exactly the same thing, it all seemed like a waste of time.

Reggie didn't have to do it anymore. He sold all his insurance through referrals. People he had already sold insurance to would tell their friends and family about him so that when he called them, he already knew that they had a need and wanted to talk. I knew he'd started by cold calling, just the same as me, but when I started, it seemed like a very long way from these phones to the office he sat in now.

I wasn't trying to sell insurance over the phone, but to get an appointment to talk to people further. When you cold call, people have no idea who you are and what you want. And you have no idea about them, other than their last names. And do they even need insurance?

This was my least favorite part of cold calling: discussing the need. When you sell a product, you have to sell the need. And with insurance, the need is always the same thing: You're going to die. It's not really something people like to talk about.

Most people would hang up the second I mentioned life insurance. I don't know if it had to do with people not wanting to think about life insurance, or they didn't like being interrupted in their daily routine, or if they just didn't like my voice. But whatever the reason, that first month of selling insurance, it seemed the only word I heard was *no*.

Then, finally, one *yes*.

I reached a young couple who'd just had a kid, and they thought they needed to at least think about life insurance. So I got the appointment and went to their house.

I told them about our policies. They wanted to know the cost. When I told them, they said that they were happy to buy, but because they were a young couple and didn't have a lot of disposable income, they wanted the cheapest premium they could get.

I tried to explain to them that the cheapest premium only meant the cheapest insurance *at the moment*. In reality, a slightly more expensive option would be cheaper in the long run. I tried to sell them on that more expensive option, which would be better for them, as best as I could.

They thanked me for my time.

The appointment was over, and I went back to the office with nothing.

How did this happen? I'd thought I was doing that young couple a favor. I'd thought that they should be educated, and that I was the one to do it. I could have sold them what they wanted and made my very first sale, but instead I went home with nothing.

It led me to a painful conclusion: When someone has their checkbook out, shut the hell up and take the money.

So I was back on the phone, cold calling again and getting more *nos*.

To Reggie, rejections were about the numbers. He told me that on average, if you call twenty people, nineteen of them will say no and one will say yes. So I shouldn't get discouraged with the nos, as each one gets you closer to the yes.

Reggie was right. It really did take about twenty calls to get one appointment. But I also learned that most appointments ended with *no*. Again, Reggie countered with numbers. He said, "Out of five appointments, you'll make one sale."

That made sense to me as well, but I didn't like it. I didn't mind getting nos on the phone, but if I got the appointment and I was in the house, I didn't want to squander the opportunity. By this time, Suzie had moved in with me. I was happy to have her there, and it's true that her steady, "real job" income as a fast food manager was keeping us stable for now, but I was anxious to start making commissions and prove to myself that I was right for having taken the leap into a new career.

So I started to think about why people were saying no. Was it because they didn't think they needed insurance? Did they think it cost too much? Did they want to shop around for a different product from a different company? I started to role-play these scenarios in my mind and tried to come up with an answer for each. Once I got into the house, I didn't want to leave without a sale. To me, a no wasn't a no; it was just a request for more information.

I started going to my appointments looking forward to hearing no, because once I heard the no, I could lead the conversation. In fact, I had more success selling to people who said no than the ones who sat there, said nothing, and then thanked me for my time.

Slowly, I became more confident. I had answers ready for anything. Whole life is too expensive? Really, it's free after a few years. Can't afford the premium now? Buy term and convert later. Want to shop around? You really shouldn't leave yourself and your family unprotected. Buy now; you can always cancel later if you find something better.

My favorite objection was, "We just don't have the money."

I would say, "What if you came home and the refrigerator was broken?"

"I'd have to get it fixed," they'd say.

"But you don't have any money," I'd say.

"We'd have to find it," they'd say. "We couldn't let all that food spoil."

And I would say, "Of course you would find the money to protect your food. Now are you sure you can't find the money to protect your family?"

I sold a lot of policies and was named Apprentice Field Underwriter of the Month, which meant that I was the best new salesman. But after a few months of this, it just didn't feel right. Sure, I thought people needed life insurance, but some of them really couldn't afford it. And frankly, few people wanted to have a conversation about death. I really liked the sales part; I just wanted something easier to pitch, like tomatoes from the back of a truck.

I remembered that my supervisor at Wendy's, Tom, had a father who was in the real estate business. So I decided to talk to him and wound up in the next stage of my career. Maybe dying was a more reliable outcome than buying land was, but people were more interested in carving out a life than they were in carving out a death.

Eight

WE ARE NOT VERY HANDY

Carl Ragan was the name of the man who pulled me from peddling death to peddling land. His office was busy; he at least was making money, and there was air conditioning. All better than life insurance. Best of all, there were no cold calls.

But *not* cold calling in the real estate business meant I had to find ways to get what I needed, namely—

Buyers

Listings of my own

I was confident that this wouldn't be much of a problem.

It was the early 1980s, and "get rich quick" was all the rage. There was information circulating everywhere. In newspapers. In infomercials. In tri-folds. In glossy magazines featuring young people eating strawberries in a courtyard, while behind them the setting sun made coral-colored condos glow. This was a time when the airways were filled with get-rich-quick guys selling courses about buying real estate. These guys ran seminars in hotel banquet rooms telling you how you could make a ton of money. Of course, it *cost* money to take these courses, both the ones in the banquet halls and the ones on the cassette tapes. But the basic idea was simple: buy run down houses for no money down, fix them up, flip them.

I wanted to get as far away from projects living as I could, and finding the right real estate opportunity might finally give me a way to do that. I knew they were out there, the real estate opportunities. And I thought I was playing it safe. After some time working for Carl and learning the ropes, all I would have to do was grab an opportunity, which would present itself to me like a low-hanging cherry on a tree.

It didn't work out that way.

Carl's business was doing so well that he had two offices. He was initially thinking about closing one of them, but seeing an opportunity, I told him I could manage it, and he let me. I knew there should be more than one person in a real estate office, so I contacted an old friend from Wendy's. His name was Wayne. He had curly brown hair and a mustache. He had a great sense of humor, and he was tired of the fast food business. When I asked him to partner with me, he said yes right away.

One of the hard facts about real estate is that if you sell a house, you have to share the commission with the listing agent. But if it's your listing, you can keep the whole commission for yourself. So the first thing Wayne and I did once we were managing the office was to run an ad in the local paper to try to get listings. We spent all of our time in the office or playing tennis, and all we talked about was how we could get our own listings—that, and how we could get rich.

One day a guy walked in who owned eight duplexes that he

was hoping to sell. Lucky, we thought. Our ads had panned out even better than we imagined. We not only had *one* listing—we had eight.

Since these were rentals, they were considered "commercial" properties. The office we worked for only handled residential properties, so the owner, Carl Ragan, saw an opportunity that hadn't presented itself before.

Wayne and I started advertising ourselves as "commercial real estate specialists." I quickly learned that if you called yourself a "commercial real estate expert," or an expert in any field, people will just accept it. We had more business than most real estate offices, who specialized in residential listings and dealt with commercial from time to time.

We thought we had found our niche. True, I was a sham. But the more listings I got, the less I felt like it.

Finally, we got an offer for a duplex, one of our many "commercial" listings. The contract was signed, and the inspection went well. We thought we were done.

But too late, we realized that when we'd told the buyer what the monthly payment would be, we'd included the principal and the interest, but we hadn't included the insurance and the taxes. This meant a couple hundred more dollars per month that the buyer hadn't considered.

The buyer was a short, stocky man who wasn't very intimidating until he stood up and started swearing at us.

"You think I'm an idiot?" he said. "You think I don't know what you're up to?" We tried to explain that the taxes and insurance were separate costs, but he didn't care. "You salesmen are all alike. Just out to make a buck. Well, I think you guys are a couple of worthless pieces of shit."

I'd never seen anyone "storm out" of a building, but that was what he did. Wayne and I sat there with our mouths open.

The deal fell through. No one was happy with us, including our broker who said you should never let a deal fall apart at the closing table. He was furious, and he made sure that we knew we had to have all the information, that we had to share the information, and that we had to make sure everyone understood that information in order to close a deal for sure.

All that work. Everyone mad at us. Our first sale gone. It was as if we'd done nothing at all.

I'd like to say our lesson was about the *principal*, *interest*, *taxes*, and *insurance* (or PITI, as it was known in real estate) and how we'd missed two of the four concepts, but it wasn't just about that. It was really about what it meant to close a deal, and how things could fall apart at the last second.

From that point on, whether in real estate or any other career, I've made it my business to make sure that I know *all* of the details and the costs. Then I go over them again, and if I have to, I go over them a third time. No one should walk away from the closing table.

It wasn't long before we were back at the closing table with another sale. This time it actually was a single-family home. We had learned our lesson about PITI with our last almost sale. There would be no surprises this time.

Or so we thought.

Just before the close, the buyer took one more walk through of the house and noticed that the refrigerator was gone. They had assumed it was included in the sale. Which is how I learned the old real estate saying "if it's screwed or glued, it stays." The refrigerator wasn't screwed or glued to the house, so if the buyer wanted it, they should have said so in the contract.

The seller said that there was no way he was putting the fridge back. At that point, everyone was ready to walk away: the buyer, his agent. I wasn't going to lose the deal over a few hundred dollars, so I asked the buyer's agent if we could take the cost of the new fridge out of our commission. The agent agreed, and the deal was done.

I went to Carl, my boss, with a commission check that was a few hundred dollars light. I thought that he would be thrilled when I told him how we'd saved the deal. He wasn't. He said that since I'd agreed to buy the refrigerator and without bothering to ask him, the price should come from somewhere else—in other words, from Wayne's and my pockets.

I'd now been to the closing table twice, and I hadn't felt like a winner either time.

A few days later, a guy came into the office and told me he wanted to sell his house. It wasn't commercial, but it was still a listing, so Wayne and I pounced. I asked him how much he wanted for it. The figure he told me seemed too low. I told him that I could probably get him more, but he said he didn't care. He wanted to sell it fast.

As soon as I heard him say that, I knew that I wanted Wayne and I to buy the property ourselves. I told the seller to think about it and to come back tomorrow in order to buy myself time to talk to Wayne.

We worked out the mathematics of the sale. The price the seller wanted was very good, but not great. Once we reduced the price by our seven percent commission, it would become a very good deal. But before we did that, we had to call our broker and tell him what we wanted to do. He wanted his share as well, so the seven percent commission went down by half. Wayne and I grumbled, loudly, with our boss, Carl. This would add over a thousand bucks to the cost of the house in addition to a down payment—money we didn't have.

But there was another way to make this sale work. It all came down to the Federal Housing Authority.

The FHA was what enabled all of us to get housing for free, since they had this thing called a nonqualifying mortgage. With a nonqualifying mortgage, all a buyer had to do was take over the seller's mortgage payments. So if you had a house for sale for $50,000 and there was an existing FHA mortgage with a $45,000 balance, you would have to put $5,000 down and take over the payments on the mortgage. To do the deal for no money down, you needed the seller to take back a second mortgage for the $5,000. Then you would have a first mortgage for $45,000 and a second for $5,000 . . . no money down. Boom! Done.

It seemed easy. But what we didn't take into account with the no-money-down part of the plan is that, at the end of it, you'd be stuck with not one, but two mortgages.

The guy came back the next day, and he still wanted to sell us the house at that low price. Wayne and I didn't have the money to buy the house, but we liked the idea of buying one with no money down.

We took a look at the property. The house was a small three-bedroom, one-and-a-half bath, single-family home. When you walked through the front door, you walked into a giant space that was the living room, dining room, and kitchen all in one. The bedrooms were on the sides. The appliances were all old and avocado green. The house needed painting inside and out, and the bathroom fixtures were worn and covered with rust. The tiles in the shower had more green stuff growing on them than the yard, and the whole place was infested with bugs. In the back of the house, the previous owners had added another bonus room, but since they really didn't want to build up the roof, they just continued the existing slope. This meant that the room started at a normal height but ended at about four feet.

In short, the house was a dump, but we thought that with a few cosmetic fixes it would be fine. Wayne and I decided to make an offer on it. Even though the price was already low, we offered less. We'd found that in real estate, no matter what the seller asks for, they are willing to take less, and no matter what the buyer offers, they are willing to pay more. This was a game you had to play if you wanted to succeed. But ideally, you'd wind up with a price that would work for both of you, and both parties could walk away feeling like a winner.

That wasn't the way it happened.

As Wayne and I expected, the seller didn't take our first offer. But that was part of negotiations. While we were going back and forth on the price, however, we had the house appraised. We were surprised that the "fixer-upper" appraised for higher than the price we were offering.

We then came up with an idea. We were trying to buy the house for nothing down, but now, with the new information about the price, we figured that maybe we could buy the house and actually put some money in our pockets. So we told the seller that we would change the price we paid in the contract to the value the house had just been appraised at. That was more than he wanted, but we also told him that we wanted him to return the excess to us at the closing for repairs. He got his price, and we got the excess: $5,000.

I'll give the money to you; you give it right back to me. We'd not only bought a house for no money down, but we got *paid* to do it. We thought we were smarter than those scam artists pushing those no-money-down seminars.

We finally owned a house. Wayne and I could move right in. Suzie would too. She had stood by me through smelling like grease every night at Wendy's, my horrific car accident, my brief life insurance career (which felt like a car wreck), and now, moving into this dump.

Once we'd moved in, Suzie's father came over for a visit. Suzie's father wasn't thrilled with me from the start. He was an engineer with a four-year degree. I was a college dropout fast food manager who was four years older than his beloved daughter. I think he had much higher hopes of who she would spend her life with. The dump wasn't going to help me win his approval.

After seeing the house, he refused to let Suzie's mother see it. He didn't want Suzie's mother to know about this dump I had their little girl living in. This place was not tri-fold material. I couldn't have found a less glamorous place if I tried.

We told ourselves that it didn't matter, because we wouldn't be there long. We would fix it up and flip it, or we'd sell it quickly and make money.

In the meantime, we'd found another good deal. In this case, the house we found had a nonqualifying FHA mortgage. That meant that we could just take over the seller's payments, and the house would be ours. No need to fill out a loan application or even talk to the bank at all.

We dickered. The seller thought that this house was worth $50,000, and he owed $40,000. Because we were trying to get the house for no money down, we offered just the $40,000 he owed. The seller wanted to walk away, but we were determined. We knew that the house was really worth the $50,000 the seller wanted, and we still had the $5,000 we'd taken for repairs on the dump we'd bought. So we offered to split the difference, and the seller agreed to take $45,000.

We now had two houses, and neither of them cost us anything. We *ruled*.

The major problem with our strategy of flipping the first house was that neither Wayne nor I was really handy. To make money on the flip, we had to do the repair work ourselves.

We called in my brother Dennis. Dennis was a year and a half older than me, and he'd moved out of our parents' house as soon as he turned eighteen. He'd saved my ass a number of times in the projects, and while no one was swinging a bat at me right now, I needed him to save my ass again. Unlike my partner and me, Dennis was very handy. He worked in construction, and he was a very good carpenter who could drywall. He also knew about plumbing and electrical.

After looking over the house, Dennis told us that we should tile the dining room to make it look like its own room, add an arch to separate the kitchen from the living room, and put mirror tiles on the wall to make it look bigger. They all seemed like good ideas, and we started in on them. The first thing we did was lay the tile floor. When my brother came in to work on the arch, he asked, "Why did you lay the floor before we put up the wall?" Now the floor would get ruined from all the work he was going to do.

We covered the new tile, but it still got massively dirty.

As for the second house, it didn't need any work. It was a nice three-bedroom, two-bath house with a two-car garage and a nice yard. It was ready for a family to move in. Suzie would have loved to live in this house, and her father would have been thrilled to show it to his wife, but we needed to live in the fixer-upper so that we could make money when we flipped it.

We decided to rent the second house—the one with no green stuff on the bathroom fixtures. We hoped that someone else paying our mortgage and tending to the place would make the house go up in value. It would take time, but we were sure we'd make money in the end. We thought it would be easy, especially when we found a renter right away. He seemed like a nice guy with a nice family: a working dad, a stay-at-home mom, and two young kids.

Did we check his credit rating? Find out if he'd ever done time? No. Either it didn't occur to us, or we didn't know how. We *did* call his employer to verify the renter had a job. Which he did, at the time.

So *that* house was covered, we thought.

While Dennis slowly educated us about how *not* to renovate a house, Wayne and I were also supposed to be working in the branch of the real estate office I managed for Carl Ragan.

This is about the time when I learned the term "fiduciary relationship" and how it applied to licensed real estate brokers. If someone comes to your office wanting to list a house at $35,000, and it was really worth $50,000, we were legally obligated to tell them that. In other words, we learned, we couldn't really do what we'd already done.

But if we didn't have our licenses, if we were a couple of guys off the street, we could buy property for whatever amount the seller wanted. Since we now wanted to be real estate investors, we decided not to renew our real estate licenses and gave up the office. Carl didn't mind—he hadn't wanted to keep the second office that I worked in open anyway. I think he was planning to sell some of his houses to us and make some commissions off of us, but after our last day of work in his office, I don't think either of us ever saw him again.

So now we had no income. Plus I had a wife.

Suzie and I had gotten married. Her parents thought she was nuts to marry me. Luckily, Suzie disagreed with them. I asked Johnson to be my best man, and I asked Wayne to stand with me as well. We had a great wedding, and then we headed to Disney World for our honeymoon. We had a wonderful time in fantasy land, but after a few days, we knew we would have to return to my own fantasy, which wasn't nearly as glamorous. It smelled like bug spray and dry rot.

Once, much later, I asked Suzie about why she had wanted to get married and stay together, given how grim things sometimes were early on. She told me that she'd always loved my ambitious nature and my can-do attitude, and that during all of the ups and downs at the start of our lives together—mostly downs—she knew that I would never give up. So she never gave up on me.

And now, thanks to Suzie's steady income from her new fast food managerial job, we could pay our bills and our half of the mortgage on the dump. She was working at a chicken-and-biscuits place at the time, and most nights we would eat whatever she brought home at the end of the day from the restaurant. Our avocado-green refrigerator was always full of chicken and biscuits.

While Suzie worked during the day, Wayne and I continued our renovations or looked around for more houses to buy, so as to expand our empire. Now the place was only *half* a dump.

The renters for our second house missed their rent payment. They said we'd have a check in a few days.

When a few days came and went, the renter said he'd lost his job, but that he'd be starting a new one in a week. He said that he would ask for an advance and pay us right away.

We had no new renter lined up, and we didn't have the money to cover the mortgage payment ourselves. What could we do but wait?

After another few days, I called the renter again. He said that the job had fallen through and that he couldn't pay us. I told him he'd have to move out, and he said he would, in a week.

He wasn't out in a week.

By now the next mortgage payment on our rental house was due. So was the mortgage on the dump we were living in. We only had money to pay one mortgage, even though we were responsible for two. So we paid the rental house mortgage, and we skipped the payment on the house we lived in.

We were in over our heads.

A month went by. We now had two mortgages due—one on the dump, and one on the rental house. Even with Suzie bringing home steady income, it wasn't enough. We alternated paying mortgages on our two properties. If we paid the mortgage on the rental house one month, we paid the mortgage on our dump the month after.

This is not what the infomercials had promised us. We didn't feel like we were getting rich quick. We were now one payment behind on both houses, and we had a deadbeat family camped out in one of them. When we realized that they were planning to stay put and live for free at *our* expense, Wayne and I went to the court house to get an eviction notice.

We thought it would be easy. A judge would see that the family was a bunch of deadbeats. Surely he'd evict them right away.

To start eviction proceedings, we learned that we first had to send the tenants a notice saying that the rent was late and that they had three days to pay it. Once the three days were up, we had to send them another notice saying that since they didn't pay the rent, they now had ten days to vacate the property. If they didn't vacate the property, we'd have to send them another notice saying that we were going to get an eviction order, to which they would have ten days to reply. Once that happened, we would go to court. Again.

We did all these things, and the renters still didn't leave, so we ended up in front of a judge. Finally, we thought we were done.

Again.

We told the judge they hadn't paid the rent in two months. We told him that our third mortgage payment was due soon. We needed the rent, and our renters weren't holding up their end. Surely the judge had to see this?

The judge asked our renter if that were true, and he said yes. He explained that he'd had a little (just a *little*) bad luck, but he had a job now and would be able to pay all three months' rent next week.

The judge gave him the week.

Of course the renters didn't pay. So we went back to court. This took another three weeks. Our third mortgage payment was now overdue by one week. But this time, when we got to court, the judge finally ordered them to vacate the property—in another ten days. The judge went on to tell them that if they weren't gone in ten days, the sheriff's office would evict them.

Ten days later, they were still there. I called the sheriff's office and told them to evict them. Did they? No. They needed a court order. I had to go back to court and tell the judge that the dead-beat renters were still living in my house.

This time, the judge gave me the order right away. The dead-beats moved out a week later. Four months after they stopped paying the rent, they were gone.

I still don't think they were trying to scam us, even though it was an era ripe for scamming. I just think they wanted a free ride at our expense. It turned into a battle—one with judges, not with baseball bats.

Stay under the bleachers until it's all clear, Dennis had told me years ago in the projects when a fight was about to get ugly.

I wasn't the same little kid any more. I'd made mistakes, and I would make more. I knew things now—especially about what *not* to do. I knew I didn't like cold calling. I knew that cranking up Elton John on the radio when you're driving home late at night won't keep you from wrapping your car around a tree. I knew not to lay tiles until the walls were complete. I knew not to let a buyer walk away from the closing table for any reason.

And now, I'd learned not to rely on what seemed an easy source of income because the people on the other side of the deal *seemed* nice.

Years later, I got into real estate again. Whenever my tenants said that for whatever reason, they wouldn't be able to pay the rent, I told them that was fine, as long as they called my mortgage company. If the mortgage company said that it would be okay for me to miss my mortgage payment, I told them that it would be okay for them to miss their rent.

But for now, the tenants were finally gone, and Wayne and I could take our first look around the rental in months. At least the tenants didn't trash the property. It was still a nice three-bedroom house with a yard. Plus it didn't smell like mildew, or have green gunk on the bathroom fixtures. Still, we had now missed three mortgage payments.

It was a nightmare, and in the end, Wayne and I decided that real estate investing wasn't for us. Since this house still had an assumable mortgage, the buyer didn't have to qualify for a loan, which meant that it wouldn't be hard to sell. (Thank you, FHA!)

However, if we wanted to sell the house, we needed to move fast. The bank had already started foreclosure proceedings on our rental property. They didn't wait around like we did, and they didn't care what our excuses were. We either had to pay the mortgage or they'd take the house from us.

It didn't quite come to that, and we finally managed to sell the house. We barely broke even on the deal. But unfortunately, we didn't break even psychologically. The ordeal took an emotional toll on all of us—me, my wife, and my business partner. Wayne was done. He told us he was going to move to Seattle to "find himself."

I thought he was being a flake. Find himself? *In Seattle?* Isn't that where it rained all the time? What kind of idiot, I thought, would move to Washington State?

Before Wayne left, I asked him what he wanted me to do with the place we co-owned, since we never got an offer on it. He said I could have it. I was now the proud owner of a dump that my father-in-law wouldn't let my wife's mother see.

I was tired of real estate as well. My father-in-law was right. We were living in a dump. We were behind by two mortgage payments. The dump had been for sale for four months now, but we had no offers. The bank kept calling about catching up on the mortgage. I asked them if there was anything we could do. They suggested I give them the deed in lieu of foreclosure. And I did.

With that, we were officially out of the real estate business.

Sure, you could buy houses with no money down, but that didn't mean they were free. There would always be PITI. There would always be lost commissions. And there would definitely always be deadbeat renters that could make all your hard work come crashing down like an archway on a newly tiled kitchen floor.

Suzie and I moved into a nice one-bedroom apartment that even my mother-in-law could see. But I needed to figure out what I was going to do next. I thought I might go back to Wendy's, so I went to talk to a friend of mine, Dave, who still worked there.

The salad bar was still there, and it looked good. I didn't know if the current manager was taking the same kind of shortcuts I once had, but it wasn't my problem anymore. I asked Dave if there were any openings he knew about, but he had a better idea.

"How would you like to open a sports bar with me?" he asked.

I thought that was a great idea.

Suzie thought, here we go again.

Nine

THE WALLS GO UP

Dave was a small man with a high voice, but he had a confidence that commanded attention, and when he spoke, people listened and did what he said. Owning a restaurant, he argued, had to be better than working at a cookie-cutter franchise.

I agreed with him absolutely. This was not a step down in my career, it was a step up. If I invested with Dave, I could run a business the way it should be run. No Operations Manual full of protocols. This time, I'd be able to make a difference.

The problem was that Dave wasn't willing to make me his partner for free. Dave thought it would take about $30,000 to open a place. He wanted a full investor. In other words, if I wanted to share his vision, I had to cough up $15,000.

I told Dave I didn't have $15,000 for my half, but that I could come up with $3,000 for a tenth of the place. I didn't know where or how I'd get it, but I knew that Dave wasn't going to let me come in for nothing. Dave was disappointed, but even if he didn't have a full investor, at least he'd have a partner experienced in the restaurant business.

We were ready to go ahead. But first, I would have to talk to Suzie.

I knew that after our failed house-flipping ventures, Suzie was looking forward to my getting a real job and bringing home the bacon—not starting a business trying to sell bacon sandwiches.

So I did what was coming more easily to me. I sold her on my vision. I told her what I thought Reggie's would be like. Always full, with neon signs and brands of beer on tap and a giant TV so that our customers could watch their favorite teams—even in the off-season, when the only things on sports TV were curling, and maybe tennis from Australia. I told her that I was sure the place would make plenty of money once we opened. Easy, right?

She gently reminded me that in order to invest, we'd have to cough up $3,000 that we didn't have.

I told her that I had that figured out: I'd take a cash advance on a credit card. Sure, I'd be paying 18 percent interest, but it would only be for a short time. Besides, the monthly payment was only about $25, and I could certainly afford that. Of course, at that rate it would take me the rest of my life to pay it off, but the plan was simple: open the restaurant, make money, and then pay off the card.

She didn't like the idea of going into debt again. After all, we'd just nearly had a house foreclosed on us. And she was right—we had no money, and I had no income. But in the end, she said, "I know nothing I say will change your mind. So go for it."

While Dave and I had plenty of experience with running fast food restaurants, we had no experience with starting up a restaurant from scratch, nor did we have any idea what it would cost. But first, we would have to find a location for our venture. We picked a large open space in a strip mall in a neighborhood in north Tampa called Carrollwood. Carrollwood was an affluent area of town, and the only other sports bar was way to the south. Location, location, location. The residents of Carrollwood needed nachos, chicken wings, and draft beer, and by God, we were going to give it to them.

We knew we'd need tables and chairs. Expensive. A built-in bar? Even more so. And that giant TV with a satellite dish to show football games and closed-circuit fights? The price tag on that was insane. But maybe the price tag didn't ultimately matter. Now that we had the location, we were sure that all we needed to do was to get the doors open, and then the sales would come in. We were sure to make the money to do the things we couldn't do right now.

For example: building walls. We didn't have the money for that. So we had one 3,000 square foot open room with tables and chairs and a fifty-foot bar with a kitchen behind it. Our customers could see everything, from the beer on tap to our antics in the kitchen. At least we had enough money for the big-screen TV and satellite dish.

Our contractors weren't cheap, either. The spot we leased came with one bathroom, but we needed two. When the plumber said that it would cost $400 to break up the floor to put in a drain, I bought a sledge hammer and did it myself.

Our plan was to sell beer and wine and salads and sandwiches. We had the money for the built-in bar, two separate bathrooms, and wide-screen TV, but we didn't have a grill. This made cooking tuna melts very, very difficult.

We also didn't have an ice machine. We thought we could just get bags of ice. Easy, right? Even though we didn't have anywhere to store it.

After two months, we ran out of money, and we knew we had to get sales going. We set an opening date, and we decided to have an open house two days before. We would invite all the other business owners in the area and feed them for free. This would expose them to the place and hopefully turn them into repeat customers, and it would also give us a chance to test ourselves before we opened "for real."

At the open house, the place was packed. The first thing everyone ordered was a drink, and since most of these people had to get back to their own businesses after they ate, they mostly ordered iced tea and soda rather than beer. So our first challenge was that we ran out of ice.

Rather than buying a grill, we were using a small griddle that took too long to grill the sandwiches that were ordered. People liked our food, but the service was too slow. Also, it wasn't good that we had no wall between the kitchen and our customers. Nobody wanted to see, hear, or smell the "process." We threw food from station to station because it was faster than walking it over, and customers could see our kitchen staff running around as I shouted orders. I cursed a lot when I shouted out orders, and my voice carried, so our customers heard everything. "What the hell did you do to that sandwich?" and "Scrape that shit off the griddle!" made them jumpy.

And then there was the smell. It's not that the smell was bad—there was just so much of it. With no walls, the exhaust vent couldn't work properly. Imagine the smell of bacon cooking, and spaghetti sauce for the meatball subs, and tuna being mixed for the tuna melts and tuna salad sandwiches. Now imagine them all mixed together.

We closed our doors at midnight, congratulating ourselves. Sure, some things had gone wrong, but the place had been packed. Surely everyone who was here would spread the word about the wide-screen TV and the tuna melts. The complaints were just a blip on the radar that we would learn from.

The next day, Dave got out his credit card, and we bought an ice machine and a better grill. What his wife thought, and whether he got the same obscene interest rate I did, we'll never know. All we knew is that we would pay it off after we opened formally and the sales started to come in.

Two days later, we were open. We had a good crowd, mostly guys who wanted to drink beer and eat nachos while watching college football on the big-screen TV.

We asked for feedback, and we heard the same thing over and over. The food was great, but the service was slow, and the place was just too large. "It's like eating in a warehouse," said one customer. On the weekends people didn't seem to care: as long as the beer was flowing and the game was on, our customers were happy. But during the week, with no sports, we were just another sandwich place with no ambience.

So while we were able to pay the bills, we didn't make the extra money we needed to finish the place with extras—like walls, for example—and business started to drop off. We needed to do something, but we had no money to do it with.

Then I remembered Rich Reinhardt.

Rich had come into the real estate office before I left. He had inherited a little money, and he thought an investment in commercial real estate was a good idea. He'd come into the real estate office because he'd been interested in a restaurant we had listed. I told him about the property: it was a small sandwich counter in an office building downtown that sold coffee and muffins in the morning, sandwiches at lunch, and was closed by 3 p.m. It wasn't exactly what he wanted. I tried to sell him on one of the eight duplexes we still had listed, but he wasn't interested in those either. In the end, I took his number and told him I would call him if something came up.

Something did come up. Reggie's needed an investor. I gave him a call.

Rich stopped by Reggie's before we were open for lunch.

He walked in and looked around. We weren't open yet, but you could see into the kitchen, see the food being thrown, and hear the swearing. The two of us sat down. Rich unbuttoned the top button on his sport coat. He had a coffee in his hand. "When are you going to get walls?" he asked.

I told him, "That's where you come in."

He could have walked away. Instead, over the course of our conversation, it became obvious to him that while we worked hard and had the manpower, we just didn't yet have the resources we needed to make Reggie's a success.

Around the same time, Dave got a call from his father-in-law from Pennsylvania. He ran a bank there, and he wanted Dave's wife to join him as a manager. She thought it was a great opportunity and jumped on it. So in the end, Rich bought seventy percent of the place from Dave, who retained twenty percent ownership; and I still had ten percent. In addition, Rich would loan the company the additional money it would need to "finish" the restaurant.

The first thing we did was put a wall between the bar and the kitchen. We might still swear and throw food, but the customers didn't have to see it. We also put in a walk-in fridge and freezer, and we reduced the size of the massive dining room by a third. We partnered with a company that put pool tables in our back room, along with video games like Pac-Man, Defender, and Donkey Kong. They would split the quarters with us. We put a wall in the back that would separate the dining room from the room with our new pool tables and games.

When we were done with the walls, the big-screen TV was much closer to our customers. The place had a much nicer feel, and the service was better once we had the right equipment. Rich also pointed out that while we were busy when a game was on, we were much slower on the other nights. So he came up with the idea of buying a VHS player, renting movies like *Star Wars*, *Superman*, and *Star Trek II: The Wrath of Khan*, and showing them during the week.

But Rich knew that while showing sports and movies was bringing in dinner and weekend crowds, our lunch business was still slow. So he came up with the idea of having us make a bunch of cold sandwiches and salads that he could take to businesses up and down the street and give away for free, so that people could try our food. He knew that the lunch crowd wouldn't be interested in things like nachos, potato skins, or other finger foods people ate with their beers. He also knew that taking tuna melts and meatball subs that would only get cold wouldn't make the kind of impression he wanted.

He was right. Soon after, the lunch crowd started drifting in. We were busy midday. Things were looking up.

We had a very good first year. We made enough to pay the bills, but not enough to pay ourselves. We hoped that we would make enough money to take a salary right from the start, but we knew that any money left over after all the bills were paid was better spent on growing the business. Things like advertising and promotion were far more important than taking any money home right now. If we invested in the business, we thought, we could take even bigger salaries later. Besides, Suzie was still working, so our personal bills were covered.

Then a new sandwich place opened across the street.

It was called The Olde Country Cheese Shop. It was one of those franchises that I disliked, with its Operations Manual and cookie-cutter style. Our customers told us that the sandwiches were great, but I said that there was no way they were better than ours. Still, over the next few months, our lunch traffic decreased.

Then the Tampa Pitcher Show, a combination movie theater

and bar, opened up a few blocks down the road. While we were playing movies that were now on video, the Pitcher Show was playing first-run movies. Our weeknight traffic slowed.

At least we had sports weekends to look forward to. Our customers loved the games, and they loved beer. As long as they kept coming around, Reggie's would be in the black.

Over the next year, we had a loyal core of customers. The same people came on Monday nights, Saturdays, and Sundays for football. But the rest of the time, there were so few customers the place looked like what it had originally been: a huge empty warehouse.

It was a lot of fun working in a bar and getting to watch sports. I'd learned from my father's example, and the only time I bought someone a drink was whenever they bought me one first. But even given all of that, I wasn't bringing home a paycheck, and Rich wasn't going to make the bucks he had hoped for from this place.

We put Reggie's up for sale. It wasn't on the market for long when a potential buyer came around. He called himself JT. He used to sell jewelry, and from the looks of him, whatever he didn't sell he wore. He had rings on almost every finger and enough gold around his neck that Mr. T would be jealous. He asked us a few questions about the sales, but it was clear that he really didn't care. Like us and probably most guys we knew, he wanted to own a sports bar. Besides, what did it matter what we were making? Once he owned it and put his stamp on things, the money would just come rolling in. We didn't tell him differently.

We didn't make money on the deal. We only had enough to pay back Rich's loan.

It seemed to me that I kept falling down. But even in my mid-twenties, it never occurred to me to stay knocked down. From my last $3,000, I'd learned the importance of walls. Plus I had another chance to think, "How do I do better? What's next?"

After Reggie's was no longer ours, Suzie and I finally went to The Olde Country Cheese Shoppe across the street to have lunch. Our customers had been right: their sandwiches were better than ours. They were bigger and had more meat, and even though they cost more, I thought they were worth it. I should have checked them out sooner. Maybe I could have responded and built a better sandwich.

But even as we were eating, I was already thinking aloud about my next project. I told Suzie that the guy who sold us our imported beer and wine had asked what I was going to do after the place was sold. He told me he could get me a job as a liquor salesman, but I wasn't sure if I wanted to go back to work for someone else.

"I kind of like being an entrepreneur," I said to Suzie.

Suzie finished her sandwich and didn't say a word.

Ten

I DON'T EVEN GET TO DRINK THE BEER

We sold Reggie's in 1983. I learned a lot about undercapitalization and understanding the competition. I also met some great people. One of them was Glenn DiMauro.

Glenn was a cobbler who worked at the shoe repair right next door to Reggie's. We drank beer together and played a lot of racquetball. Glenn talked about how he wanted to own his own shoe repair shop. Soon I considered him a friend instead of a just a business neighbor.

I remembered a conversation that I'd had with him in front of the big screen at Reggie's. He told me about the shoe repair business. Did I have any idea how much ladies' heels cost wholesale? I did not. He told me they were nine cents. "And after I repair the shoes with that nine cent part, I get $3.50," he said. That stayed with me.

Around the same time we sold Reggie's, Glenn decided to quit his job and move back to Cleveland to pursue his shoe repair dream. We kept in touch, and I knew we would see each other again.

At the same time, I met another person. I don't remember his name—maybe because I'd like to forget what soon came out of meeting him—but he was about to have a big impact on my life.

He was a salesman for Tampa Wholesale Liquor, the company where we got our wine and imported beer. When we sold Reggie's, he asked me what I was going to do next. When I told him I didn't know, he asked me if I had any sales experience. Of course I did. He told me that there was an opening for a salesman at his company and that he would give me a recommendation.

So the next day I went to Tampa Wholesale Liquor and applied for the job. In some ways, it felt like a step backward to be going to work for someone else again, but what else was I going to do? For the first time since I'd started working in real estate, I had no irons in the fire, and I thought it might be nice for Suzie if I started making some money for a change while I figured out what to do next.

Tampa Wholesale Liquor was in the industrial part of town. On the outside, it looked like all the other warehouses, but when you went inside there were rows and rows of shelves as far as the eye could see. The place was divided into sections. One had bottles of wine from every country of the world. Another had every kind of liquor you could imagine, and then there were shelves and shelves of imported beer. Tampa Wholesale Liquor didn't stock domestic beer like Miller and Budweiser because those brands had their own warehouses and their own separate accounts. But imported beer? *That* we had. We stocked beer from Germany, England, and Canada. And the Canadian beer they sold the most of was Molson Canadian Ale. I may have forgotten the man who introduced me to the job, but I definitely remember the Molson.

I met the manager in a forgettable office. He asked me a lot about my sales experience, and I answered all his questions. But though I didn't tell my interviewer this, I didn't know why you would need any. When it came to liquor, the law in Florida was simple: only one wholesaler could sell each brand. If Tampa Wholesale Liquor sold Bacardi, nobody else could. If you wanted Bacardi at your restaurant or bar, you had to buy it from us. While there was competition about which "well" brands a bar might carry—well brands being the Brand X versions of liquors like vodka and gin you would get if you asked for a "gin and tonic" instead of a "Tanqueray and tonic"—wholesalers in Florida had a virtual monopoly on top-shelf brands. Bacardi rum. Patron tequila. Stolichnaya vodka. Baileys Irish cream. If a restaurant wanted to stock these brands—and of course they wanted to—they had to go through Tampa Wholesale Liquor. Who needed sales experience?

I was assigned a very good area around Tampa. My job would be to drive around and meet with the various restaurant and bar owners and "sell" them liquor, wine, and beer.

The first week, I called on all my accounts. About half of them said that they didn't need to see me, which surprised me. They were happy just to call in their order every week. That was fine with me because I still got the commission.

This was a great job. I got to drive around, talk to people, and sell them beer, liquor, and wine. At the restaurants, I was usually offered something to eat, and when I would call on the bars toward the end of the day, they always offered me a drink. I never had more than one, though, as I didn't want to meet any more trees with my car.

I also made great money. On average I was pulling down $400

a week, which was a lot of money in the early eighties—especially when your rent was only a couple hundred dollars a month. Suzie and I ate out a lot. We went to movies.

I was as far from my childhood in South Philly as I could get, and that was just fine by me.

Then one late afternoon I got a call from one of the restaurants in my territory that would change everything.

The restaurant was out of Molson Canadian Ale. I told them I would have the truck bring some tomorrow, but to hold them over, I would drop off a couple of cases on my way home. I had the guy in the warehouse put two cases in my trunk, and I stopped by the restaurant on my way home to drop them off. I reached into my trunk and, without bending at the knees, grabbed both cases, and lifted them out. As I did, I felt a slight pull in my lower back. I thought nothing about it, and I carried the cases into the restaurant and went home.

The next day I couldn't move. My back was killing me, and there was pain shooting down my right leg. I called in sick, put on a hot pad, and hoped it would get better.

It got worse. I called in sick again the next day, and Tampa Wholesale Liquor gave me the name of a doctor who they thought could help me out. I didn't worry about missing work or losing income: Since I was injured on the job, they put me on workers' comp right away.

I went to the doctor. He immediately suggested that my injury was just a muscle pull.

"I think it's much worse than that," I suggested. "I'm in pretty serious pain."

"It's *my* job to determine what your injury is," he said, stiffly. Okay, fine, I thought. Doctors are typically skeptical of people claiming that back pain is preventing them from going to work, and this one was no exception. But after many tests and x-rays over the next few weeks, they determined that I had ruptured a disc in my back and I would need surgery.

For those of you fortunate enough never to have had back problems, the vertebrae are bones that stack to form the spinal column. A disc is the fleshy tissue between the vertebrae that acts like a shock absorber, cushioning the load on the spinal column. After lifting the case, one of these discs in my lower back had bulged and ruptured. The doctor's solution at the time? Since the disc was out of alignment, all he had to do was shave it, shape it, and everything would be fine.

Only as I found out, it wasn't. We have discs in our backs for a reason, and preservation of those little shock absorbers is vital.

I had only been with Tampa Wholesale Liquor a few months. Suzie and I had been married for two and a half years. It was a couple of weeks before my twenty-eighth birthday, and I was going under the knife. We were both worried about what was, in those days, a major surgery, but the doctors told me not to worry. I was young and in shape, so I would be back on my feet in no time.

I believed them.

As soon as I woke up from the operation, the doctor remarked on how bad the damage had been, much worse than he had thought.

"You must have been in serious pain," he said.

"I told you before that I was in serious pain!" I told him. "You should've believed me at the time!"

"I guess so," he said, dismissively. "How do you feel now?"

"I'm *still* in terrible pain."

"Give it time," he told me.

But time didn't help. I was in the hospital for a week following the operation, and after that I went into physical therapy. They told me I would be back to work in a few weeks. Those weeks went by, and not only did I not get better, I got worse. The doctors put me on muscle relaxers and narcotic pain killers like Percocet and Vicodin. They helped to dull the pain, but they dulled my brain as well. I thought that while I was laid up I could at least read or study some new things, but I was so doped up I could only sleep.

After a few months of this, I confronted my doctor. "Right after the surgery, you know how bad you said the pain must have been?" I asked him. "Well, the pain is worse now."

Finally, he redid the x-rays, and he performed a test called a myelogram. The myelogram was a very painful experience. I was in a standard hospital gown—you know; the one that your butt hangs out of? And they lay you on a cold metal table, stomach down. There is a big x-ray machine above you, and it takes a few x-rays of your back. Then a doctor puts a very large needle right into the spinal canal—which runs next to the vertebrae and which contains the vital nerve roots that control bodily functions—and fills it with dye to see if the bulging discs are compressing the spinal canal. As your entire spinal canal fills with this fluid, you feel the pressure and plenty of pain. This test took over thirty minutes, and I was awake for every excruciating minute of it.

I spent the night in the hospital. The nurses told me that I had to sleep with my head propped up or I would get a massive headache. I slept with my head propped up, and I got a massive headache anyway.

The test revealed that the damage to my lower back was worse than anyone had thought. Now the doctor said that there might be a problem with the disc above the one they'd worked on. I would need a second operation.

I wanted to ask him, *This time, will I really get better?* But I didn't, because it wasn't as if I had any choice. So only four months after the first surgery, I went back into the hospital for another.

Financially, we were doing okay. I was getting workers' comp, and my boss at Tampa Wholesale Liquor was calling on my customers for me until I was finally well enough to work again. And Suzie had her job managing Wuv's Chicken and Biscuits. None of it added up to as much money as I had been making at Tampa Wholesale Liquor, but we weren't going out for dinner or to the movies now, so we didn't need a lot of money. But it still bothered me that Suzie had to go off to work and take care of me. I didn't have any problem with her working when I was trying to make my fortune with real estate or the bar—at those times, we were in it together. But I no longer felt like I was pulling my weight.

Still, the doctors told me—again—that I would be on my feet and back to work in just a few weeks. Again, I believed them.

After the surgery they put me on morphine. To me, this was a miracle drug. One minute I was in serious pain, and then after a shot of morphine, I was on the top of the world. I felt warm and safe.

I'd known that my father was an alcoholic, and I'd known that he was addicted to opiates. I knew that addiction could run in the family, as well, and I'd had my own run-in with drinking too much, which ended with my car accident. Don't get me wrong: I really don't think that there was any similarity between us, and I never worried about hereditary addiction. But suddenly, after taking morphine, I understood how people could get hooked on drugs, and that scared me.

The morphine regimen lasted a week.

After I was released from the hospital, I was put on Vicodin and Flexeril, the muscle relaxer. I spent my days studying financial planning and a little bit of Italian, and once again, I was sent to physical therapy three times a week. For the first few months, my back was starting to feel stronger, and I was able to walk more and more each day. At one point, they had me lifting weights on a machine, and the doctor even brought other patients in to show me off as one of his success stories.

But weeks turned into months and months, and then a year. Even at my best, I never really got to where I had been before that first operation. Soon, though, I realized that not only was I not getting better: I was getting worse.

So I went back to the hospital for another painful myelogram. Again, the news wasn't good. I'd had discs clipped and shaved and cut, and it was painful. But now the discs above those weren't working either. They couldn't take the additional pressure or strain from the discs missing from my lower back. The doctors said that the only thing they could do was a back fusion.

"You've had your chance," I told my doctor. "You've had two. Why should I trust you?"

He tried to explain what was happening in my back. I'd developed degenerative disc disease—or "failed back syndrome." (I've always assumed that he meant that I'd have had this problem eventually anyway, and that the initial injury just accelerated it. But some doctor reading this may disagree.) Because of the disease, I was inevitably going to have to have a fusion done, and it might as well be now. The fusion would stop the degeneration, he said. Soon I would be on my feet and back to work.

I got a second opinion from an orthopedic surgeon whom I'd heard good things about. He agreed that the fusion was my only option. I convinced him to do the surgery, working together with my initial doctor (a neurologist.) My initial doctor wasn't happy about this, but I told him that if we were going to do this, we'd do it my way.

I even got a third opinion. Suzie's mother worked for another orthopedic surgeon in California, so I flew out to ask his advice. He studied the films I'd brought, and after thinking about it, he told me that he didn't know whether the fusion would make me better or not. "But if you're not getting any better," he told me, "you should think seriously about it."

I wasn't getting any better. What's more, I'd learned that my boss at Tampa Wholesale Liquor had hired someone to replace me. That wasn't as serious as it sounds—because of the way workers' comp laws worked, he'd have to give me my old job back, or one comparable to it, as soon as I got better. But it definitely helped to convince me that if I wanted to get better, and if physical therapy wasn't helping me anymore, the back fusion was my only choice.

Plus, I was only twenty-nine, I'd been in treatment for a year and a half now, and I was tired of being in pain and on drugs. So again, I decided to trust my doctors. I told them to do it.

In 1985, when doctors were performing a back fusion, there were no titanium rods, no minimally invasive techniques with small incisions and arthroscopic tools that reduced the amount of damage to the muscles and tendons. Instead, they made a six-inch cut in my back and removed the four bottom discs from my spinal column, and then they augured out bone from my pelvis. Imagine you just pulled a carton of ice cream from your freezer, and that ice cream is very hard. You take your ice cream scoop and you lean in and push down into the frozen block, but you are only able to scrape out a little at a time. That's what they did to my pelvis, and as they scraped out a little bone at a time, they used it to build a bridge connecting the four lower vertebrae.

They might as well have been hacking at it with a machete.

This operation lasted over eight hours, and afterward I was in intensive care for days. I spent a couple of weeks in the hospital, and then I was home. Physical therapy wouldn't start for a few weeks, giving the bones a chance to fuse. I was taking a lot of drugs, so I wasn't in much pain, but all I did was sleep.

I started physical therapy, but my back did not get better. Finally, after a few months, I asked my doctors what the next step would be, the next treatment we could try to achieve a full recovery.

But the doctors gave up before I did. They told me they had done all they could, but I had degenerative disc disease—failed back syndrome—and my back would now always hurt. They told me that I would probably never work again, and that I should apply for disability.

Failed back syndrome? It sounded more like failed *doctor* syndrome to me. But the state of Florida agreed with them and notified me that they could no longer send me weekly workers' comp checks. They would pay for any medical bills relating to my back for as long as I needed it, but they would be sending me a one-time check to settle the compensation portion. I was currently receiving $200 a week from them, so they would send me three years of payments up front—$40,000—and then they would be done with me.

I thought that was a lot of money. When I think about it now, I realize it wasn't much for someone in his twenties who was never going to work again.

I was depressed, and I was taking plenty of drugs. I slept and took pills, and I quit going to physical therapy. What was the point? I was twenty-nine years old and I was never going to work again. I wasn't going to play tennis or racquetball, and I wasn't going to fulfill any of my aspirational dreams about the life I wanted for me and my wife.

My mother, who I'm sure thought she was helping, would talk to Suzie about her life taking care of a disabled husband and how it had all worked out fine. I hadn't yet told Suzie about how bad things were in the projects, and I didn't tell her now. I had been disabled for two years now, and so far, Suzie had stuck with me. I wanted to keep it that way.

And for a long time, I had told her—and believed—that this was only a temporary setback, that soon I would be back on my feet and working again to achieve our dreams. But now, here I sat, ready to apply for Social Security disability and maybe even food stamps. Hell, maybe there was even a housing project in Tampa I could move into.

This was not my plan.

So one day I sat in my bedroom, ready to take my pain pills. The financial news was on, and there was a segment playing about the life of some rich person. I lay there and watched it, thinking, *I was going to be one of those rich guys. Now here I am, going the opposite direction.*

That's when I suddenly decided: I wasn't going to be my father. This wasn't the life I wanted, and Suzie certainly didn't deserve it. I wasn't ready to give up.

So I called to Suzie. I gave her my mountain of pills.

"Flush them," I told her. "Flush them all. I'm getting the hell out of bed."

Eleven

SHOE REPAIR, MORE REAL ESTATE, AND A HOUSE OF CARDS

After Suzie and I flushed away my narcotics, the first question that occurred to the two of us was, what's next?

My mind went back to Glenn DiMauro, my friend from Reggie's who'd gone off to Cleveland to open a shoe repair store. In one of our regular phone conversations, after I'd given up on hack doctors and narcotics, my mind went to the markup he'd mentioned on heels: from nine cents to $3.50.

"Do you think you could use a partner?" I asked him.

Glenn quickly mentioned that I didn't know how to fix shoes, but I told him I knew plenty about sales and marketing. Glenn went on to say that he didn't think I'd be willing to move to Cleveland, but that if I were, he'd be happy to have me join him in his business there.

I really wasn't interested in moving to Cleveland. Glenn had ties there to his family and his in-laws, but I had none. Plus, it was freezing there. So I asked him: why didn't he just come back to Tampa, where it was sunny, and we'd open a shoe repair shop of our own?

After very little thought, Glenn and his wife agreed. They thought it was cold in Cleveland too, and they missed the sun of Florida. They were coming back.

Slowly, since I still wasn't able to do much, I scouted locations for our new business. I could only spend an hour a day driving before I had to lie down.

But I knew what we were looking for. Instead of leasing a large space and hoping that the customers would come, like I'd done with Reggie's, I looked for something small. I found a space available in a new shopping center in an area just north of Tampa called Carrollwood. It was a corner shop that was 400 square feet, about the size of an average bedroom. By comparison, Reggie's had been 3,000 square feet.

When Glenn and his wife arrived a few months later, I had the space almost completely set up, including a lounge chair (the cheap woven plastic kind that rusted in the rain) behind the wall that separated the counter from the shop. I needed a place to lie down, but I didn't want the customers who came in thinking that business was so slow I could take a nap. Behind the wall, I could work and recline during the slow times that I hoped wouldn't come.

All we needed was the shoe repair equipment Glenn brought with him. If you've never been in the back of a shoe repair, you have no idea how big and bulky this equipment can be. I don't think it's changed much in a hundred years. There are motors and belts that move wheels with sandpaper on them to grind down the rubber and leather on a shoe, and there are other wheels that trim the excess. If you didn't know the machines were for fixing shoes, you would think they came out of some medieval dungeon.

Glenn knew how to use all of them. What's more, he was not only a craftsman but a flirt. He had curly dark hair, a beard, and a swagger that made all the counter girls swoon. His wife was a good-looking blonde with windswept hair who didn't seem to mind Glenn's charm when it was directed at other women.

Initially, the two of them seemed like a happy couple. But Glenn's wife was superstitious. And unknown to us, she had consulted a fortune teller, who told her that a chaotic influence—or as I learned later, a *snake*—would come into her life. Glenn thought it was funny, because he thought he was the chaotic one.

Later, we learned that Glenn's wife hadn't seen her fortune that way. She thought the snake was me. Soon enough, we'd all find that out.

As Glenn set up his equipment in the back, I started advertising. I ran an ad in the local paper, *The Carrollwood News*, with a special: *Ladies' Heels Repaired for 99 Cents . . . No Limit!!!*

On the day we opened, women were lined up out the door. They had bags of shoes. Some of them told us that they had planned to throw them out, but for 99 cents, why not get them fixed?

It was 1986, when women's shoes tended to be cheaply made and gaudy. But "cheap" didn't describe our clientele. Our business was in a well-heeled part of Tampa, and "well-heeled" was what we got. That doesn't mean we didn't get some cheap shoes. We charged so little that ladies brought in bags of the cheap stuff. But we also got plenty of Ferragamos and Jimmy Choos, the kinds of shoes that at this point in my life had seen and done more than I was still dreaming about.

Glenn knew this was a chance to build the business from the start, so he decided that he wouldn't just replace the heels, he would also fix anything else that was wrong with the shoe. If the leather was torn around the heel, he would glue it down. If the color had faded, he would polish them and bring the color back. When people came to pick up their shoes, they thought they had brand new shoes again. We started saying that at DiMauro's Shoe Repair, we "made the old new again for a fraction of the cost."

Our business took off. No other shoe repair advertised, and they certainly didn't run the kinds of specials we were running. Soon we had more business than our little shop could handle. We had to hire counter help.

Glenn was in charge of that, and he hired the youngest, cutest girls he could find.

I asked Suzie to join us, and at twenty-five years old she was the oldest girl there, but she didn't work the counter. She'd finally had enough of counter work, had enough of Wuv's. Glenn's work was a good fit for her. She already knew how to sew and use a sewing machine, but the kind of sewing you do in the shoe repair business requires much bigger needles and a commercial-grade sewing machine that could sew through the leather used to harness Clydesdales like the ones we'd seen in Busch Gardens. Glenn taught her how to use them, as well as how to do rip and tear work on shoes and other leather items.

We had been in that small corner spot for about a year when a bigger spot about three times the size became available. We didn't even have enough room to store the shoes we had to repair in that small shop, so we decided to move.

Once we were in the new store, Glenn hired more cute young counter help and a shoemaker's apprentice. We were making more money than we dreamed possible, but we were also working sixteen hours a day, seven days a week. Of course I spent most of that time lying down, but I could do the books, write ads, and even shine shoes from my lounge chair. It may have been cheap, but it kept the pressure on my back to a minimum.

Business was so good that we decided to expand the shoe repair to a second location. A few miles north of our neighborhood, Carrollwood, was a town called Land O' Lakes. A lot of our customers came from there. We thought we might get even more business if we had a shop right in town where they could drop off and pick up their shoes. The Land O' Lakes location had no equipment, just a counter and a person to staff it.

There were a few hiccups in our drop-off service, and it never did as well as our Carrollwood location, but it still did well enough to pay for itself and add some additional profit to the business.

It was the middle of the Big Eighties. Women permed their hair and wore clothing with shoulder pads that made them look like linebackers. Men were trading in their disco attire for linen suits and pastel T-shirts like the ones on *Miami Vice*. On MTV, Dire

Straits was singing, "Money for nothing and chicks for free." If you'd told me when we first started expanding that the two concepts in that song would bring us tumbling down in the end, I would've laughed in your face.

Our business was not only thriving, but we were expanding. If we wanted to keep expanding, we knew we might at some point have to borrow money from the bank. So we made sure we showed every penny of income in case we ever needed a loan.

And I kept good books. Personal computers were becoming more and more popular. I'd never stopped being intrigued by them since Johnson and I had studied how they worked in his room after school. So I kept up with new software like Lotus 1-2-3 and WordPerfect, and I used both to help manage the business and keep track of our sales and profits.

This came back to bite us big time when we filed our first tax return, but hey, we were happy to be in the bracket that we were in. Still, we thought about how we could invest this money. Ideally, we'd invest it in a business that had a favorable tax treatment.

That's how I got back into real estate. It seemed like the right thing to do. Besides, I'd had experience. I knew what mistakes to avoid, didn't I?

As our sales increased, it became more and more urgent to find a house to invest in, and soon we found our first. It was a nice three-bedroom, two-bath house in a good neighborhood. It had an assumable mortgage, and the seller needed to move fast due to a job transfer. The house was listed at slightly below market value, but I didn't care about that. I cared about the terms. I told the seller that I would give him his full asking price, but I wanted him to take a second mortgage—that is, I wanted to buy the house for no money down. I also asked him to pay the closing costs.

He turned us down, but I knew he didn't have a lot of time, so I told him that if he changed his mind, he should give me a call. Two weeks later he did, and we had our first house.

Now we needed a renter.

Neither Glenn nor I had the time to manage the house, so we hired a real estate management firm. They charged ten percent of the rent, but they said they would handle everything. That is, not only would they find the renter, they would collect the rent and deal with any issues. When a toilet overflowed in the middle of the night, the tenants would call the management firm, not us.

The only problem was that the rent the management firm told us we could get was about $300 a month less than we were paying for the two mortgages. After thinking about it, we decided that this was okay. The shoe repair could cover the negative cash flow and create a tax break at the same time. Besides, we weren't trying to make money off the rent: For now, we just wanted the tax benefits. The appreciation would come later.

Our accountant told us we couldn't do it legally. The shoe repair was a business, and we were buying a house. The shoe repair business couldn't pay for our house and take a write off—unless, of course, we were willing to form corporations.

So that's what we did. The shoe repair became Cobbler's International Incorporated, and the real estate business became Saint Mauro Incorporated, after Glenn's last name and mine. (After all, *Santino* in Italian means *Little Saint*.) Cobbler's International owned Saint Mauro. Now we were legal.

Glenn was the president of both corporations. He was a great guy, but he had an ego. He loved being president. He loved that the shoe repair was called DiMauro's.

I was only the vice president, and that worked for me. I didn't need my name on the sign; I just loved taking money to the bank. Besides, as the vice president, I always had the "out" of telling salespeople and others that I would have to clear things with the president before I could give them an official answer.

In the second year of our business, things continued to expand. We opened a third location of DiMauro's Shoe Repair in the Town 'n' Country neighborhood of Tampa, and we bought more houses for the tax breaks. By the end of the second year, we owned five houses. We had yet to put any money down.

We also never qualified for a single mortgage. Every time, we bought fully assumable FHA and VA mortgages. Our cash flow on the houses was negative, but we were making tons of money in DiMauro's Shoe Repair to compensate. Besides, we didn't need cash—at least not then. We had plenty of that.

Some of these houses needed work, so we hired my brother Dennis to do it. When we drew him in, we formed our third corporation, Brothers Three Incorporated. Before long, we had seven houses, three shoe repair shops, and three corporations: Brothers

Three, Saint Mauro, and Cobbler's International. It seemed like the more we expanded our house of cards, the more we succeeded.

And we were sure that once we got the appreciation—that is, once these houses went up in value and we could sell them for a profit—we could reduce our massive negative cash flow.

Then one of our houses sat vacant for a while. The real estate management company wasn't making that empty property a priority. We knew we'd have to make a change.

My uncle Joe was also in real estate. He said he could manage the properties for us. Uncle Joe was one of the few people at my father's burial, and he had been the first person my mom had called to help her when my father died. He did a great job helping my mother, and I knew he'd do a great job keeping our houses rented. Plus, I loved keeping money in the family.

By the end of the third year, we owned fifteen single-family homes along with our three shoe repair shops. We were all working together, and we had my brother and uncle in the business, too. Our businesses were doing well, and we were finally living the good life.

Glenn and his wife lived in a great two-bedroom condo with a loft, and Suzie and I lived in a three-bedroom house on a large corner lot with a pool and a hot tub, as well as plenty of space inside for me to lie down. Glenn and Suzie loved sports cars, so we bought each of them a Datsun 300zx Turbo. Suzie loved driving that sporty car, which was low in front to hug the road and higher in back. It was shaped a little bit like a lady's shoe.

In short, this was what I'd dreamed about when I was a kid in the projects so many years ago, when something as simple as going to the movies required me to help someone home with their groceries or shovel someone's sidewalk to earn enough money for a ticket. Now I could go to theaters whenever I wanted.

Then the house of cards all came crashing down.

Glenn and his wife started to have problems. I don't know when I first heard Glenn talking about her in derogatory terms. It could've been any time—after all, Glenn and I were not only business partners, we were still good friends, although I could no longer play racquetball with him because of my back. But we still went to sports bars together, he always told me about his personal life, and I told him about mine.

I remember one night when Glenn was complaining. "My wife wants me to work fewer hours. I told her we were trying to build a business. She said I spent more time with you than I do with her. So I said, 'Screw you!'"

At first I didn't think much about it—every couple has their ups and downs. But it quickly became apparent that there wasn't going to be another "up." Their marriage was falling apart, and fast. I tried to step in and be the voice of reason, but his wife didn't want to hear anything I had to say. After all, she thought I was the "snake."

Finally, she wanted a divorce. I knew we were in no position to liquidate any of our assets, so I told Glenn to offer her a settlement—in the form of a note, of course. We had some cash, but we needed it to cover the negative cash flow from our properties. But she wouldn't go for what we were offering.

Once they both hired lawyers, I knew that our businesses were in real trouble.

Ours was a very simple business plan. The shoe repairs made the money. The houses lost the money, but the shoe repair covered those losses. At some point, we would start selling houses and our investments would pay off. But before then, if any one of these things changed, we would be screwed.

I told that to Glenn's lawyer. He, in turn, told Glenn's wife's lawyer, but they didn't care.

Shortly after, Cobbler's International was hit with an injunction, which meant that Saint Mauro's was hit with an injunction as well. We could no longer funnel money from the shoe repairs to pay the mortgages for the houses. Again, I tried to tell Glenn's lawyer that the rent from our properties didn't cover the mortgages, but he didn't care. At this point, I don't think anyone other than me understood the kind of trouble we were in—not even Glenn.

Some divorces can be amicable. This one was not.

I was called as a witness to the divorce proceedings. They called me because I was keeping the books. Fortunately, I had been doing my job, and I knew they were in perfect order. Of course, I remembered the last time I was in court, when I was trying to get rid of the deadbeat renter. Even though we were in the right, the judge still gave the people more time to squat in our house for free. I hoped that this judge would be different.

But then the judge asked me about the revenue for the shops. I told him that everything was there in the books.

"What about the revenue not in the books?" he asked.

"We've showed everything," I said.

"No cash business shows all its revenue," he said. "Therefore, I'm going to assume your sales are twice what you're showing."

Shocked, I tried to reply, but Glenn's wife's lawyer objected, and the judge dismissed me from the stand.

I didn't understand. We were trying to build a business that employed a lot of leverage, and I'd been scrupulous about showing all our revenue. And now I was being told that no one does that? I thought that this time, we were finally screwed.

I had no idea.

The next week, Uncle Joe told me that one of our tenants didn't pay the rent. I had been through this before, and I knew that even if we moved fast, it would be months before we could get that tenant out and another one in. So I told my uncle to put the house up for sale.

Immediately, Glenn and I were summoned to court again.

"It has come to my attention that you are trying to sell one of your houses," said the judge.

"It's true," I said, "but you don't understand our situation."

The judge said, "You can't sell anything until this divorce is settled."

I tried to explain the negative cash flow, and pointed out that because of the injunction, the money from the shoe repairs was going into escrow rather than helping to slow the cash leak. If we couldn't use the shoe repair money, and if we couldn't sell a house whose tenants weren't paying us rent, our business was going to unravel, and soon.

"I guess the parties should be very motivated to settle quickly," said the judge.

But Glenn and his wife weren't.

To make matters worse, we were being stalked. Glenn's wife's lawyer had hired a guy to watch the stores and count the customers to try and come up with their own revenue numbers. But how would they know whether someone was picking up a pair of ladies' heels they'd just paid ninety-nine cents for or men's soles for thirty dollars?

It wasn't long before the house with the nonpaying tenant was behind in mortgage payments and in foreclosure. Glenn's wife's lawyer accused us of hiding money and of letting the house go into foreclosure to somehow hurt her. Her lawyer called for an audit.

Sadly, it took the auditors months to discover that we weren't lying when we said that if we couldn't sell our properties, we had nothing. By then, a few more houses were in foreclosure, and more were vacant. The judge finally came up with a settlement. Glenn's wife would get the house they lived in, plus a few more—in particular, the ones that weren't in foreclosure yet. Glenn would keep the shoe repair shops, but for a while, he'd have to pay her half of the profits.

But it was too late. There was no money left after legal fees and negative cash flow. We never got to sell a house, and since we'd only owned them for a few years, we didn't get the appreciation we'd counted on.

There was nothing we could do but shut it all down. And the only way to do that was by declaring corporate and personal bankruptcy. We lost everything. I even heard that Glenn's ex-wife declared bankruptcy. Her lawyers never got paid.

It was a hell of a ride. We went from nothing, to being on top of the world, to nothing again. I had been poor before, but, I'll tell you, it's worse being poor after you've been rich. When I grew up in the projects, I could only dream about the kind of life I wanted. While we were building our empire, I felt like I finally had that life.

But the feeling you get in the pit of your stomach when someone is pounding on your door to repossess your stuff, or seeing the look on your wife's face when they take away her cool car, is something I'll never forget and something I never want to feel again. We could no longer afford our house with the pool and space for me to lie down. When the creditors were done with us, all Suzie and I had left was our furniture and one car—and not the sporty one.

I had to come up with a plan, and fast.

Twelve

GET OVER IT

When Suzie and I had been married for five years, she began to talk about starting a family. I didn't think it was a good time, not with us trying to start the shoe repair business with Glenn, so I bought her a dog.

A while back, I had seen a man walking a Sheltie down the street. Thinking it was a collie, I asked him how old the dog was.

He said, "Seven years."

"Seven years? Then why's it so small?" I asked.

He told me that the dog was a full grown Sheltie. I thought that was cool and told Suzie about it, and ever since then we'd wanted one. So when we were ready to look for a dog, I looked in the paper for a dog breeder who had Sheltie puppies, and Suzie and I went there to pick one out. She named him Mikey, and he was a very smart, playful puppy. Suzie took him on walks and taught him tricks, and for a while, she stopped talking about starting a family.

Mikey satisfied Suzie for about two years. Then she asked me again about when we were going to start a family. We were still involved in the shoe repair business, and I thought that this wasn't a good time either. So I bought her another Sheltie. This one she named Tanya. Both Mikey and Tanya were purebred Shelties, and when Tanya was old enough, we started to breed them. Suzie loved having the little puppies around and was always sad when we sold them.

Tanya had a couple of litters, and we decided to stop breeding her, but we kept one of the puppies from her last litter. We named her Brandy, bringing our total number of dogs to three.

Our three dogs kept Suzie busy, but it wasn't long before she asked about us starting a family again.

"And don't buy me another dog," she warned.

Our shoe repair business was falling apart, and I pointed out that we would probably end up bankrupt, but Suzie didn't care. She said that if we waited until everything was perfect, we would never have a kid. So at the beginning of 1989, in spite of my disability and being bankrupt, we decided to try to have our first child.

We also decided to move to California. Suzie's parents lived out there, true, but I had another reason in mind. In the years since he'd left the military, my childhood friend Mark Johnson had never left my life. He and I were learning a lot about computers and software, and I was using that knowledge to help manage all of our businesses.

According to Johnson, an area called Silicon Valley was beginning to develop, and there were lots of opportunities in the tech industry. Why not head west and get one of those jobs? I certainly wouldn't have to be on my feet all day like I was in the fast food business. A job sitting behind a desk working with computers sounded like the next logical step.

We'd lost everything and were starting over again. This sucked, but I'd been knocked down before, and I wasn't ready to give up on my dreams of building a successful life for Suzie and me.

I'd always wanted to be successful, even when I was selling tomatoes from the back of a truck. But it was even more important to me now that I had a wife and a back problem that wouldn't go away. Suzie had stood by me through three start-ups by this point, and as a result, she had watched her car be repossessed. I wanted to give her and our future family the financial security we deserved. And our best shot to do this, I thought, was in California.

Our immediate problem was this: How were we going to get there? With my mauled back, there was no way I could drive a truck across the country. We had no money to hire movers. Then Glenn solved our problem. He said that now that everything was gone—his wife, his business, and his counter girls—he had no reason to stay in Florida. So he decided that he would go with us, and he could do most of the driving.

We rented a twenty-six-foot U-Haul and loaded what was left of our furniture. We also rented a flatbed trailer to pull behind it that we would put my car on, and in that car we would put our three Shelties. We would make many stops along the way to let them out to run and play. That was the theory, and at least the dogs seemed happy about the plan while we were still in the driveway.

The first thing we discovered about the trailer was that it had sides. Makes sense, right? You're traveling with a car on a flatbed, you don't want the car to fall off the side. But when I'd made this plan, I'd thought that the trailer would have movable sides so that you could open the car door. Instead, the sides blocked the door from opening altogether. I didn't figure out how much of a problem this would be until I drove the car onto the trailer and tried to get out. I had to squeeze myself through a window. For the entire trip we would have to reach through the partially open window with a stick and open it the rest of the way in order to get the dogs out.

We were finally ready to start: Suzie, Glenn, and I in the front seat of the truck, everything we owned in our twenty-six-foot U-Haul, and the dogs in the car being pulled behind us. We headed west across the panhandle of Florida in our modern-day equivalent of a wagon train.

Soon, we came to the Mississippi River.

Since she was a kid, Suzie'd been afraid of driving over bridges. She'd never refused to go over one, but then again, she'd never had to go over the bridge that went over the Mississippi River. This bridge looked as if it went straight to the sky, and it was so long that we couldn't see the end. Suzie had a look of terror on her face that I had never seen before.

When she saw that massive structure, she yelled, "STOP!"

Glenn, who was driving, said, "Stop and do what?"

"Go around," Suzie said.

Go around the Mississippi River? I didn't think so.

Even though I didn't realize it at the time, Suzie was already pregnant. If I'd known that she was pregnant, would I have told

Glenn to pull over and negotiated? Would I have asked Suzie what we could do to make this easier for her? No. Because the fact is that when you're crossing the country, you can't go around the Mississippi River.

I said, "Sorry, Suzie, you'll just have to close your eyes. Glenn, punch it."

And over the river we went.

Next we had to get to Texas, where my sister Madelyn lived and where we were going to spend the night.

Before we got there, I decided to try driving, even though I had never driven a stick before. Especially not in a twenty-six-foot U-Haul truck that was pulling a car containing three Shelties. Glenn talked me through it pretty well at first, but he was napping when we hit the border of Texas. Suddenly, we saw a sign telling everyone to pull over, and I had to downshift. I had no idea how to do that.

I yelled at Glenn, napping in shotgun, to get up to talk me through downshifting to a stop. By the time Glenn woke up and talked me through it, I was panicked and yelling. Glenn yelled back as we rolled to a jerking, violent stop. What we didn't know was that the border guards were watching.

One of them approached the car. "What's all the yelling about?" he asked.

I didn't think we needed to tell him about driving stick. Instead, I asked him why we were being stopped by border guards. "We never left the country," I said. "What's the point of a border stop?"

"What country are you from?" he asked.

I was confused, so I said, "This one."

"And which one is that?" he asked.

"America."

"What part of America?"

"Are we in Texas?"

"Yes."

"Then this part of America."

I don't know what part of my confusion he found threatening, but he did not look amused as he asked me to get out of the truck and show him my ID. After looking at my driver's license, he shoved it back in my face.

"See here," he said. "You're from Florida, and that is in the *United States of America*. The next time someone asks, that's what country you're from."

I felt like asking if I was still in the *United States of America*, but I thought I'd better not push my luck. Glenn took over driving for a while.

Soon we were at my sister's house in Houston. We were hot and tired when we got there, and we still had 2,000 miles to go before we reached Suzie's parents' townhouse in San Jose.

We spent the night and woke up refreshed. As soon as we were all packed up and loaded, Glenn gunned the engine of the truck. There was a large bang. We got out of the truck and opened the hood. The radiator had exploded, and green fluid was everywhere.

We had to spend another night in Houston while the closest U-Haul garage replaced the radiator.

The next day we were on our way again. It took us almost a day to cross Texas, New Mexico, and Arizona before we hit the California border. Suzie even tried to drive a little, but she had been getting carsick—or so we thought. We would learn in a few weeks that she was actually pregnant with our first child.

Once we reached California, the border police stopped us again. I was driving, but I had finally mastered downshifting to a roll without fishtailing or stripping the gears. And I knew that this time, when he asked what country I was from, I would be ready for the answer.

Instead, he asked me if we had any fruit with us.

"I have an apple we bought in Arizona."

"You can't bring that into California," he said.

"What can I do with it?"

"Either throw it away or eat it."

"If I eat it, I'll still be bringing it into California." I said.

He didn't see the humor in that. "What's in the back of the truck?"

"Furniture?"

"Did you pick up any people? Are they in the back?"

"No."

I don't know what he could've seen in us other than complete cluelessness, but he asked us to open the truck anyway. By now we had driven over 2,000 miles with our stuff in the back of the truck, and it had moved around during the trip. When we started to open the back, a box spring started to fall out, and then a lamp to its right fell over.

The cop yelled, "Close the truck before the whole thing comes crashing out!"

It would be years before I heard the word *coyote* used to label something other than the canine, and before I learned that we probably could have made extra money picking up people from Mexico and hiding them behind our poorly secured furniture—if we'd wanted to, of course. As long as we didn't bring any fruits with us.

Once we were in California, we still had about 500 miles to go to Suzie's parents' townhouse. None of us had showered in a while, and we were all tired and stinky.

The route had us taking I-5 north until we got to 152, where we would head to Gilroy across mountains called the Diablo Range— a name which was much more prophetic than we realized—and then north to San Jose. We thought about stopping at a rest stop before getting onto 152, but we had learned along the way that a fully loaded twenty-six-foot truck pulling a trailer with a car on it didn't go very fast over hills and mountains, and we were so close that we just wanted to get there.

But we had no idea what was going to happen on the narrow mountain pass. This was a very steep grade, and even with the gas pedal all the way to the floor, the fastest we could go was fifteen miles an hour. It was dark now, and this was a one-lane road. The cars behind us were backing up for miles.

Just before we reached the top, another lane came onto the right side of the road. We assumed it was a shoulder where we could pull over so that the cars could pass. We were relieved, and we pulled over just in time to hear a loud horn. A yellow Volkswagen beetle passed us on the left, and then a large semi that had been merging into our lane abruptly swerved back into the left lane, almost hitting us. We weren't on the shoulder—this was a short, temporary lane that trucks were supposed to pull into while cars passed on the left. But the trucks were supposed to keep moving, not stop—as we learned the hard way.

Months later, when we returned in the daylight, we finally saw the steep cliff by the turnout. I had been in car accidents before, but the drop to the canyon below still took my breath away, thinking about what had almost happened to us and our caravan of furniture and dogs. This treacherous pass deserved the name *Devil*.

Finally we arrived in San Jose. There was a parking space large enough for us in front of the townhouse where Suzie's parents lived. It was the first thing that had seemed to go right for us during the entire journey, and we pulled right in.

When Suzie's father saw where we had parked, he said, "You can't leave the truck there. That's the bus stop."

"They can tow us," I said, and all three of us found a guest bedroom or sofa and crashed.

Thirteen

SHOULDN'T YOU BE LOOKING FOR A JOB?

After a very nice sleep in a very nice bed, we were ready to get moving again.

We had no place to live in San Jose, but Suzie's parents had a second home in a little town called Angwin. Angwin was in the mountains about 1,600 feet above the city of St. Helena in the Napa Valley. It was a sleepy little town with one gas station, one grocery store, and Pacific Union College.

The town was quiet except for the birds, and the view of the valley from the balcony of the house was magnificent. Western sunsets from the deck; rows and terraces of grapevines. There were enormous evergreens that made the air smell like pine. There were birds in the bird bath in the back yard. It was easy to sit and forget that there was a world outside the mountain slope.

This was the house my in-laws were going to retire to some-day, but for now, they told us we could stay there until we found a place to rent of our own and a job in San Jose. Suzie's parents would stay in Angwin on the weekends, but we would have the place to ourselves during the week. So we put our furniture in the garage (the house was already furnished), and we moved in.

We should have been looking at help-wanted ads in the newspaper. But we had just been through an ordeal, we told ourselves. In fact, we'd been through several, counting the trip west, the bankruptcies, and my back surgeries. We needed to decompress, we told ourselves. And we were in the Napa Valley, the home to some of the best wines in the world.

So instead of looking for jobs, we started to explore. This was 1989, before the tourist trade had completely taken over the valley and before wineries started to charge for tastings. So tasting is what we did. We went from winery to winery, and Glenn and I would drink and eat the crackers and cheese they put out. Suzie didn't drink, so we always had a driver.

No drinking and driving for me. I learned that lesson.

Sadly, after a few weeks Glenn's father took ill, and he had to go back to Cleveland. Glenn had been a very good friend and a very important person in my life for a while now. He would return briefly to California after visiting his father, but he would eventually return to Florida and later to Cleveland, where he would once again own a shoe repair business. This time, I hoped things would go better for him with the counter girls.

Even though Glenn was gone, Suzie and I still didn't start looking for jobs. I still needed decompression time, I figured. Suzie was two months' pregnant and carsick even now that we weren't in a car.

Our days were simple. Get up and have breakfast, lightly clean the house, head down the hill to the wineries, and then head back up to sunbathe in the backyard and take a nap. It was a pretty good life. For the first time since I'd lifted that case of beer in 1984, my back felt pretty good, and I didn't need any meds. Who needs narcotics when you have a view like ours?

Soon the weeks turned to months. During their weekend stays, Suzie's parents started to ask us about our plans for the future. "Where are you going to live?" they asked, and "Shouldn't you be looking for a job?"

We didn't want to think about that. We had just been through a *terrible ordeal*. We needed time to *decompress*. We knew that a baby was coming, and we knew that at some point we'd have to provide for a child, but for now working seemed abstract.

Eventually, Suzie's father, Bill, "suggested" we rent a house in San Jose from a friend of his. This friend was being transferred out of state, but he wasn't ready to sell it because he knew he would be back in a few years. So he offered the house to us for rent at a very good rate, especially for California. Bill gave us the *good* news, and like that, our three-month vacation was over.

Once my pregnant wife, my three dogs, and I had all moved into our new rental in San Jose, we started to fix up the place. Suzie and I were mowing the lawn one morning and dumping the clippings into the trash bin, just as we'd done in Florida, when a neighbor strolled up. I remember him as being an old guy, but in retrospect I think he was younger than I am now.

"You can't do that," he said.

"Can't do what?"

"Put the yard waste in with the trash."

I asked our helpful neighbor, "What do we do with it, then?"

"Just dump it in the street," he said.

Not in a container at all. According to our new neighbor, the city sent out a truck that scooped the stuff out of the street and took it away to turn it into dirt. So we followed his advice and put our yard waste in the street.

On the morning the truck came to pick it up, the driver knocked on our door. "We can't take your yard waste," he told me. "There's too much dirt in it."

I pondered this. Too much dirt. In the yard waste.

"What do you do with the yard waste?" I asked.

"Compost it, and then sell it as dirt," the yard waste guy said.

"Okay," I said. "Then why is it a problem that there's dirt in the stuff you're taking away and turning into more dirt?"

"You can't put dirt in the street," he said.

It didn't seem like much of an answer, but it was the best answer I was going to get.

"All right. How do we get rid of our dirt?"

"Put it in your trash can," he replied, and he moved on.

I thought there couldn't be anything crazier than trash canning extra dirt instead of putting it in the street with the stuff that they were going to turn into dirt. But then I had an encounter with the San Jose Animal Care Center.

Everyone has a story about the service they get at the DMV. It's slow. You have to take a number. The counter workers are indifferent or outright hostile. Your picture never turns out the way you'd like it to, but by the time you get around to asking for a retake, the DMV employee has already called, "Next!"

But the normal DMV experience? That's nothing compared to the treatment you get when you try to register three Shelties in Santa Clara County.

The San Jose Animal Care Center was a small building that looked like the DMV, with a couple of tired-looking people working a counter. I took a number and waited in a functional, government-issued chair. When it was my turn, I walked up to the counter and said, "Good morning. We just moved to San Jose, and I would like to register my three dogs."

The lady at the counter said, "You just moved here, and you're already in trouble. You can only have two dogs in Santa Clara County."

I don't get intimidated very easily, and I didn't in this case either, in spite of the fact that the clerk behind the counter was a very large woman who, in her uniform, looked like a state trooper. And when she said I was in trouble, she said it with such authority that I thought she would be pulling out the handcuffs next.

I said, "I'm sorry; I didn't know. But I have no intention of getting rid of one of our dogs, and we don't plan to move. Can I at least register two of them?"

The lady behind the counter pulled herself up and forward in her chair, making herself look even bigger and more ominous. "What do you plan to do about the third?"

"I have no idea, but I'd like to get two of them registered today, at least."

"You can't register only two of your dogs if you have three."

She wasn't picking a fight. I'd seen people picking fights. She was reciting facts, the way she probably did all day every day for most of her life. These were the rules, and she was here to enforce them.

I didn't move. She didn't move. We were at an impasse.

Then, instead of stepping aside so that she could call the next customer up, I asked, "How do you know if a person has three dogs if they don't tell you?"

Blank stare.

"Based on where the dogs get their mail," she finally said.

"My dogs don't get a lot of mail."

"They get mail telling them it's time to renew their tags every year," she explained. "If we mail out three renewal notices, that means there are three dogs, and there can't be."

I thought about this. "If you have two dogs, can a third dog visit?"

She seemed puzzled, as if I'd stumped her on a quiz show. "Of course."

"Can they have a sleepover? Like kids do with their friends?"

"Sure, I guess."

"All right. Two of my dogs will be getting their renewal notice at my house. The third is their *friend*. That dog gets her mail at my in-laws' house in San Jose. But she might have a lot of sleepovers."

More staring. "Fine. I'll need both addresses."

She handed me some forms. We were done.

Even before we lived in San Jose, I hated the statement, "We do it this way because we've always done it this way." Where's the room for growth? For productivity?

I didn't blame the trash guys for telling me to put the dirt in the trash can. Nor did I blame the woman who told me I could have three dogs as long as one of them got their mail at another address. It seems hilarious now, but to me, asking questions about the process—*any* process—is just the logical thing to do. But how many people cave in when confronted with bureaucracy, even if it doesn't make any sense? How many people say, "Yes, sir, I'll do a better job with my dirt next time," or, "Okay, I'll get rid of my third beloved Sheltie even though my pregnant wife will cry"?

The truth is that it never occurred to me *not* to question these ridiculous policies. Would things have been different if I'd finished basic training? I don't know. I *do* know that it's the responsibility of all of us not to let the person behind the counter dictate the way we live our lives—especially if they're doing the same thing over and over again and expecting it to yield different results.

If there's a better way to do something, why not advocate for it? Why not stand up for logic and reason things out?

But whether or not the San Jose government bureaucracy was logical, there was one thing I knew for sure: I still needed to find a job. I was going to be a father.

Suzie was now three months pregnant and wanted a job with flexible hours. Her mother, Lucy, who worked at a doctor's office, told her about medical transcriptionist work. Lucy told her that after a doctor saw patients, he made notes by talking into tape recorders and handed the tapes to someone else to type up. The person doing this at the office where Lucy was working wanted to take time off. Suzie could take her place, and she could transcribe from home. So Suzie had a job before me.

Don't get me wrong: This was not a competition. But for a good portion of our married life, Suzie had been the breadwinner. When I'd started up businesses and failed, it was her salary we'd fallen back on. And when I couldn't work because of my back? Suzie provided for us then as well. Given all that, even if she hadn't been pregnant—and even if I hadn't been acutely aware that we were no longer just providing for each other, but for a child—I *still* would have thought that it was Suzie's turn to put her feet up and my turn to provide for us.

I did what I set out to do in San Jose. I looked for a job at a computer or software company. There were plenty of them. I didn't think it would take long to be hired, since I knew a lot about computers, including how to build them from scratch, and I knew all of the top software products of the day: WordPerfect, Lotus 1-2-3, dBase, and DOS. In a lot of ways they're just lingo now, but in the late eighties, they were the currency of the trade.

I got the Sunday paper, and on Monday I started to apply. In most cases, the ads directed applicants to mail a résumé, but I never thought that dropping a résumé in the mail where it would get combined with all the others was smart. How much can you tell about someone from a piece of paper? Instead, I went to the business personally and asked to see the hiring manager; if for no other reason than to hand them my résumé or fill out an application in person. I wanted them to put a face with the résumé.

I started to hear the objections. I'd learned from my sales days that an objection is just a request for more information, so at first I wasn't concerned when I heard, "You can't work for us. You don't have a college degree."

I would say, "No, but I have years of business experience."

And when I heard, "But you have no formal training in

computers or software," I pointed out that many companies were started in the Silicon Valley by people with no formal training or experience. I thought that this would work, but I was competing with kids straight out of college who had degrees in computer science. I was a thirty-three-year-old balding man with a résumé that included shoe repair and fast food management. No one would take a chance on me.

We had a little money coming in from Suzie's job. Not only was she covering for the medical transcription lady, who needed time off, but she also picked up more transcription work from a few doctors on her own. She also applied with an office temp agency who gave her some assignments. So we could pay our bills, but we still had a baby on the way and no insurance.

When Suzie was four months pregnant, I knew I had to take drastic measures. The tech jobs just weren't rolling in like I'd planned. So I applied for a job I knew I would get: a manager at Wendy's. This was not what we'd come to California for, but I had to start bringing home a paycheck.

The Wendy's in San Jose turned me down at first: I was *over-qualified*. That was a new one for me. Sure, I'd heard "underqualified" a lot recently from the tech industry, so often I was tired of hearing it. But *overqualified*? Wendy's was supposed to be my backup plan. I didn't understand why they would reject me. I thought then (and still think) that if you're building a team, you should hire the best people you can find. It shouldn't matter if their experience is throwing a ball or flipping burgers. You shouldn't turn someone down because they have more skills than you need at the moment. Isn't it the manager or employer's responsibility to make sure that their employees stay motivated, challenged, and productive? Would you hire an employee and only teach them the minimum they need to do the job so that they don't become overqualified and therefore bored?

I wouldn't think so. As your employees get better at their jobs and acquire new skills, it is better for them and better for your company. Just make sure you put those skills to good use, or else they *might* move on. Not because they became overqualified, but because, just maybe, their manager or supervisor is actually *underqualified.*

I was honest with the hiring manager at Wendy's. I told them that I had already looked for other things and that they didn't pan out. I said I had a lot of experience and at age thirty-three much more maturity than most of their employees. I would not be going to discos (or "clubs," since it was now the eighties) every night and trying to drive home drunk. I told them that I knew my way around the salad bar.

They finally agreed and gave me the job.

I was thrilled to be working and to have insurance again. But all those months hanging out on the deck at my in-laws house after wine tastings had made me forget how hard manual labor could be for a man with fused vertebrae. Sure, I could work at a shoe repair shop where I could lie down when I needed to, but there was no lying down at Wendy's. This was a job where I would be on my feet all day, and I hadn't done that in years.

The job was exactly the same as it had been, and I was very productive almost immediately. But three hours—that was all it took during that first day at Wendy's before my back started to flare up. There was Tylenol and Advil available in the first aid kit by the sink, but they did nothing for my kind of back pain. All I could do was gut it out.

I only put in six hours because I was in training, but when I got home I had to go straight to bed. I was in agony.

I went to the doctor my mother-in-law worked for the next day. He told me that I shouldn't be on my feet, and he gave me a prescription for Vicodin and Flexeril. I couldn't take these while I was working because they made me groggy, but I took them as soon as I got home. I wasn't happy about being on drugs again, but I needed this job.

This went on for a couple of weeks. I would go to work, and by the end of the day I would be in serious pain. Then I would go home, pop some pills, and go to bed. The next day I would repeat the same thing. I would get two days off per week, but never back to back. I would spend each day in bed, my wife working, my three dogs digging in dirt that I couldn't put in the yard waste.

Suzie saw what this work/pill routine was doing to me, and she knew it couldn't last. I went to the doctor again, hoping there was something they could do to help, but I heard the same thing I'd heard years before.

"You shouldn't be working at all," he said. "You're disabled."

NO I WASN'T! I WAS NOT MY FATHER! I WAS GOING TO WORK AND PROVIDE FOR MY FAMILY!

I lived like this for a month. Then I was fortunate enough to get my two days off at the same time. I spent the entire time in bed, taking narcotics and muscle relaxers. At the end of the second day, I was so doped up that I couldn't make it to work, so I called in sick. I couldn't believe that I was *that guy* again, on drugs and unable to function. I knew I had to take the meds or I wouldn't be able to rest at all, but I was trading my brain for my pain, and given the choice, I would take being able to think over being pain-free.

I didn't take pills during my sick day, and I drank a lot of water to flush the drugs out of my system. On the fourth day, I felt ready to go back to work. I was sure I would get through my shift, but in the first hour my back started to tighten up. Soon after, the pain was worse than ever.

I had only been at Wendy's a month, but it felt like a lifetime. I didn't know what I would do next, but now I knew that I couldn't do this.

I went straight home after my shift was over. Suzie and her parents were in the kitchen having dinner. I hobbled in the door, unable to mask my pain. I spoke before they could say anything.

"I'm quitting my job," I said, and I went to bed.

I could hear their muffled voices from the bedroom. I couldn't make out what they were saying but I could tell no one was happy. And me? I was the least happy of all. Was this it? Was I really done? Was I really disabled?

The next day I went to the Wendy's office and told them I was quitting. I hadn't told them about my back before I got the job, but I told them now. I was amazed at how understanding they were. They said that they didn't want to lose me, but I explained that I just couldn't be on my feet like that. They told me that I could lie down in the back whenever I needed to, but I told them that the place was always busy, and I just couldn't leave the counter while everyone else was working so hard. I wasn't built that way. Still, I thanked them for the offer and said I would consider it after some time off, when my back had recovered. After all, I didn't want to burn the bridge.

So I was unemployed again. I took the next week recovering in bed without narcotics, and then I started looking for that tech job again.

But the second time looking for jobs in the tech industry was no better than the first. I was hearing the same things: no formal training, no experience in tech, no college degree. I was getting desperate. There were a lot of jobs in tech, but there were a lot of people applying for them—people with college degrees and experience.

Then I saw an ad in the paper that mentioned *testing*.

Fourteen

PRINTERS, PLOTTERS, AND CAMERAS

The ad said, "Device Testers." I didn't know what a device tester did, but it was in the computer section of the want ads. I used a lot of software products and had worked on a lot of computers, and one thing I knew I could do was find problems. This might finally be it, I thought.

I called the number in the ad and reached the Avery Temporary Agency. They were looking to place contractors at a tech company. I didn't know what company it was yet, but I knew it was in tech, and that's where I wanted to be. So I asked about the position.

The woman I spoke with sounded pleasant enough.

"We're looking for device testers. Do you have any device testing experience?"

The true answer was "no." But so far, the truth had gotten me a job at a fast food restaurant that had almost killed me. What's more: I knew that I could do any job in the tech industry. Since the first personal computers had come out, Johnson and I had been building them from scratch. But none of these people would give me the chance. The second they heard "no experience," the conversation was over. And I needed the job to support my wife and my child on the way: I couldn't let the conversation be over.

"Yes," I told the woman on the phone. "Yes I do."

"That's great!" she said. "So what kinds of devices have you tested?"

What kinds of devices had I tested? I didn't even know what she was talking about. But I was in now, with no turning back.

I said, "You and I know that there are many kinds of devices. Rather than me listing them all, why don't you tell me what devices *you're looking for?*"

"That's a great idea. We're looking for someone to test printers, plotters, and cameras."

"Printers, plotters, and cameras? Did you say printers, plotters, and cameras?"

"Yes, why?"

"That's amazing. My last job was testing printers, plotters, and cameras." Not quite the truth. Of course I knew about printers; I used them all the time. But cameras? What did cameras have to do with software? And what the hell was a plotter?

"Wow! That's great! Our client was looking for someone who had some experience testing printers, plotters, *or* cameras, but they never thought they'd find someone who'd tested all three."

Did I go too far? Was I in too deep? My heart was pounding so hard that I was sure she could hear it on the other end of the phone. I was even beginning to sweat a little. But I knew I had to see where this would end. The worst that could happen is that I wouldn't get the job, and that would have already been the case if I said no.

Then the news got better. She told me that the company looking for testers was Ashton-Tate. Ashton-Tate was the company that made dBase, and I knew that product well. If this job had anything to do with dBase, I'd be fine. Plus, the commute to Ashton-Tate from our house was only ten minutes—not a trivial consideration in San Jose.

I really wanted this job.

"It looks like they're taking interviews tomorrow," she told me. "Send me your résumé, and I'll set you up."

God, not the résumé. *Fast food. Shoe repair. Didn't finish college. No tech experience.* I had to think fast again.

I said, "It seems like these people are anxious to get someone in there. Why don't I go there and take them my résumé directly?"

She thought that was a good idea, and so I was set.

The next morning I went to Ashton-Tate. I "forgot" my résumé.

Ashton-Tate was in a three-story, light-colored building at the top of a hill. After coming from Florida, I was still amazed that not everything was completely flat—not the scenery, not the architecture. I went inside and told the guard that I was here to see Keith, the test manager.

Soon Keith appeared. He was a young guy, probably no more than twenty-four or twenty-five, with short blond hair. Everything about Keith seemed friendly, from his casual polo and khakis to the smile he extended me along with his hand. Of course I was anxious about not having a résumé, but everything about him made me feel welcome.

I reached out my hand and said, "Pleased to meet you. I've been using your company's software for years." At least *that* much was true.

Keith asked me to come back to his office. His office was in the back of a large room filled with people working at individual desks, each of them typing away feverishly. I would learn later that these were the "developers," or the people writing code for the product I would be working on.

He said, "So you're the guy with all the experience testing printers, plotters, and cameras."

Rather than repeat the lie, I answered, "This is a really nice location you have here."

"Do you have your résumé?" Keith asked.

I had rehearsed this next line: "I thought I was supposed to mail it to the Avery Group."

"No problem. I'm sure they'll forward it to me. Let me take you to the room where you'll be working."

Huh. The room where I'd be working. I hadn't even been through the interview yet. Maybe the interview would happen there—in other words, maybe he was going to ask me to demonstrate my testing ability. I hoped he couldn't hear my heart pounding.

We walked down the hall, and he opened a door. In the room there were four long tables. On each table were five computers. Next to each computer was either a printer, which I recognized, or another device—large, with an attached metal arm holding a pen for some reason—which I assumed was a plotter.

Keith handed me a time sheet and told me that every day I should fill in the time I came in and the time I left. He walked to the door, turned to me, and said, "If you need anything, let me know." And he left.

There I stood, wondering what had just happened. I didn't even know what they were paying me. I didn't dare ask for fear of starting a conversation that might lead to a discussion of my *experience*. The bottom line, though, was that after almost six months in California, I had the job in high tech I came here for.

I had no idea what the job was, but I had it.

I walked over to the first computer. Attached to it was the same printer I had at home. When I checked out the computer, the only thing installed on it was a program called Applause. I was hoping to find dBase, since I knew that product, but it was nowhere to be found.

I launched Applause. It was a presentation program, like PowerPoint, although I hadn't heard of PowerPoint in 1989. Few people had. In any case, Applause looked like an easy program to learn. Of course I had no idea what to do with it, or with these printers, plotters, or cameras.

There was another door leading from the room. I opened it and found dozens of printers, plotters, and cameras on the floor of the next room. It was like a minefield.

I went back in the main room and sat down. I really had no idea what I was supposed to do, and I had no intention of asking Keith.

After a couple of hours of checking out the software on the different computers and looking around the space, Keith showed up, wanting to know if I wanted to come to lunch with him and some of the guys.

I still didn't want to get into a conversation. "My house is only a few minutes from here," I said. "I told my wife I'd come home for lunch."

"Cool. See you later."

I would soon learn that tech guys say cool a lot.

So I went home. When I opened the door, I heard the familiar high-pitched screech of our printer. Suzie was in the office, doing her job as a medical transcriptionist. Even though she was now six months pregnant, she was still putting in plenty of hours making the money that the two of us needed to survive. I was so excited to tell her my news and hopefully take some of the pressure off of her. I figured that after having supported me through all my back surgeries and bankruptcies, it was *her* turn to relax.

When she heard me come in, she came out of the office. "How'd the interview go?"

"There wasn't any interview."

"No interview? How will you know if you get the job?"

"I've already got it."

She was thrilled and plainly relieved. "So what exactly does a device tester do?"

"I have no idea. I think I bit off more than I can chew."

"What are you going to do?"

"I'll just have to figure it out. No way am I losing this opportunity."

Before I went back to work, I called the Avery Group to let them know that I had the job. The lady I talked to said that she'd already heard and that Keith was very impressed with me. Impressed with me? How the hell did I impress him? (Of course I didn't say that out loud.) Then she told me I would be making $10 an hour. Not bad, considering that minimum wage was $3.35. As a manager at Wendy's I was making $30,000 per year, so this was about a third less, but at least I wouldn't be on my feet and in chronic pain all day.

It was 1:00 p.m. when I got back to the testing room, and I decided that I would learn how to use Applause. I hadn't had any guidance, but I was sure that whatever I was going to print, plot, or take a picture of was going to come from this application.

I was working on this at 3:00 p.m. when a guy walked in the door who would save my ass. More importantly, he would become a friend, one that I still have today. His name was Chris Burroughs.

Chris was a stocky guy with long blond hair and a beard. He came in, sat down at one of the computers in the back row, and started to print something. This was a guy who knew what we were supposed to be doing, so I walked up and introduced myself. I told him I was a tester. Chris was not. He worked in PSS, or Product Support and Services. These are the guys you talked to if you were to call the company for support with Ashton-Tate's software.

"If you're in PSS, what are you doing here?" I asked him.

"They give us a chance to earn some extra money after our shifts," Chris explained. "You know—testing printers, plotters, and cameras."

When I knew that Chris wasn't someone in my reporting chain, I felt comfortable enough to ask the question that had been on my mind all day. "What are we supposed to be doing in here?"

It ended up being pretty simple. All we were supposed to do was use Applause to create a presentation, which is just a series of slides, and then print those slides using a printer, plotter, or camera. We then looked at what we'd printed and compared it to what was on the computer screen. (This is where I first heard the term WYSIWYG, pronounced "wisiwig," or "What You See Is What

You Get.") If what was printed looked different than what was on the computer screen, we had a bug, a defect, and we'd write it up in a report that would go to the software developer, who would fix it.

I already knew how to attach a printer to a computer, and it turns out that you connect plotters and cameras the same way. (The plotter, I learned, was indeed the device I'd seen with the arm holding a pen: When you printed something on it, the arm would move back and forth and "draw" whatever you were printing.) Plus, since I'd spent a couple of hours that day learning Applause, I already knew how to make a presentation.

Chris said, "Remember, the job is to *find* bugs. We're supposed to prove it *doesn't* work. So make sure you create all kinds of charts and graphs. Stress the device. Break it."

This sounded like a lot of fun, and for the first time all day I relaxed. I went back to that first computer and created a couple of slides. I then sent them to the printer. One of the printouts showed a line over the graph that shouldn't be there. I showed it to Chris.

"You found your first bug," he told me.

It felt kind of good.

I worked for the next couple of hours, and in that time I found a few more bugs. I was really starting to feel good about this. That night I went home and told Suzie about Chris and how he'd saved my butt. Suzie asked, "Do you still think you bit off more than you could chew?" I could only smile.

The next day at work, Keith told me that he was really impressed with the bugs I found. "It's great to have someone of your experience on the team," he told me.

"I appreciate the opportunity," I said, avoiding the issue of my experience. "I like the operation you have going on here."

Keith left, and I went back to work. But before I did, I told myself that I was going to make these guys glad they hired me.

A few minutes later Keith came in the room with a couple of guys. He told me that he had hired a couple more testers, but that they had less experience than I did. "Could you show them what to do?" he asked. I said that I was happy to, and I began to show them exactly what Chris had showed me just the day before.

For the rest of the week I tested the output from printers, plotters, and cameras with Applause. Every day, the other two guys and I would sit at our computers, create a presentation, and then send the output to a printer. When that printer was done, we would switch it with another printer, plotter, or camera and do it all again. If there was a bug, we would fill out a form and place it in a box that the developers would pick up and fix. Once the bug was fixed, we'd get a new version of the software and test it again to see if the bug was really fixed, or if the developer had broken something new when he touched the code.

It didn't take me long to figure out that if you tried to print something simple, it almost always worked. The more complicated your output to the printer, the more likely you were to find something useful to the development team. Add a picture, some color, shapes, broken lines, a graph or two, and try to print multiple copies of everything. I took what Chris had said to heart: I tried to break everything.

As a result, I was finding a fair number of bugs and getting through a fair number of devices. But I still knew I could do better. Plus, although creating the tests was always interesting, there was a lot of monotony in the job: setting up the print jobs, waiting for the old dot matrix printer to screech out the prints, et cetera, et cetera. I knew that these parts of the job could be better, too. Plus, I wanted these guys to be happy that they hired me—and even though I had only come in as a contractor, I now wanted a permanent job at Ashton-Tate.

The other guys always took the last two computers in the back row by the door. I took the first computer in the first row, closer to the other printers. This left most of the computers in the middle of the room unused. So one day, thinking about how I could test more efficiently, I decided to remove all of the chairs except one. Even with my bad back, I could sit and slide from computer to computer, printing something from each one as I slid by. I would try to get all the printers running at the same time, and once they were, I would slide back on my chair to check the output. If there was a bug, I would write it up and then move to the next device.

I tried to set a personal record for how many bugs I found in a day or how many devices I could get through. I'm sure the younger guys wondered why I was busting my ass this way. I think they were like a lot of people: They put in their required hours, and then they went home. In their minds, we got paid by the hour, so it didn't matter if you tested one device in that hour or ten: You still got the same ten dollars. I was thinking beyond that.

In the process, I made my job fun again, and Keith noticed the results. My contract was only for one month, and at the end of it Keith called me in and said that he thought I was doing a great job. In fact, he said that I was getting through more devices and finding more bugs than the other two guys put together by far. He wasn't planning to renew the others because he thought I could handle the workload by myself. He asked if I'd like to stay for another month, and I said of course.

"You know, I never got your résumé," he said, wiping the smile from my face.

"Really? I'm sure I sent it to the Avery Group. Let me call them and see why they didn't send you a copy."

He could have easily asked me to just bring him a copy the next day, but thankfully he didn't, and back to work I went. Now I had the entire room to myself, so I removed the last row of chairs and went about setting new records for devices and bugs.

I went home for lunch to tell Suzie the good news. When I got there, she told me that someone from the Avery Group had called and wanted me to call them back as soon as possible. I thought, *Oh no, they're going to ask me about that résumé*. But I had no choice; I had to call them.

They didn't ask about my résumé at all. Instead she congratulated me on getting my contract renewed and told me that Ashton-Tate was thrilled with my work. Further, I was getting a raise to twelve dollars an hour. Wow! A twenty percent raise in one month.

In retrospect, I guess it would've been possible to make up a fake résumé to give these people. But at the time, I never considered that to be an option. No one was pressing me that hard about it, and lying on a résumé would mean creating a permanent record of the lie. My real résumé, with no tech experience on it, was still there waiting for the time when I'd inevitably have to show it. At that time, my real résumé would be the truth that would expose the lie.

I just hoped I'd be able to prove myself worthy of hiring before that time ran out.

I had a great time racing my chair around the room and finding all of these bugs in the devices, but from time to time I would find bugs in the software as well. It was interesting, so one day I asked Keith about whether he needed anyone to test the software as well as the output.

Keith said that he already had a team of software testers. "But do you have any *experience* as a software tester?" he asked.

This time I didn't lie. I told him I didn't have any experience.

He said, "I'll tell you what. Your number one priority is device testing, but if you want to get experience testing software, I'll let you do it nights and weekends. I'll pay you time and a half for the overtime."

Time and a half worked out to eighteen dollars an hour. I'd love to work overtime.

I was thrilled, and I couldn't wait to tell Suzie. She wasn't thrilled that I would be working so many hours, but with our first child only a couple of months away, she knew we needed the money.

It was now January of 1990, and my contract was up again. This time, Keith said that the product was almost done, but that he would like to keep me until the end. This was good and bad. I was glad to stay, but I didn't like the word *end*.

I asked him about a permanent job, but he said he wouldn't be hiring for a project that was coming to an end. There was another guy, though, who was in charge of testing for this division of the company. His name was Bob Turner, and Keith said that he would introduce us.

Bob was a very nice guy who really liked to talk. That worked out well for me, because when I was introduced to him, he told me all about his experience in software testing. All I had to do was listen and nod. Every now and then I said things like "of course" and "that makes perfect sense."

At the end of our talk, Bob said, "You really seem to know your stuff, and Keith has nothing but good things to say about you. I'm not hiring right now, but I'll be putting together a new team next month that I'll consider you for. Do you have a résumé?"

"Not with me."

"Don't worry. I'll get a copy from Keith."

Was I screwed? Only time would tell.

Looking back, it was strange that I'd never met Bob before this introduction, because suddenly he always seemed to be turning up in the lab. We worked together a lot as we finished up Applause, finding the last few bugs and getting the product ready to ship to the public. We got along great, and we even became friends. Chris would also help us test from time to time, and we started to go to lunch together a lot, something we continued to do many years later.

I was doing more and more software testing, but I was still testing devices as well. The project was winding down, so there was no longer any need for overtime. The cut in pay hurt.

Fortunately, I got another call from the Avery Group. They told me that another company was looking for a device tester who would work weekends. Power Up Software was about an hour's drive north of where we lived, but they were willing to pay *twenty* dollars an hour. I said I'd do it.

My contact at the Avery Group reminded me that she'd never received my résumé, and that Power Up would need to see one.

"No problem. I'll take it with me."

Nobody asked for it on site, and I went to work right away.

I worked every day of the week—Monday through Friday at Ashton-Tate, Saturday and Sunday at Power Up Software—but these were both very temporary jobs. I was in the tech world where I wanted to be, but with the knowledge that at any day the project would end and I'd be left with nothing for me, my wife, and the baby that was on his way any day now. Between us, Suzie and I were working three or four jobs, but any or all of them could end at any time.

So I decided that I needed to start pushing for the permanent job at Ashton-Tate. I asked Keith if Bob had talked to him.

"He did. He really liked you. He asked for a copy of your résumé. I'm sure you know that I never got one, but that's between you and Bob now."

Did Keith know? Did he care? Would Bob care? Yes, I was worried. But I'd have to deal with that later.

I went to Bob and asked him if he was ready to build his team. He told me that things were getting a little tough at Ashton-Tate and that he could only hire one person full-time. He said he'd like to interview me.

By now I had been doing device and software testing for four months. I'd learned a lot in that time. I'd also read a number of books about software testing, so I thought I was ready for an interview.

The next day Bob and I talked for over an hour. At the end, he told me, "I knew you knew your stuff. The job is yours if you want it. I just need your résumé for the file. Bring it by whenever you can."

There was no getting around it. I was going to have to give him my résumé.

The next day I went to Bob's office. He wasn't in yet so I placed my résumé on his desk and went to work.

About an hour later Bob came to me and had my résumé in his hand.

He said, "What is this?"

"It's my résumé," I said.

"You gave me the wrong one. This is for some fast food manager who apparently also worked in the shoe repair business."

I said, "That's my résumé."

He looked at it again. "Where's all the experience testing printers, plotters, and cameras?"

"I don't have any," I told him.

Bob furrowed his brow, confused. "You mean to say you don't have any experience?"

"Only the experience I got here."

"So how do you explain the fact that you told us you had all this experience?"

The moment I'd dreaded was staring me in the face. And I stared back at it. I needed this job; I wanted this job—not only for me, but for Suzie and our child. I wasn't afraid. Bob was a man who held my future, but he was a decent guy whose worst vice was that he liked to talk. He was not someone from a rival gang in Philly. He was not my father. I was sitting, but I sat tall.

"I lied," I said without hesitation.

"You *what*?"

"I lied."

Bob was getting upset, struggling to understand. But he didn't seem angry. So before he could reply, I asked, "If I showed you guys that résumé before I started, would you have hired me?"

Bob looked me in the eye. I could see him thinking about it: Was his priority to be angry about the lie, or was it to hire the person he knew would do the best job for the company going forward? I looked right back at him.

"We wouldn't even have talked to you," he finally said.

"I believe you. So now that I've been here four months, are you glad you hired me?"

"Yes."

"And you're offering me a permanent job. If you forget the résumé, do you still think offering me that job was the right call?"

Bob didn't hesitate. "Yes."

"There you have it."

"There I have what? You *lied* about your experience. Are you saying the end justifies the means?"

"Yes! Yes, absolutely the end justifies the means. I wouldn't have gotten this job otherwise, and you wouldn't have gotten a guy who's doing a great job and who'll continue to do a great job as long as he works for you."

Bob looked at me as though I were a difficult equation that he could almost wrap his brain around.

"All right. Just promise me you'll never lie to me again."

"Of course," I said. And I meant it.

Later, when I was a manager at Microsoft, I would find that a lot of people felt as overwhelmed on their first day as I did. *I don't belong here*, they'd think, even though they'd gone to excellent schools and gained top-notch experience—the kinds of things that look good on résumés.

My bosses at Ashton-Tate did not expect to get me as a worker—a shoe repairman, a fast food manager. They expected someone with experience with printers, plotters, and cameras— not someone who'd lived and worked and failed and tried again.

You could say that I'd lied by omission and that I had no business being in the tech industry to begin with, because that was how a piece of paper described me.

But I was not a piece of paper. I was a person who'd used the opportunity given to him to learn and excel. When the other temps spent time in that one corner with their one machine each, I set my workspace up so that I could roll down a line of computers and devices, looking for expected behavior and flaws. And when

I was done rolling one way, I rolled back the other, always checking: *Is this what's expected? And this? And this?*

I gained experience, I gained knowledge, and I proved my
work ethic. I was the right person for the job. After four months
of experience I knew it, and just as importantly, Bob knew it too.

And even if Bob had decided to fire me over the résumé issue,
at least by then I'd have had four months of experience testing
printers, plotters, and cameras to fall back on.

I told Bob that in my case the end justified the means, but of
course I don't think that's true for every case. What I do think is
true is this: Whether or not you have a thin résumé hanging over
your head, when you get a job that you like doing, with coworkers
you like, instead of sitting in a corner and working timidly, you
should learn to prove yourself. Learn to roll. Dedicate yourself
to that job. And when you think you're done? Roll back to the
beginning and do it again.

Fifteen

FINDING THE RIGHT BUGS

It was the morning of Saturday, February 24, 1990. I would start my permanent position at Ashton-Tate the following Monday. In the meantime, I had my temp job at Power Up Software to go to. So I left the house for work, not knowing that by the end of that day, my life would change forever.

Suzie had gone to work as well. She'd been working at a temp assignment, but today would be her last day, as Nicholas was due in a couple of weeks. She wanted to make sure that she had plenty of time off of work to get ready before he arrived.

At noon, her water broke.

Suzie drove herself home. She even took a shower before she drove herself to the hospital. She had tried to call me, of course, but she couldn't remember the name of the company where I was working. There were no cell phones then, and she had no idea how to contact me. Instead, she left me a message on our own answering machine. Of course I was oblivious to this as I continued to toil away testing printers at Power Up.

I worked until 5:00 p.m., and then I started the hour-long drive home. By the time I got home at 6:00 p.m., Suzie had been in labor for six hours. I noticed that she wasn't home, but I just assumed she was at the store. After a few minutes, I thought to check the answering machine messages.

"George, this is your wife," said the message. "I'm at the hospital having your son."

I jumped in the car right away. As I drove to the hospital, I went over the things we'd learned in birthing class: breath coaching, massage. I arrived at the hospital, all smiles, and asked her: "Are you ready to breathe?"

I was saying this to a woman who was in a great deal of pain (she had a fear of needles, so she'd turned down a spinal block), and who'd been in labor for six hours with absolutely no idea of my whereabouts.

"Where have you been and what took you so long to get here?"

I tried to explain that I had been at work, but I didn't get the feeling that she really wanted to talk. "Would you like a massage?" I finally asked.

She wasn't interested in that either. She pointed at a chair on the other side of the room. "Why don't you sit there and be quiet?"

Suzie wasn't one for barking orders (except when it came to driving over big bridges), so I sat. I moved the chair closer to her, but I sat.

I must tell you that watching a woman give birth is both a beautiful and disgusting thing. There was so much blood that I asked the doctor, "Is Suzie going to be okay?"

The doctor said, "Don't worry, that's not Suzie's blood."

"Oh no. Is that coming from the baby?"

The doctor said, "No, the baby's not bleeding."

"So whose blood is it? *IS THERE SOMEBODY ELSE IN THERE?*"

The doctor was too busy to humor me after that comment, and he went back to work.

A few hours later, our first son, Nick, was born.

I don't know how Suzie did it. She had our first child through natural childbirth, and in spite of the pain and the yells of "NEVER AGAIN!" during the birth, by the very next day, she was already saying she would of course have another child. I don't know what hormones get secreted during childbirth, but they must work very well or no woman would ever have a second child.

I was amazed at how small Nicholas was, though I'm sure Suzie thought he was huge. He was wide awake, and he was looking around as if he was taking it all in. He didn't cry at first, and I thought, *This is where the doctor slaps the baby*. And then, *If that doctor hits my kid, I'll floor him.* I was amazed at how protective I suddenly was.

They started to take Nicholas out of the room, and I asked, "Where are you taking him?"

A nurse said, "We take him out, clean him up, and do some measurements."

"I'm going with you," I said.

What had come over me? Do men also have some hormone that gets secreted the second they become a dad? I don't know, but I knew that I was his dad, and my job was to protect him.

After they washed Nicholas, they took him to Suzie. As Suzie held him, I thought about all the things that I had tried and failed with in my professional life so far. At those times, I always knew that no matter what Suzie and I did, we would be okay in the end. But it was no longer just Suzie and me. There was another person now who was totally dependent on us. There could be no more fast food jobs where I had to take narcotics to stay on my feet. There could be no more start-ups where I learned about the importance of walls between a kitchen and a dining room. There could be no more bankruptcies. I couldn't fail again.

Monday was the first day of my new full-time job at Ashton-Tate, a job that felt far more important today than it had on Friday. I showed up for work first thing Monday morning. Suzie was home with Nicholas, and her mother had come over to help. Nick was still the size of a football, but Suzie and her mom never seemed to want to put him down. If that baby made any kind of sound, one of them picked him up.

I shouldn't have been surprised that Suzie was such a good mother. After all, she'd taken care of me through all those years of back operations and debilitating pain. Besides, this was something that Suzie had wanted for a long time, and after almost ten years of marriage and three dogs, she'd finally gotten it. She seemed delighted.

When I arrived at the office on Monday, the first thing Bob asked me was, "How was your weekend?"

"We had our first baby Saturday."

He stared at me. "Why are you even here?"

"No way am I gonna miss my first day of work."

Bob was a very nice guy. He told me to meet with HR, fill out all of the new-hire paperwork, and then go home for the rest of the day. Which I did.

The next day, I returned to Ashton-Tate to work as a software tester on a new version of Applause that was being designed for Microsoft Windows.

I was getting very good at finding bugs, and I was having fun doing it. I remembered what Chris Burroughs had told me: My job was to prove that the product *didn't* work. So I would find as many ways as I could to stress the system. In the end, software testing wasn't much different than hardware testing: Just as I tested the printers and devices by taking simple text presentations and complicating them with color, charts, and anything I could think of, I tested the software part of Applause by imagining something simple that a user might actually do, and then trying every combination or variation of that action that I could think of.

Additionally, I bought books on software testing and studied them as much as I could. When I learned that knowing a little about the way code worked would make it easier to work with the software developers, I decided to take a coding class at De Anza Junior College in San Jose. My plan was very simple: learn all I could, work hard, and get ahead.

I put in a lot of hours doing all of this. Soon my part-time job at Power Up was done, and I had my weekends back, but I wanted to make more of a commitment to turning this new career into a success. So I talked to Suzie about going in to Ashton-Tate on Saturdays and continuing to try and impress Bob. They had taken a chance on me, I told her, and I wanted them to be proud that they had.

I was very aware of what I was asking of her. Six days of work a week. Unlimited hours. A wife at home with a newborn.

I don't know if she was tired of the upheavals in our financial circumstances, or if I just scored big time by marrying an excellent, supportive wife. But whatever the reason, Suzie agreed that I should do it.

And so I vowed to do my best on my part of the bargain. Not only did I owe it to Ashton-Tate—I owed it to my new family.

Soon, I had my first opportunity to really prove myself. The new version of Applause was ready for printer testing, but Ashton-Tate didn't have the money to buy the printers, plotters, and cameras it needed to test. They said it was because they didn't *want* to spend the money, but soon I realized that it was because they didn't *have* it. So I was asked to call the companies and see if we could borrow the devices we needed to test.

Of course I got pushback. After all, these companies were in the business of selling printers, not loaning them out. They told me no: If we wanted to test their devices, we'd have to buy them.

But this time, instead of taking "no" as a request for information, I took it as a need for a plan. I had to come up with a reason for them to loan us their devices.

After thinking about it, I proposed things to the companies this way. Applause was a minor product, but dBase was a major one. So I told them that if they agreed to loan us devices instead of charging us for them, Ashton-Tate would contract a developer to create the code that would make our software, Applause, compatible with their hardware. Since a lot of the "printer driver" code would be the same for similar programs, I would try to get the developer to write a driver for dBase at the same time. That way, the device companies would get support for two of our software products, including the one with the very large install base. In other words, they could try to sell us one device, or we could help them sell many.

The hardware companies seemed to like this idea, and soon we had more printers, plotters, and cameras than I could test.

Since we needed more people to test all of the devices we were getting, Bob asked me if I wanted to be a test lead. Bob said that he'd looked again at my original fast food/shoe repairman résumé. This time, he was impressed with the amount of management experience it listed. He wanted me to hire and manage a new team of device testers.

Of course I was thrilled. I had only been with Ashton-Tate a few months, and I was already a manager. All that hard work had paid off.

Since Ashton-Tate wasn't hiring full-time employees, I had to hire contractors. Of course I called the same contracting agency that had sent me to Ashton-Tate in the first place. The Avery Group was thrilled to hear that I was doing so well. They were even more excited when I told them what I wanted.

"Hey, listen. I need some contractors. And don't even think about sending anyone over without a résumé. You have a bad rep for doing that."

"You! That was just *you*, George!" the agent on the phone said.

We had a good laugh remembering what fun they had trying to get a résumé out of me, and soon I hired three people from them.

The next thing I did was to take the old bullpen, where the first version of Applause had been developed, and turn it into a large printer lab. I surrounded the room with racks to hold all of the printers, and I filled the room with tables.

Once the lab was built, I invited the few companies that didn't loan us their hardware to see the lab. When they saw all of their competitors' devices, they realized that they needed to have their devices there too. Soon, they started to loan us the devices that we didn't already support.

Bob was thrilled with what we were doing, and he gave me my own private office next to the lab. This was unheard of. You had to be at Ashton-Tate for quite some time or be a high-level manager to get your own office. It was a very nice pat on the back from Bob.

I had a lot of management experience at this point, and I definitely knew what kind of manager I wanted to be and what kind I didn't want to be. In particular, I wanted to make sure I avoided hiring anyone onto my team who behaved like the guys I'd worked with initially in the printer lab. They weren't bad guys, but they didn't have any higher goal beyond finishing out their hours and going home. Maybe that was because they didn't have anyone telling them that they should have had one.

Any time I hired someone throughout my career, I tried to find out exactly why they were looking for work at my company and what they hoped to do there. I didn't just ask them about where they saw themselves in five years. That's an interview question, one where people try to prepare an impressive answer in advance. Instead, I turned the interview into a conversation. In a conversation, people tend to relax, and I could figure out what they really hoped to accomplish. Once I knew that, I could show them how working at the job could get them to that goal, but only if they were willing to put in some serious effort.

When I started managing people on Applause, I tried to motivate them to find all of the bugs they could. I would hold contests and give out rewards for finding the best bugs. In the process, we found some really arcane ones, problems that would take a ridiculous number of steps to reproduce: Suppose a user typed a letter into an edit box, hit Enter 100 times, and then crashed their system. When we took bugs like this back to the developers to fix, they'd usually counter: "But no user's ever going to hit Enter 100 times like that. Why should we waste our time writing code for situations that aren't ever going to happen?"

"I don't care how unlikely it is," would be my typical response. "The system should never crash. How hard could it be to write an error message?"

They told me I was being unreasonable, and thinking about it now, I guess I was. But I thought everything was working really well until I had a chat with a guy named John Nicol.

John had been Chris Burroughs' supervisor in PSS, but now he was in charge of program management. John was a tall, thin, athletic man who was a little younger than me. He was very friendly, and he had always been very helpful. Like Chris, John remains a friend to this day, over twenty years later.

One day, John was coming down the hall when he heard me and my team cheering about how many bugs we'd found. Later that day, he expressed his concern to me.

"You seem to be finding a lot more bugs than the developers may have expected," he said.

I told him what Chris had told me my first day on the job: that it was our job to prove the product didn't work.

John said, "Yes, but we also need to *ship* it. Look, I'm glad you're finding bugs, but tell me about your relationship with your developers."

Here's what I wanted to tell him: *We swear at each other a lot.* We swore at each other just as much as they did on construction sites. At first it had surprised me that the tech world used the *f*-word as much as they did, but hey, I didn't back off from using construction-site language either.

"Adversarial," I told him. "I don't mind. We're telling them their product is buggy."

"Don't you think developers care about quality, too?" he asked. "If you worked together, instead of thinking of yourselves as being at odds, we might not only find more bugs, but we'll start to find the *right* bugs—the ones that impact our customers the most."

He was right. So I told my team to start concentrating on the more important bugs—the ones that crash the system or damage the user's data, not the ones that happen after 100 presses of the Enter key. Soon my team and the dev team were working much better together, and John and I became very good friends.

At home, Suzie was enjoying being a new mom. Nicholas was a great baby. He took naps every afternoon and slept through the night almost from the start. Suzie was able to go back to work as a medical transcriptionist, and she was already talking about having a second child.

I thought it was a good idea. After all, I had a good job with good insurance now, and we also thought it might be a good idea to have the two children close together in hopes that they would be friends and enjoy the same interests. So just before Nick's first birthday, we decided to start trying, and almost immediately Suzie was pregnant with our second child.

That's just about when things at work started to become strange.

The company wasn't making as much money as it used to. The last version of dBase, Ashton-Tate's flagship product, was buggy, and the company took a long time to ship an update. The testing team for dBase in the Torrance office had apparently been so worried about shipping another buggy version that they took far too long testing the update. By the time they finally shipped it, a lot of customers had moved on to competitors' products like Borland's Paradox.

I really knew things were getting tough when I tried to order an eight-dollar printer cable and was told I would have to wait until next quarter—two months away. I finally paid for it out of my own pocket.

Soon after, the rumors started that we were either going out of business or being sold. We continued to work on the new version of Applause, but the first version wasn't selling. We were up against products like Harvard Graphics, Lotus Freelance, and a new product that Microsoft had just acquired called PowerPoint.

Finally, in July 1991, the company announced that we were being bought by Borland. Borland was also in the database business, but they were once much smaller than Ashton-Tate. We were the big fish, but they still swallowed us whole.

The acquisition process would take months, and in the meantime, while the business and legal issues were being negotiated, Ashton-Tate wasted no time in laying off employees to ensure that they remained a viable, streamlined company. I had never worked for a company that laid people off. Morale was low all over the office. Bob told me not to worry: He would make sure I had a job as long as he could. That felt good, but I was still worried. It seemed like every day I said good-bye to another good employee.

Plus, I couldn't help worrying for my own family. Suzie was now about six months pregnant with our second child, and this month marked our tenth wedding anniversary. While Suzie's parents watched Nicholas, we had planned to take a trip to Las Vegas, where we'd never been. But I didn't think that now was the time to be spending money, so we cancelled and went to dinner instead.

I had to imagine that Borland would keep some of the Ashton-Tate employees on after the acquisition. But then the next round of layoffs came, and Bob came to talk to me. I thought I was gone, but Bob told me that I was now the test manager. "They laid *me* off," he said.

I felt very bad for Bob, but I was glad to still have a job. My relief was short lived, though: Soon after, we heard that Borland only planned to keep the PSS employees after the merger. That meant my friend Chris would have a job, but not me. It was just a matter of time.

John stopped by my office to tell me that I had a month before I and everyone else besides the PSS employees would be laid off. John was going to stay around to complete Applause.

"What do you plan to do?" he asked.

"I guess I'll have to find another job."

"Do you have a résumé?"

"Yes." I was never going to play that game again. Besides, now I had experience as a device tester at Ashton-Tate and Power Up, as well as experience as a software tester and lead.

When he looked at my résumé, though, John wasn't impressed. I hadn't revised it since Bob had told me never to lie to him again. John said, "This looks like you're a fast food restaurant manager."

He helped me spruce up the fast food section of the résumé by emphasizing my management experience, and we added the new skills I had acquired in the tech field over the past two years, as well as my new test manager title. When we were done, I thought it looked pretty impressive. And I'll always have John to thank for that.

September and October of 1991 were very stressful months for everyone at Ashton-Tate. The layoffs were now happening on a weekly basis. Every Friday, a few people were called upstairs to HR and let go. I made it through the month of September and into October, but my stress level was always high: Our second child was due on October 16, and I knew the final date for the merger with Borland was October 11.

On that day, the few of us who were left got the call to come to HR, and I received my severance package. I received three months' pay, and my insurance would continue for three months as well. The insurance was a welcome surprise, because in the early morning hours of October 16, right on time, my second son, Steven, was born.

Unlike with Nicholas, I was home for this one. I remember Suzie calling out from the bathroom: "George, you need to take me to the hospital now."

I, still half asleep, asked, "Why?"

"Because the baby's coming!"

"Are you sure?"

"Come in and see for yourself!"

I went to the bathroom, and I was shocked to see a baby already starting to come out of my wife, right there in the bathroom. Luckily, the hospital was only five minutes away, because Steven was born just a few minutes after we got there. He was only a little smaller than Nick, he had a full head of dark brown hair, and he started crying the second he was born. As with Nick, I didn't leave his side until they returned him to Suzie.

So there we were: Suzie and I had our second child, and I was once again unemployed.

Sixteen

MICROSOFT'S ARROGANCE VERSUS MINE

When I was still working for Ashton-Tate, some of my employees asked if I had applied to Microsoft. I had no intention of applying to Microsoft. In the first place, I didn't want to move to Seattle, and in the second place, I *hated* Microsoft.

I wasn't alone in that hatred. Most people in tech—except, of course, those working for Microsoft—hated Microsoft too. Initially, IBM had been the 800-pound gorilla of tech, but Microsoft had taken them on and won, and now they had become just as powerful. They owned the operating system, DOS, which ran most PCs, and this meant that they dominated the market. What was more, two of my favorite programs, WordPerfect and Lotus 1-2-3, were being quickly destroyed by Microsoft's Word and Excel. Only Apple gave them any serious competition, and with their new operating system, Windows, which resembled the Mac user interface, they were poised to give even Apple trouble. They were the evil empire. Why would I want to be part of that?

But then I listened to all of my testing team tell me, one by one, that Microsoft's Menlo Park office, just north of San Jose, had turned them down. My entire testing staff was considered beneath Microsoft's standards. These were good testers. Microsoft would be lucky to have them.

At the time, I was still waiting for the final layoff from Ashton-Tate. I had already been passing my résumé around and getting some responses, and I knew that I would have at least a few months of salary coming as part of my severance package. I also knew that I would get job offers and that I would have some time to decide between options. So for the first time in a while, I had a little bit of opportunity to have some fun.

I thought, *the arrogance of these people, turning down all of my people*. I'd show *them* arrogance.

All of my staff had interviewed with the same woman at the Menlo Park office, the test manager for Microsoft PowerPoint. We'll call her Agnes. My staff gave me her contact information.

I got Agnes on the phone. "My name is George Santino. I'm the test manager at Ashton-Tate. I understand that you've interviewed all my employees and turned them down. I'd like to apply for a job so that you can turn me down too. That way you can say you batted 1000."

She paused for a moment. "Batted 1000?" she finally asked.

"If you turn me down too," I said, explaining the reference, "you can say that you turned down all of the testing staff from Ashton-Tate when they asked you for a job."

She hesitated and asked me to repeat who I was and why I was calling.

"George Santino. Test manager at Ashton-Tate. I want you to turn me down for a position at Microsoft."

I could hear what sounded like a "hum" or an "um" before she spoke again. "I'm not sure what you're asking me. Are you applying for a job?"

"Yes, but I want you to turn me down for it."

"If you're serious, please send me your résumé."

She didn't sound particularly enthusiastic, but I didn't care. I sent her my résumé, formatted nicely and with new tech-industry-professional experience.

A week later I got a form letter from Microsoft saying, "Thank you for your interest. We currently do not have any openings that fit your experience. We will keep your résumé on file."

They turned me down without even an *interview*? Now I was even more pissed. I called Agnes back.

"I got your letter," I said. "You turned me down without an interview."

She said, "Aren't you the guy who said you wanted to be turned down?"

"Yes, but I'd think you'd at least have to interview me to know I'm not a fit before you send me a rejection."

"If we interview you and make you an offer, would you take the job?"

"Of course," I lied.

She asked me if I could come in the next day.

Suzie made no secret of the fact that she thought I was wasting time and screwing around. But I wasn't really risking anything. By this point, I already had offers from other software companies, and I had more interviews scheduled for the next week, with the possibility of more offers. I wasn't sure which offer I should take, and I wanted to see how the interviews went first. As soon as I had all of my *serious* offers, I was going to compare the salaries and the benefits of each. I knew that wherever I went next was where I wanted to make my career, so it was important to be careful.

I also knew that I had no intention of working for a big, evil company like Microsoft. But I was going to the interview anyway. I'd show them up for their arrogance. I didn't know what to expect, and I didn't care. I didn't even prepare.

Microsoft's Menlo Park office, where the PowerPoint team was based, was located in an area of rolling hills and woods on a street called Sand Hill Road—some of the most expensive real estate in the area.

The Microsoft waiting room was really nice. They had better chairs then I had in my home, and there was art on every wall. I had to look back at the sign on the door to make sure I was at Microsoft and didn't make a wrong turn into a gallery.

My first interviewer was a tester in his midtwenties, about ten years younger than me. He led me to his own private office. That was my first experience with culture shock. A kid this young with his own door that he could close? The Ashton-Tate guy in me said, This kid is too young. He should have to be in a bullpen and then work his way up.

He asked me testing questions and a few of the logic questions that Microsoft had already become famous for. *Why are manhole covers round? How many gas stations are there in the US?* The point of these questions was not to see whether you knew the answer, but how you went about figuring it out. For instance, to figure out how many gas stations there are, you might first want to figure out how many cars there are. You might be able to figure that out by starting with how many people are in the United States and then guess how many cars there are for so many people and how many gas stations might be needed to service that number of cars.

The manhole question was easy for me: Manhole covers are round because they are heavy, and this makes them easy to move. Apparently the interviewer also wanted to hear that square covers could fall in the hole, but it was still enough to let me move on to the next part of the interview. So the first interviewer ushered me out to the lobby to wait for the next interviewer to come through.

By the end of the day, I'd been interviewed by four testers, one developer, and finally Agnes. All of them were younger than me. I left the building thinking that I'd done well. I was sure that they would make me an offer. Once they did, I would get to turn them down, just like they'd turned down all of my people. End of fun distraction, on with my life.

A few days later, I got a copy of the same rejection letter.

What? I knew I'd done well in those interviews. What could the problem be? I called Agnes again.

"Why didn't you make me an offer?" I asked.

"Well, you don't have a college degree."

"College degree? *College degree?* Have you heard of Bill Gates?"

"Of course I've heard of Bill Gates."

"I assume you know *he* doesn't have a college degree."

"Are you comparing yourself to Bill Gates?" she asked.

"No. My point is that not having a college degree shouldn't be the only reason to turn someone down. After all, Bill Gates doesn't have one, and neither does Steve Jobs. When I was in college in the early seventies, personal computers didn't even *exist*. If I stayed in college, I would have gotten a degree in business management. Instead I went out and got seventeen years of business management experience."

There was a pause on the other end. Normally I might've worried that I was being too pushy. But I was still planning to walk away and find a real job. This was just a game to me. Wasn't it?

She hummed a little like she was confused again, but she understood. "Good point. Would you be willing to come in for another interview?"

By this point, I had four serious job offers from tech companies. Why wasn't Microsoft one of them? Who did these people think they were?

"Absolutely," I told Agnes.

At the second interview, the Microsoft testers asked me a bunch of hardware questions—an area I knew well, thanks to my time at Ashton-Tate and my afternoons with Johnson spent pulling apart computers to see how they worked. They also asked me about networking (the server kind, not the social kind), which I knew nothing about. I didn't come out of this set of interviews as confidently as I had the first, but I thought I'd done well enough to get an offer.

Two days later I got the same form letter.

These people had to be kidding. I couldn't imagine what they wanted, and I'd have to call to hear this new objection. As furious as I was by now, my days as a salesman had taught me that it was important not to minimize or ridicule objections, even Agnes'. I may have thought they were lame, but that attitude got me no closer to my goal: having an offer from Microsoft so that I could turn it down.

I'm told that a lot of people would've accepted the third "no" and moved on, looking back and wondering what would've gotten them through the door.

That's not the way I was built. I always wanted to know things, and I was never afraid of asking. That way, even if a situation didn't go my way, I could look back knowing that I'd gotten everything I possibly could from the experience, and that the extra information I'd gleaned might help me next time.

Since I assumed Microsoft's latest objection was going to be about my lack of network knowledge, this time I prepared. I did some role-playing in my head. If Agnes asked me a question about networking, I would reply, "How much network knowledge do I really need?" I knew this was a job to test PowerPoint. I had spent the last two years testing a product just like it, and while we did have to install a Novell network to do some testing, that installation certainly didn't require the in-depth knowledge of networking that they'd asked me about in the most recent interview. If they told me that the job actually did require network knowledge, then I would counter with, "I have complete confidence in my ability to learn what I don't know. I assume you have the same level of confidence in your ability to teach."

Ready with my responses to their possible questions, I called Agnes again.

"I got your latest form letter. I still don't understand why you rejected me. It's my third rejection, by the way."

Agnes said, "We're concerned about your experience."

"Network experience, right? Let me ask you something: How much experience do I—"

"Windows experience."

"What do you mean?"

"We're looking for people with at least five years of Windows testing experience."

This was in 1991. Windows 2.0 had been released at the end of 1987, and many companies had yet to get on board with it. Five years ago, when Agnes said I'd have to have started testing Windows applications, was 1986. In 1986 most people felt lucky to have access to a computer at all, and those who had a PC were treated to a black and orange or black and green display and had to save their work on 5.25 inch floppy disks. Few people outside of the main Microsoft campus in Redmond, Washington, had seen or used Windows in 1986.

"Are you kidding? Five years? Who has five years Windows testing experience? You guys just came out with Windows 3.0.

I can't imagine many people were using Windows before that, including you."

Don't get me wrong. I didn't say this in a mean way—I think I even laughed when I said it. But I knew I was right, and I was pretty sure she would agree.

"You have a good point," she told me. "But I still don't think you're what we're looking for."

This was going to be my fourth rejection. What could her excuse possibly be? *Not what they're looking for*. That wasn't only insulting, it was *vague*. By now this had become a Microsoft versus George smackdown, and I was more determined than ever to win. So I ran through the list of all possible objections with her again.

"Look, I have two years of experience testing Applause for Windows. That's one of the few products outside of Microsoft being developed for Windows. I have plenty of people management experience. I built the test lab for Ashton-Tate from nothing. No one will work harder than I will."

The phrase "test lab" seemed to hit a chord.

She said, "I might have an idea. Could I call you in a couple of days?"

"Fine. But I have other offers, and I have to make a decision soon."

"I'll get back to you."

I guess that wasn't technically a rejection. Still, it was a *maybe*, and a maybe isn't a *yes*.

And something had changed, I could tell. When I'd started this process, I had no intention of going to work for Microsoft. But after three nos and a maybe, I was fed up with them. Now I *did* want to take a job with them—if only to show them, by becoming one of the best hires they'd ever had, just how wrong they were to take so long to offer it to me.

A couple of days later, one of the companies who'd made me a job offer said that they were at the point where they needed to make a hiring decision. If I wanted a job with them, I'd need to let them know now. It was a job I was definitely interested in taking. Suddenly, the time I could spend having fun by screwing around with Microsoft was running out.

Later that day, Agnes called me back.

She said, "I thought about what you told me about the lab you built at Ashton-Tate. We have a test lab and need someone to take care of it. Would you be interested?"

I said, "Lady, I will take a job sweeping the floors if that's what it takes to get in there and show you people that you were right to hire me."

"Funny you should say that," she countered, "because keeping the lab clean *would* be a part of your responsibilities."

I didn't care. I wasn't worried about cleaning a lab as part of my entry-level position. Experience had told me that if I worked hard and well, it wouldn't matter where I started, but where I finished.

"If you're making me an offer," I told her, "I need it fast. I told another company that I'd give them an answer by tomorrow."

"We'll courier it over this afternoon," she said, and the call was over.

That afternoon, the offer I'd worked so hard to be able to turn down arrived. It was disappointing. Of the four other offers I had on the table, the Microsoft offer was twenty percent below the lowest.

I called Agnes. "Your offer isn't good enough," I told her.

"That's the offer. Take it or leave it." There was that Microsoft arrogance again. I was wavering now, wondering if I shouldn't just take the best offer of the four and kiss Microsoft good-bye, but then she went on to say, "Did you notice the number of stock options?"

"Sure, I see them. But I can't buy food for my family with stock options. Why don't you keep your options and give me more salary?"

And then Agnes surprised me. "You don't know what you're talking about. Be quiet and take the offer. Trust me. You'll be glad you did."

I just had to see what she meant.

When John and Chris heard that I'd accepted a job at Microsoft, after telling them for weeks that I had no intention of doing so, you can bet they were shocked.

"You hate those people," Chris reminded me.

And I did. But now, I wanted to show them how much I hated them by proving just how wrong they had been to delay hiring me for so long—after multiple interviews, and after they'd rejected every other qualified person on my staff—only to put me in an entry-level job that would involve cleaning up a lab. It was the three-ring binders all over again—must have five years' Windows experience, must have college degree—and the best way I could make a difference at Microsoft, I felt, was to prove just how faulty their hiring scripts were by how well I'd perform.

And again, I wasn't taking any risks. I still had my severance package, and if the job sucked, I had plenty of other offers on the table. I could quit at my leisure. But soon enough, I realized just what Agnes had been trying to tell me about those stock options, and there was no reason to look back.

This episode in my life begs the question, "So? Who won?" I've always looked at this exchange as a challenge, and I still do. But now, twenty-five years later, it also seems like a negotiation.

Like most negotiations, this one had two sides, each trying to get what they wanted. In the beginning, Microsoft didn't know what they wanted, and I knew what I definitely didn't want. If I had been less persistent, or if Agnes had stopped taking my calls, we both would have lost.

Instead, I like to think that we both won. They got a hard working employee who wasn't afraid to ask questions or be specific. And I got what I didn't realize I'd needed when I first called Agnes and asked her to reject me: an excellent working environment where my skills and persistence would be assets.

I was starting as the lab coordinator, having taken the job for all the wrong reasons. But once I was there, I focused on doing the best job that I could. And in a very short time, I realized that my aspirations had become higher—much, much higher.

Seventeen

PRESENTING MYSELF

Here's how Microsoft was structured when I started with them in October 1991. Every tester began as an individual contributor, or IC. Above IC was test lead, and then test manager. Test manager was about as high as most testers usually climbed in their career. Above that was the product unit manager, or PUM, and above that was general manager. A general manager could also be a partner, or not. Above that was vice president, and at least when I started, above that was the one president of the company.

I started out as a lab coordinator in the PowerPoint group at Microsoft. One of my responsibilities was to help keep the lab clean. Everything I've just described was still above me.

PowerPoint was one of the smallest business units at Microsoft, with only about one hundred people at that time. It was the only product they developed in their Menlo Park office. I would be their lab rat. It was a job I didn't want, but it was the job that changed my life.

My first goal was to get out of that lab. This wasn't so much because the lab was a bad place. In fact, it was a much better lab than the one I'd had at Ashton-Tate. The room was large, with tables along the walls and more in the center of the room. There were no windows, but the room was well lit and packed with all the latest hardware and software. Unlike at Ashton-Tate, I wouldn't have to reach into my own pocket to buy a printer cable here. But I didn't come to Microsoft to work in a lab.

Not that the job as lab coordinator was hard. I knew the hardware, and I didn't mind keeping the lab clean either. But the lab was a dead end. I had no direct reports like I did at Ashton-Tate. Here I was an army of one, an entry-level peon with aspirations. Microsoft was a software company, so if I wanted to move up, I had to become a software tester.

After my first day, I went home and told Suzie my plan.

"From this point forward, I have two jobs," I said. "From 9:00 a.m. until 6:00 p.m. Monday through Friday, I'll be the best damn lab coordinator they have ever seen. But from 6:00 p.m. until 9:00 p.m. Monday through Friday and 10:00 a.m. until 4:00 p.m. on Saturday, I'll test PowerPoint." It was my plan to find more bugs than their software testers, so that when they needed a new official tester, I would get the job.

Suzie had just had our second child, Stevie, less than two weeks ago. Nick, our first child, was only eighteen months old. She had dealt with my working long hours at Ashton-Tate as I tried to move ahead, but that was with one child. Now we had two.

But as had become her habit in the ten years we'd been married—through real estate and restaurants and surgeries and narcotics detox and cross-country moves and one bankruptcy and repossessed car—she gave me her full support. Not the first time,

I couldn't believe how lucky I was to have a wife like Suzie in my corner. We agreed that she would put all her effort into the home front, and I would concentrate on my career.

A lot of people used the lab. Mostly it was testers finding bugs and programmers trying to fix those bugs, but even sales and marketing people came in to see how the product was progressing. I made sure to talk to everyone and learn all I could about the way things worked within Microsoft.

One thing I had heard from a number of people was that Microsoft was all about results. The entire review system and one's progress up the ladder had everything to do with what you accomplished. Microsoft also was a place that didn't listen to people who said, "Give me that opportunity and I'll show you what I can do." No: You had to *show* that you could do it first, and then they'd trust you with the opportunity.

I had no problem with that. I wanted to be a software tester, and I was willing to demonstrate that ability *before* I had the job.

Over the next few months, that's exactly what I did. I made sure my lab met the needs of the testers and developers as my day job, and I found bugs as my night and weekend job. I made sure my bug reports had all the information the developers needed to reproduce the problem, and when they had questions, I made sure to respond quickly. Soon I was entering more bugs than many of the testers.

In the meantime, I realized exactly what Agnes had meant about the stock options included in my low-salary offer. Since I'd been hired, Microsoft stock had gone up fifty percent, and the company had just announced a stock split. As I said, there was no looking back.

About three months after I started, I heard from some developers working in the lab that the testing team needed to hire more testers. This was my chance. I planned to talk to Agnes the next day, since she was the PowerPoint test manager and would be the one to make the decision.

But before I could say anything to her myself, the reputation that I'd been working to build paid off. Agnes mentioned to a couple of developers that she was preparing to run an ad in the paper for two more testers. Both developers that she talked to said that they would prefer for me to test their code.

"You know he's the lab coordinator, right?" she reportedly said. "Not a tester."

One of the developers told her, "I think you're wasting his talent in the lab."

The next day, Agnes came to me and asked if I wouldn't mind leaving the lab to become a full-time tester. I, of course, said that I would. "I told you I would make a good software tester."

"I always knew you would," she told me.

Before I could disagree with her memory, she went on to say, "Aren't you glad you listened to me about the offer?"

I had no choice but to tell her, "You were right on that point." At least we'd learned to communicate with each other, if only to disagree.

I got to go home that day and tell Suzie that I'd accomplished my first goal. I was out of the lab and into software.

But this was only the beginning. Now that I was a software tester, my next goal was to become a test lead, and after that, a test manager. To do so, I would have to continue to work the long hours I was getting used to. This time, I would be the best software tester I could be from 9:00 a.m. until 6:00 p.m. Monday through Friday, but from 6:00 p.m. until 9:00 p.m. Monday through Friday and 10:00 a.m. until 4:00 p.m. on Saturday, I would start to do more leadership things. That is, I would look for opportunities to improve the processes we used and to try and lead the other testers by example.

I wasn't the only one working long hours. Microsoft was great at hiring smart people who were willing to work hard. And Microsoft was great at rewarding those people. I had already had my first review, and I got a double-digit percentage raise. I also had stock options and would get many more over the years.

Stock options were one of Microsoft's smartest ways of keeping employees. When you were hired and during your performance review, you could earn stock options. But although the number they were willing to give could be large, you didn't get them right away. They would vest over time. These options were affectionately known as "golden handcuffs."

One thing I noticed was that a lot of people tended to exercise these options as they vested, spending the money rather than leaving it in place to grow. Everyone knew that when an employee showed up with their first new car, they had most likely just experienced their first vesting.

Personally, I still drove the car I'd brought with us on the flatbed from Florida. It wasn't in great shape, and the windows leaked, but it ran. Suzie was driving a car we'd bought from her grandfather. We both would've liked a new car, but Suzie and I agreed that we would not touch my stock options. They would either be worth a lot some day or nothing, but in the meantime, we would live on my salary, which would get better with every review.

Microsoft also had other investment programs, including an employee stock purchase program and a 401k, into which they put matching money. That matching money and the discount on employee stock purchases was free money, so I participated fully in both.

But as I said, the next step in my plan was to move into management. This is where I knew my skills really lay. So I started working with the other testers.

One of those other testers was Dan Hoffman. Dan was younger than me, but so were most people at Microsoft. Dan also wanted to be a test lead. So shortly after we became friends, we started a period of what has since become known as "coopetition." Basically, we cooperated as we looked to bring about change, but we also knew that we were competing for the same career opportunities.

We started to do things like "buddy testing," where we and the other testers looked at one another's areas while someone was out sick or on vacation so that the area wouldn't get too buggy while they were gone. We also did something that I called "tag team testing" where we would test an area together. There is an old testing saying: Bugs nest together. If you find a bug in your kitchen, you can assume there are probably more and get out the bug spray. Likewise, if you find a bug in code, you know there are probably more in the same area. So when Dan or I found a bug, the other person would suggest other, similar ways to break the product. These fresh eyes on the area helped to find many good bugs.

Everything was going well, and I was well on the way to showing Agnes what I could do, when one day a very heavy printer was scheduled to arrive at the lab. They delivered it to my office while I was out at lunch. Had I been there, I would've just asked them to take it to the lab directly, but here it was on my floor. Without thinking about it, I bent down to pick it up, and suddenly pain shot into my back as if I'd been stabbed. Soon my whole leg was in pain, and I was on the floor.

Even though I'd never recovered completely from my beer-lifting injury and my back hurt all the time, some days were worse than others. There were days when I could get so engaged in what I was doing that I could even forget that I had a bad back. Toward the end of those days, my back would suddenly remind me about that fact, so much so that I had to lie down *immediately*.

Which is what happened—and worse—after I lifted that heavy printer.

How could I have been so stupid? I asked myself. *I just got this job.*

I didn't tell my coworkers anything. I hadn't told them about the surgeries when I'd been hired, and no one had seen the accident happen. As far as they knew, this was a new injury. So I told them that I had tweaked my back, and I asked one of them to drive me home.

The next day I could hardly move. I asked Suzie to take me to the hospital. They did an MRI, and the doctor told me that my back was beyond repair. He said the disc above my fusion was starting to tear, and that he could prescribe some Vicodin and Flexeril for the pain, but that was all. I said that I didn't want the drugs, so he told me to stay off my feet for a few days. He went on to say that he didn't know how I was even able to work, and that I definitely shouldn't be putting in the hours I was.

I had heard this all before. The only reason I went to the hospital was to make sure that I hadn't done any real damage, like fracturing my fusion. Since that wasn't the case, I was back to work in a few days. I spent a lot of time lying on the floor with a keyboard on my lap. I took all the aspirins I could find in the first aid kit in the Microsoft kitchen, and though it took a couple of weeks before I could put in the same crazy hours, I was still leading by example. Soon, I knew it would pay off.

PowerPoint was continuing to grow as a product, and we were adding more and more features in order to increase sales. This required hiring more developers, and more developers meant more testers. Soon Agnes had twenty people working for her, and her boss, the product unit manager, said that it was time to hire test leads. He told her that with twenty testers she should have four test leads reporting to her, with four people reporting to each test lead.

She told him that this was no problem, and that she'd hire four test leads.

He told her, "Don't you mean three? I assume George is already a lead."

He was *almost* right. I was a leader, but now I was officially a lead.

Agnes picked three other leads, but sadly Dan Hoffman wasn't one. I asked Dan to work on my team, so he asked Agnes if he could be assigned to me. But Dan and I both knew it was only short term. Dan was as ambitious as I was, and there was only so high you could go in Microsoft if you wanted to stay in California. Once the leads were picked, there wouldn't be an opportunity for anyone else here to become a lead unless one of the existing ones left or was hit by a bus. Dan knew this, and soon he was presented with an opportunity to move to Redmond, Washington, where Microsoft was headquartered and where they developed all of their other products. One of those products was Microsoft Word, and Dan became a lead there.

We stayed in touch, which would eventually bring about my next move. But before that happened, I had a team to build in PowerPoint.

I was assigned a few testers on my team, and I wanted to make sure we got more than our fair share of work done. I continued to lead by example by finding plenty of bugs, but I realized that we could do so much more. We had a system of testing the product as a whole, as well as the areas of the product we were assigned, but it was a manual process that was very repetitive, labor intensive, lengthy, and boring.

Here's an example of a manual test for something like Word. I click to open the application. I start a new document. I type in some text, and then I make some of it bold, italic, whatever we're testing. I try to print it out. If I find a bug, I assign it to the developer. They fix it and make a new build of the product. Once I verify the fix, I run all my tests again. I do all of that over and over. After hours of this, everyone's brain was shut down from tedium. This meant that we weren't thinking about new and innovative ways to stress the product; we were too busy finishing our repetitive tasks to think.

It was the three-ring binders all over again. I had to find a better way. We needed automation.

I explained it to Agnes. Instead of performing all the test steps ourselves, I could write programs that would perform those steps for us. The program could even be set to run on a timer, so that in theory, all of us could be testing software while home in bed.

She said, "If you automate everything, then what would the testers do?"

"Design new test cases," I said. "That way we're not only doing the testing we'd normally be doing, but we're doing *more* testing, and we're doing it in a smarter way."

She just didn't understand: To her, testers ran the tests. That was our job. So I decided I needed to show her how this would work, and I knew just the guy who could help me with this: my old friend, Chris Burroughs.

Chris was the guy I met at Ashton-Tate who told me how to test those printers, plotters, and cameras. Chris was also a very hard worker who was always looking for ways to improve processes. If I intended to be a successful manager, I needed to surround myself with good people, and Chris was one of those people.

Chris had gone to work for Borland after Ashton-Tate, and like me, he hadn't been a big fan of Microsoft. After coming to work at Microsoft, I learned that I was wrong about the supposed "evil empire," and now I had to convince Chris of the same thing. I gave him a call, and as I expected, he wasn't really interested in coming to work at Microsoft. I didn't give up. I talked to him about how a results-oriented guy like him could do well here, and I talked to him about all the great things we could do. It took a few calls and a lunch or two, but I finally convinced Chris to apply.

A few days later, Chris came in for his interview. He talked to five people, and I was one of them. Of course I said I wanted him. In fact, I think everyone did except for Agnes.

"I'm not sure he has the skills," she said.

"You thought the same thing about me, remember?" I said.

"But he doesn't have a college degree."

And here we go again.

"Are you kidding? I know he doesn't have a college degree. Are you seriously bringing that up? Am I not working out well?"

"I don't want to get into the habit of hiring people without degrees," she said.

"I know you have a hang-up about only hiring college grads, but every now and then you find someone who truly can add value to a team with or without a degree. I was one of those people, and Chris is another."

She relented, and Chris was hired, but not before Agnes said, "If he doesn't work out, I'll hold you accountable."

I think she meant it as a threat. I didn't find it threatening; I knew that Chris would work out great. Besides, I already knew that I was accountable for every decision I made.

I already had a few good people on my team, but with Chris, we were really going to add value. We immediately got started on automating our tests. Agnes didn't approve it or like it, but I decided I'd ask for forgiveness later instead of permission now, and we kept writing automation.

But soon enough, we realized that even creating these automated tests was a bit monotonous. All of it was "black box" testing—testing through the user interface, with each tester acting as an end user—and setting up black box tests took almost as much time as it might've done to run the tests the hard manual way. We needed to be smarter.

That's when another piece of the puzzle fell in place. A résumé crossed my desk from a guy named Anil Mehra. Anil was from India, but he was a PhD candidate here in the states. I was impressed that he was working on his PhD, and I had him in for an interview. He was a down-to-earth guy, and he had some interesting ideas about testing, which he viewed as an interesting personal challenge. I was talking to him about our black box tests, and soon I realized that he had ideas for bypassing the user interface altogether and using his knowledge to test directly from the program code. I liked the way he thought, and I wanted him on my team.

Once Anil joined, all the puzzle pieces were in place to truly change the way we tested. Soon, Chris and Anil had come up with a brilliant automation plan, one that not only worked for Power-Point but for other products as well.

It was time to reveal what we'd done, and we set a meeting to show our work to Agnes and to her boss. Agnes wasn't a fan, but her boss was thrilled.

One thing I've learned about being a manager is to be quick to give credit and slow to lay blame. In fact, I always say that the successes belong to my team, but the failures are mine. My superiors know that some of the credit is mine and that not all of the blame belongs to me, but I don't have to say it.

I've also always been a big fan of making sure my bosses—whoever they are—get plenty of credit. My attitude is simple. The more your boss puts things that you and your team get done in their own performance reviews, the better the reviews for you and your team will be as well.

So now—after we'd built a new automated testing system virtually from scratch, over the objections of our test manager—I thanked Agnes publicly for all of her support. The business unit manager congratulated her for her foresight.

During the months and years that had passed, things went well at work and at home. Though I worked six days a week—sometimes seven, if we were about to ship a product—I usually got to spend Sundays at home with Suzie and the kids. I tried to make up for the heavy workload by spending maximum quality time, reading them stories and playing with them. I was probably the only father out with them and the neighborhood kids, running around our cul-de-sac on Sunday mornings when other dads were still reading the newspapers.

One time, Suzie told me that the other fathers in the cul-de-sac were always home for dinner with their families, while I was late. I told her to think about the stock options we were making through the company because of my hard work. "In ten, twenty years," I told her, "those other fathers will all still be working, hoping that Social Security doesn't run out before they retire, and I'll be home for breakfast, lunch, *and* dinner."

Life is full of trade-offs, and I have no regrets. Even my back held up pretty well, though I did tweak it a couple of times by horsing around with the kids. (Not by lifting printers—I learned that lesson.)

At work, my team and I continued to get great reviews. My salary had more than doubled, and I'd received many more stock options. Microsoft stock continued to go up, and it even split a second time since I'd joined the company. I was beginning to realize that I'd probably be with Microsoft until I retired.

But my next goal was still ahead of me. Now that I was a test lead, I wanted to become a test manager. And I knew I couldn't do that at Microsoft in California.

I had no real desire to move to Seattle. I heard that it rained there all the time. (Of course, any time I went up there for the company meeting, the sun was shining and the place was beautiful. I was starting to think that they just told the California people it rained all the time to keep us from moving there.)

But if I wanted to keep working for Microsoft, I knew I needed to start making some contacts in Redmond. Dan Hoffman was there and was a start, but I needed more.

Every year in San Francisco, there was an event called Software Quality Week. This was a weeklong event that allowed testers—or "software quality assurance engineers"—to come together, share ideas, and take classes and seminars. A number of testers and test managers from the Microsoft main campus in Redmond would always come down for the event.

This year, I decided to plan an event of my own. I talked to

Agnes about having a barbecue at our office. We'd send a bus to San Francisco and bring down some of the testers, test leads, and test managers visiting from Redmond to show them our site and some of our work. Agnes loved the idea.

At our site, not only would we have food, but I would have Chris and Anil demo their automation program. It was my hope that it would leave a lasting impression. It did just that, and after the barbecue and our automation demo, I had the chance to talk to a number of people from Redmond.

One of those people was Jeanne Sheldon. Jeanne was the test manager of Microsoft Word and my friend Dan Hoffman's boss. Jeanne was well known throughout Microsoft not only as a great test manager, but a great people manager as well. I had heard about her, but I had never met her until Dan introduced us. Jeanne and I had a great talk, and I found her very impressive.

"If you ever consider coming to Redmond," she told me, "give me a call."

It was the summer of 1994. I had been with PowerPoint for almost four years. During that time I went from lab coordinator to software tester to test lead. I received good reviews and nice salary increases and stock option grants, but my next goal was test manager, and I knew that wasn't going to happen in Microsoft's small California location. I had to talk to Suzie.

I knew Suzie wouldn't be happy about the idea of moving. Her parents had moved to California when she was eighteen years old, and while they'd really wanted her to go with them back then, she'd decided to stay in Tampa and continue to date me. That worked out very well for me, but Suzie missed her parents and sister, as well as all of her aunts, uncles, cousins, and grandparents. Aside from me, she'd been alone for almost ten years. But for the past six years, her whole family had all been together again in the same state. More importantly, our children were being raised around them. When I talked to her about possibly moving to Redmond, she told me that she wasn't sure she wanted to give all of that up.

What's more, Suzie would soon be pregnant again with what we thought would be our third and last child. Nicholas was four years old now, and Steven was two. Suzie really wanted a little girl, and had either Nick or Stevie been a girl, I think we would have stopped at two. I just wasn't a big fan of three kids. With two, we were even: We could play man-to-man defense, but with three, we would have to play a zone.

But as Suzie pointed out, I was the one going to work seventy hours a week while she was the one taking care of the kids. She said she would be fine taking care of three. So we agreed that there would be three, but not four. If the third child was also a boy, we were done.

Although we agreed on that, however—three kids, not four— we weren't yet agreed on Seattle. Suzie didn't want to go, and I wasn't totally sure I wanted to either, despite the career advantages. But that fall, Suzie's parents went on vacation and spent some time in Seattle. When they came back, they told us that they thought the place was great, with good schools and cheap real estate compared to San Jose. They told us that it was a great place to raise kids, and they thought it would be a good idea for us to move there.

Suzie and I were surprised. "But we won't see you as much," she said to them.

They told her they would be there for all of the kids' birthdays and for Christmas every year. Suzie was still concerned, but she felt better about being farther away, and I felt better about my ambitions.

That November, just after my fourth anniversary at Microsoft, I told Agnes that I was moving to Redmond. I didn't have a job there yet, but once my mind was made up, I saw no point in waiting. I told her that Chris Burroughs could take over my team as lead, and she agreed.

I set a date for being in Redmond right after the first of the year. Now the only problem was to find a job.

The first person I called was Dan Hoffman. Dan told me that Jeanne, the manager whom I'd met at the barbecue, was looking for a test lead on the Word team at the Redmond campus. That sounded interesting, but I wanted to check out some other jobs as well. Just as I'd done with my prior job search, I wanted to see all my options spread out on a kitchen table and carefully compare each one before coming to a decision.

I talked to the Microsoft internal recruiter, and she set me up with interviews with three groups, one of which was Word. I flew up to Seattle that next week.

When I arrived on the Redmond campus, I was told that I would interview with two groups one day and then Word on the second day. After that, I would return home, and they would call me. I wasn't worried at all about these interviews. I had been working for Microsoft for four years now, and in total I now had six years of testing experience.

But on that first day of interviews, the interviewer started with one of Microsoft's famous logic questions. Hadn't I been through this before? Hadn't I been vetted years ago? It seemed like a waste of time.

"So now you know I know why manhole covers are round," I told him at the end of the interview, after a number of logic questions had passed, "and how to get a fox, a chicken, and a bag of corn across a river. But you have no idea if I can test."

He didn't respond, but instead took me to the next interviewer. This one had more software testing questions for me, but he also wanted to talk a lot about why I didn't have a college degree.

"You know I already work here, right?" I asked him. I honestly thought that I was past all this. I had been here for four years, and I had accomplished quite a bit. I thought that I had earned some respect. But this guy didn't know me, and he didn't care about what I'd accomplished with PowerPoint.

The rest of the day didn't go much better. I was once again faced with that Microsoft arrogance that I had started to forget about. As an insider, Microsoft is a great place to work, filled with great people. To an outsider, though, some of them can be real pricks, and for some reason I had become an outsider again.

At the end of the day I met up with Dan Hoffman, and we went to dinner. I told Dan about my day, and he said, "I don't know why you're even bothering with these other groups. You should just take the test lead job in Word."

"I haven't even interviewed with them yet."

"Don't worry about that. Jeanne and I both know you, and we know you'll do a great job."

The next day I went to the Word offices, as part of the official interview process, but it went very differently than the first few rounds of interviews with the different groups. I talked to six different people. Nobody patronized me; nobody was an arrogant prick. Nobody asked me about manhole covers.

At the end of the day, Jeanne asked, "So, are you going to come to work with me?"

I found it interesting that she said *with* me and not *for* me. I told her right away that I would be thrilled to, and then I went to call Suzie.

Eighteen

THE WORD IS CHANGE

Moving from California to Seattle was a lot easier than moving from Florida to California. Microsoft took care of everything. They assigned us a relocation specialist who hired packers and movers. There was no U-Haul truck or bridge to go around. We would fly up and stay in an apartment that Microsoft provided. They even hired a realtor to help us find a house.

The first week of January 1995, we were in Washington State.

Remember when I said that it rained in Seattle all the time, but that I hadn't seen any rain on any of my visits? Well, on the day we arrived it was raining, and it rained every day of the first three weeks we were there. It kind of sucked, but we'd made the move, and there was no going back.

I started work in Word the day after we arrived. Suzie worked with the realtor to narrow down the search for houses, and when she found a couple she liked, I took a look. Suzie was about two months pregnant and wasn't feeling very well. With her other two pregnancies she'd had morning sickness, but this time, it seemed a lot worse.

A couple of weeks after we arrived, I decided that it would be neat to take Suzie, Nicholas, and Steven up to the mountains so that the boys could experience snow for the first time. Suzie wasn't a big fan of the cold, but she thought it would be fun.

On the car ride up to Snoqualmie Pass, Suzie started to have some serious morning sickness. When we arrived, she said that she would stay in the car for a little while. So the boys and I went into the snow and started to have a snowball fight, and then they started to slide down the hill. The kids thought this was a blast. We even started to build a snowman, but the boys got carried away, and soon they had built a base bigger than they were.

After a while, we decided to check on Suzie. When we got to the car, she wasn't there. We searched for her, and there, behind a nearby snowbank, we found Suzie lying in the snow. Suzie who hated the cold.

"I needed to lie down," she said as soon as she saw us.

We decided to head home. That night, I asked her, "This is just morning sickness, right?"

"It's much worse," she said.

The next day, Suzie went to see her doctor while I stayed home with the boys. About two hours later, she walked into the apartment with a strange look on her face and a greeting card in her hand. She gave me the card, and when I opened it she pulled out an Instamatic camera and took a picture of the expression on my face as soon as I read the words on it. *Congratulations! You're having twins!*

That's right: twins. We were going to have four kids after all.

Not everything, it turns out, is in your control.

Suzie had been seeing an OB/GYN in San Jose who hadn't said anything to her about twins. In fact, this new OB/GYN assumed that she already knew. During her visit, he'd asked her how she was feeling, and she'd said she felt bad. He told her that it was normal morning sickness. Suzie pointed out that she'd had two other babies, and while she did get sick, she didn't get *this* sick. This new doctor said, "But you didn't have them both at the same time, did you?"

Suzie said, "Of course not."

"Well," he said. "You're twice as sick because this time, you're having two at the same time." That's how she found out.

So now we knew we would have four kids. But the big question was, would Suzie be dogpiled by a houseful of boys? Or would she get the girl she'd always wanted? (Either way, we both knew that after four kids, we were definitely done.)

We scheduled an ultrasound to find out our answer. The problem with this test was that while they can tell you the sex of the baby, that wasn't the main focus. They wanted to check out every inch of each of these babies, and there was an order in which to do it.

So Suzie lay there, holding my hand, while the technician ran the wand over her belly. The foot looked good, the ankle, the leg. It took almost fifteen minutes before we heard, "And baby number one is . . . a boy."

Suzie went from holding my hand to squeezing it pretty hard.

Of course she immediately asked if the other one was a girl. But they couldn't tell her that yet. They had to finish looking at all the other parts of baby number one, and then they could start on baby number two.

It was the longest twenty minutes of my life, and the circulation in my hand was completely gone by the time we heard, "And baby number two is . . . a girl."

Thank God.

Three months after moving to Washington, we moved into the new house that Suzie had found for us in Woodinville. It wasn't far from Microsoft, and it had good schools and a small wine community that reminded us of Napa. But we didn't dare say the word "wine" around Suzie, who was still barfing from twice as much morning sickness as usual.

Not only did we now have a nice house, we also had great neighbors. When we first moved into our new place, they all came over one after the other with cookies, cakes, and pies to welcome us to the neighborhood. Suzie said, "I guess I won't have to cook tonight."

I said, "I'm not eating any of this food. I don't know these people."

You have to remember that I was from the projects. I wasn't used to nice neighbors bringing me food. Even in San Jose, where we'd lived in a nice neighborhood, people kept to themselves. Here, people would ask you how you were doing while you were walking down the street, and they'd really want to know the answer.

Over the years, I got over my suspicion, and we would become good friends with all of these people. We would have neighborhood

Easter egg hunts, pumpkin carvings, and fantastic Fourth of July block parties. And they really came through for us in ways that we couldn't have foreseen before the twins were born.

At work, Jeanne Sheldon had welcomed me to a strong team of people. Word was much bigger than PowerPoint. While PowerPoint had twenty testers, Word had sixty. I was one of eight leads. My goal was still the same as it had been: to become a test manager. Jeanne knew that, and she was willing to work with me toward that end. She was not only my boss but a mentor, and she really knew a lot about testing and managing people. She continued to teach me a lot as I grew as a lead.

My first assignment was to manage the workgroup feature team. I had about six people working for me. One of those people was a young man by the name of Quentin Clark. Quentin was brilliant, and he was working on a new way to open websites through Word. At the time, if you wanted to use the Internet, you'd have to know the IP address of the web page you wanted to visit, using software to connect your computer to an address like *184.168.47.225*. Quentin was working on technology to allow an address like that to be given in a much more user-friendly format—for example, *georgeasantino.com*—which you could then open in Word. The stuff he was doing was so cool and innovative that Bill Gates even came to his office once to see it.

I knew that Quentin would go far in the company, but for now, he was the top guy on my team. Quentin didn't need a lot of management from me. While I was his lead, I was more of his mentor, and he worked on his project in a very independent way.

I spent my time managing the rest of my people. Word had a lot of processes in place, so initially, there wasn't a lot of opportunity for me to bring about the kind of change that I'd brought in PowerPoint. Soon, though, a chance presented itself.

One of the test teams in Word worked on automation tools. One day, the lead of that team decided to leave Microsoft. Jeanne came to me and asked if I knew anyone who could take over the team. I said I would.

Jeanne asked, "Who will run your team?"

"I'll run that one as well."

"This'll mean more hours."

"Not a problem."

I still had that deal with Suzie. From 9:00 a.m. until 6:00 p.m. Monday through Friday, I would be the best lead I could be, and from 6:00 p.m. until 9:00 p.m. Monday through Friday and 10:00 a.m. until 4:00 p.m. on Saturday, I would do everything I could to prove that I could be a test manager. So I took over the automation team. I now had the workgroup team, the automation team, and the project that Quentin was working on.

I knew that if I wanted to be a test manager, I had to do things that benefitted not only Word, but the rest of the products in what was becoming known as Microsoft Office: initially, Word, Excel, Access, and PowerPoint. The automation we had created for PowerPoint was going well, and our automation tool—TCG, or Test Case Generator, the program that built and ran the automatic test cases we came up with for PowerPoint, but also theoretically for any application you could think of—was even being used by a couple of groups in Redmond. So I decided to contact Chris and Anil and talk to them about helping me get it adopted across Office. They were happy to do so.

One of the people who now reported to me on the automation team was Juan Beaufrand. Juan was a very sharp developer, and he knew code and testing. He was my liaison with Chris and Anil in California to help implement TCG across Office. He was a very tall guy from Venezuela, about 6' 3", and he was very smart, but he was also very quiet. I told him many times that if he wanted to be heard in a meeting at Microsoft, he'd have to learn how to interrupt people. But he was never comfortable with that.

We made pretty good progress with adapting the tool, and we were finally ready to take it to the testing teams for the other products. Here was the problem, though: When we'd developed TCG for PowerPoint, there was no preexisting automation tool that we were replacing. But Word and the other Office products already had their own automation and tools in use.

Some groups within Microsoft had a phrase that I learned around this time: "not invented here." To me, this was more of that Microsoft arrogance, except now it was product unit arrogance. If *my* team created it, it was good; if *your* team did, it probably wasn't. In this case, we were the other team. Word was willing to adopt our methods, but Excel and Access weren't ready to admit that what we did, as outsiders, was actually better than their own internally developed tools.

There was no easy way to break this logjam. So rather than argue about whose tool was better, we started to talk about the benefits and shortcomings of each testing tool. As a result of those discussions, we decided to form a virtual team and work together on a new tool that we could all claim ownership of.

That's not to say it was all smooth sailing. But the concept of Office rather than the individual programs being the product was beginning to catch on, and the powers that be were thrilled to see us all finally working together.

Around this time I was also getting a reputation for building great teams and weeding out people who weren't performing well. Jeanne noticed this and started to move underperformers to my team. You would think that people would start to be afraid of being moved to my team for fear of being managed out, but it turned out to be exactly the opposite. I've always said that any idiot manager can fire someone, but it takes a good manager to turn a person around.

Any time I was given one of these challenge employees, I would sit down with the person and try to find out what the issue was. Sometimes it was just that they didn't have the skills they needed. If that was the case, I would make sure they got whatever training they lacked. Sometimes they were just in the wrong job altogether. If that was the case, and if I thought they would be successful in a different role, I would help them find it.

I would never transfer a problem to another team. If I wasn't sure that an employee would be successful, they would stay with me. I found that people who aren't doing well usually aren't happy in general. Usually they're also under a lot of stress in their current situation. But even though they're unhappy, they don't want to lose their jobs: A lot of people fear change, and it's better to have a job you hate than no job, right?

One time, I had an employee who'd initially seemed excellent on being hired, but who'd since been promoted and who was underperforming. After talking to him a while, we figured out the problem: As an entry-level tester, he was only required to find and report on bugs, which he could do very well. At the level he was currently, he was expected to know how to code and write automated test cases, and he didn't yet have those skills. I told him he had a choice. He could stay at his current level and try to learn the skills he didn't have yet, but in the meantime he'd get negative performance reviews. Alternately, he could take a demotion back to entry level and learn the same skills, but while meeting the expectations of his job. After thinking it over, he agreed with me that the demotion was the better choice. A year of studying and hard work later, when he was promoted again, he had the skills he needed to succeed at the higher level.

In a few cases, however, it turned out that I had a person who just wasn't going to be successful at Microsoft in any role. Whenever I reached that conclusion, I made sure that the employee and I always arrived at it jointly, after having worked together for a while. I did have a few of those over my years at Microsoft, and I'm glad to say that most of them landed in a better place. Once these people were in their new roles, their stress level generally went down and they were better off. A number of them came back and thanked me for the push in the right direction, even if that direction was out of the company altogether.

Another thing I noticed from underperformers is that they often didn't get the feedback they needed in order to adjust. Sure, Microsoft had their review process, but that was a formal way to get feedback on your goals and objectives twice a year so that you could be rewarded for your successes. And of course, that only happened if you had successes.

For some of these people, the twice yearly performance reviews were the only times they were getting feedback. Sure, it is easy for managers to say "good job," but few people like confrontation, so they save the comments that essentially say "bad job" for the review. The problem with this, however, is that it's too late. No one wants to hear how they could have done better at a task months after the fact, when the rewards are being given. They need to hear this along the way, when there's still time to do something about it.

I decided that on my team, we would do this differently. Every week, I would meet with my direct reports in one-on-one meetings. This meeting was mostly to talk about the issues of the day. Additionally, at the first one-on-one of the month, we would sit down and discuss the employee's goals and objectives, as well as how they were doing. This way, I could give people timely feedback that they could adjust to, if they wanted.

Not everyone wants to work hard, and that's fine. But they at least have the right to know what it would take to be considered exceptional, and therefore to get exceptional rewards. Only then can they decide if those rewards are worth it.

In my opinion, life is full of trade-offs. During my career, I chose to work hard and put in long hours. I did this in the hope of putting forth exceptional results and therefore getting exceptional rewards, the kind that could change the lives of my family and me forever. And this worked well for me, but I missed some school plays and weekend soccer games along the way. I had some people on my teams who said that they would never work a weekend or take away from their time with their family. That's an okay choice too.

I remember one lead saying to our manager at review time that it wasn't fair that George and his team got better rewards than he did. We worked weekends and created tools because our team thought it was fun to do that. He thought it was fun to hike on weekends, and he thought he should get rewarded for that. Sorry, that's not the way it works.

It was now the summer of 1995. It still mostly rained all the time, so I certainly didn't mind putting in all the hours. But one day, I arrived at work to find the place like a ghost town. I asked the first person I saw where everyone was, and they looked at me kind of strangely and replied that the sun was out. I guess I hadn't really taken notice. But the sun was out, the mountains were visible all around, and everything was green. Suddenly I understood why people put up with the rain. Once it stopped, this place—the Evergreen State—was beautiful.

Suzie was feeling better than she had been when we'd first moved here, but she was very pregnant, and she was ready for these two babies to get out of her. They weren't due until September, but we were told that twins sometimes come early. We weren't prepared for how early, though, because on July 22, 1995, Suzie began to give birth.

The first one to be born was Joey. Madelyn was next, but her water hadn't broken, so the doctor had to go in to get her. We didn't know it yet, but the fact that Madelyn's water hadn't broken saved her from what Joey was about to go through.

Joey ended up with an infection. It seems that a lot of mothers have this bacteria, and in most cases it doesn't infect the baby. From what we were told, however, premature vaginal births increase the chances of the infection being passed to the baby. It didn't infect Maddie, but it did Joey.

We didn't know this at first. Joey was born and taken off to be cleaned and checked like they do with all newborns. Maddie was born next and taken away, too. Since both of them were premature, they would have to be placed in incubators for a little while, after which they would let us hold them.

Finally, there we were: Suzie was holding Maddie, the little girl she'd always wanted, and I was holding Joey. As I looked at Joey, I noticed he was changing color from a nice new baby pink to purple. I said to the nurse, "Is this normal?"

She grabbed him from my arms and ran out of the room with him. Suzie and I just looked at each other.

"Should I go with the nurse?" I asked.

Suzie said, "Yes!"

But when I tried to get in the room where they were working on Joey, they told me to go back to Suzie's room. When I got back, Maddie had been taken as well. Suzie was very worried, as was I, but we couldn't do a thing.

Soon a nurse came in and told us that Maddie was fine, but that she would have to stay in an incubator for a few days.

"What about Joey?" we asked.

"He has an infection," the nurse told us. "His lungs also aren't fully developed, so he's having trouble breathing."

They also said that they weren't set up to deal with this issue, and that they would have to send him to Seattle Children's Hospital in an ambulance. We wanted to go too, but they said there was nothing we could do, nor would they know anything until tomorrow. They told us we could both drive over there the next day.

This made for a very difficult night.

Suzie had to stay at our current hospital, Overlake in Bellevue, and while she could look at Maddie, she couldn't pick her up. Nicholas and Steven were home with one of our wonderful neighbors in Woodinville, who'd come over to watch them when I took Suzie to the hospital.

The next day, Suzie checked out of Overlake and went with me to Seattle Children's Hospital to check on Joey. Maddie would stay in the hospital in Bellevue. When we arrived, we were told that Joey was in the intensive care unit. "He's in no pain," they said, "but be ready: He's not going to look good to you."

No amount of warning, though, could prepare us for what we saw. There was our little premature baby with tubes everywhere and bandages over both his eyes, a bright light shining on him. We were told that they were doing everything they could, but that we should prepare for the worst.

We were devastated. How could things have gotten so bad so fast?

For the next week we had the same routine. We would get up in the morning and have breakfast with Nick and Steve. One of our neighbors would come over to watch them, and then Suzie and I would visit Maddie in Bellevue. We would drive over a floating bridge that spanned Lake Washington to visit Joey, and then we'd drive back over that same bridge to visit Maddie before we headed home. Suzie still hated driving over bridges, but she wasn't going to let anything stop her from visiting her child.

Fortunately, Maddie was soon able to come home, but Joey would stay in Seattle Children's for a while longer. One day the doctor said they wanted to take Joey off the ventilator in order to see if he could breathe on his own. If he could, there was hope for his recovery. They said that they would try it that night and that we would know something in the morning. We came back the next day, and Joey was back on the ventilator. The doctor said that things hadn't gone well.

It was the midnineties, and personal use of the Internet was fairly new. I didn't know much about how to use it, but Quentin Clark knew more about it than most people. I decided to ask for his help to do some research on what was wrong with Joey. I wish I hadn't: I learned that ninety percent of the babies with Joey's problem died, and of the ten percent that didn't, fifty percent had severe developmental problems. I didn't dare tell Suzie.

But then, slowly, Joey started to get better. Over the next week, he became able to breathe on his own, and they were able to stop giving him drugs to keep him under. Soon, the tape came off his eyes. The doctors stopped assuring us he was in no pain. There was no need.

His skin turned pink, and Suzie got to hold him.

Finally, a month after he was born, he was out of the hospital. And despite all dire predictions, Joey continued to grow and develop at a normal rate.

Altogether, I ended up taking a month off from Microsoft, which was one of the great benefits they offered people when they had a child. Suzie was doing much better now. Nick wasn't quite five years old, but he was a lot of help, and he really enjoyed the babies. The neighbors were amazing as always, bringing us food and even offering to take Nick and Steven for a few hours to give Suzie more time with the twins. All of our neighbors had kids either Nick's age, Steven's age, or both, so the boys had friends to play with while we were away.

A few months after everyone was out of the hospital, we were visiting our friend John Nicol when one of his neighbors stopped by. Coincidentally, she had been one of Joey's nurses at Seattle Children's. She asked how he was doing, and when we told her that he was fine, she admitted that they had all been certain that he wasn't going to make it. She talked about how they saw us come in every day and felt bad, knowing what we were going through and what we were about to go through when he died. *When* he died, she stressed, not *if* he died.

Looking at Joey twenty years later, you'd never think of him as the kid who couldn't be taken off the ventilator, or the kid for whom we had to prepare for the worst. He may be six feet tall and in college, but he's still our miracle baby.

After my paternity leave was over, I found things in Word going very well. Jeanne ran a great team and had great processes in place. There wasn't a lot of change I could bring about, so I continued to demonstrate my test manager abilities by managing multiple teams. I already had the automation team, the workgroup team, and Quentin's project when another opportunity presented itself.

Another team at Microsoft had been working on a commercial automation software product, but they had decided it didn't fit their plans. Jeanne was asked if her team could take it on, and of course she brought it to me. I remember she said that she was going to continue to give me work until I told her I had enough on my plate. I told her to bring it on, because I would never say "enough." So I took on another project.

This project was more of a development project than a test one. I had managed testers who wrote code for tools and automation, but this involved a lot more than that, and it was more than I could personally do. But I always thought one didn't have to be able to rebuild the engine of a car to run a car company, and I didn't think I had to be a coder to manage a coding project. Besides, I had Juan, who would be doing most of the coding and testing, which meant that I had little to worry about.

In order to manage my four teams over the next year, I knew that I would need help. While I was the lead, I asked Juan to take a technical leadership role over the automation team and the development project, and I also asked Quentin to take a technical leadership role over the workgroup test team in addition to his own project. This let me focus more on coordinating the groups overall and making sure that our contribution was useful across Office.

Basically, I had taken two of my team members and trained them to the point where they were functionally serving as leads under me. In other words, I was doing the work of a test manager already, without the title. As I well knew, at Microsoft you didn't ask for opportunities; you proved you could do the work already, and I was engaged in doing that toward my next goal. Jeanne liked what we were doing, so I got great reviews on her team. (And at the same time, Microsoft stock did another two-for-one split.)

My time in Word went quickly. About eighteen months after I'd arrived, we shipped the first and only version of Word that I worked on. Close to the release date, the product unit manager of Publisher realized that she was in need of a new test manager and asked Jeanne if she knew of anyone who could do the job.

I'll always remember Jeanne's reply. She said, "Yes, I know someone. In fact, he's kind of a junior test manager already."

I was in Word for less than two years and only worked on one release before I was on my way to becoming the test manager of Microsoft Publisher. This was another case where I did exactly what it took to move ahead at Microsoft: I started to demonstrate the ability to fill a role before I actually had it. It worked before, and it had worked again.

Nineteen

TESTING THE LIMITS

Alex, the product unit manager of Publisher, told me the great things Jeanne had said about me, and she wanted me to meet the people whom I was going to work with. She said she wanted to make it clear: This meeting wasn't an interview. Unless there was some real conflict between me and the people I was going to work with, the job was mine.

I wasn't worried about conflict. I thought I could get along with anybody.

A little bit more about Microsoft structure: Now, assuming that I didn't have any conflicts with anyone on Alex's team, I was a test manager. Testing, however, was only one of three branches involved in a project: The others were development and something called program management, headed by the group program manager (or GPM). The GPM managed the schedule and the features of the project, coordinating with the program managers under the GPM to write the specifications for the features that the developers would code to. In other words, these guys designed what the developers would build, and what the testers would ultimately test.

Imagine hiring someone to create really elaborate wedding cakes with fruit filling and layers of ice cream, all decked out with roses. If you don't want the whole thing to go splat on your big day, you'd want someone to design the whole thing before you had your bakers and frosters work on it, wouldn't you? (And of course you'd want testers to taste it for you.)

Jerry, who I was now talking to, was the GPM for Publisher. At first, his meeting seemed just like the others I'd had with the people on Alex's staff. But then he asked me, "What would you do if I told you I needed to release a product before it was ready?"

This was an extremely strange question to ask. "I wouldn't release anything that didn't meet my quality bar," I told him.

He said, "What if I told you that the schedule was more important than the quality?"

I said, "While I know that shipping is a feature too, people will wait for quality." I told him about my fast food days and how no customer cared how fast they got cold fries.

Then he said, "What if I told you that you had no choice?"

I didn't like the way this conversation was going, and at this point, I had to seriously think about how badly I wanted this job. My old job with Jeanne on Word was waiting for me, I knew, if I didn't take this. It'd be better to wait for something better to come along than let myself be pushed around this way.

So I replied, "As far as I know, I don't work for you. We're peers and my decision weighs the same as yours."

And I thought that was the end of my opportunity to work on Publisher.

The next day, Alex called me and asked if I could meet with her later that day. I was prepared for bad news, but I was surprised when she said that everybody liked me and the job was mine. I wanted to say thank-you and get out of there, because I knew you never stuck around after the sale was made, but I had to ask. "Really, everyone? Even Jerry?"

She said, "Yes, Jerry most of all. The last test manager he worked with was a marshmallow, so he wanted to test you out— see whether you'd cave under the pressure of a ship date. And he loved the way you were willing to fight for quality."

Cool.

Testing is a weird way to rise to the top of the software industry. Most people you think of as visionaries are either developers or program managers. But testers? No one wants to be told that they're not ready to release a product, or that there are bugs in their code.

For that reason, a lot of testers in the 1990s burned out. They weren't ready for the fights that were part of the job, such as the one that I'd had with Jerry or the ones I'd had with many developers before, when I would insist that a bug had to be fixed and they would try to explain the product's behavior away. I remember saying to a few of them, "I'm glad *you* can explain why the product acts that way, but unless we're shipping *you* in the box, there won't be anyone to explain it to the user."

I'd been with Microsoft for six years now, and I had achieved my goal of becoming a test manager. But the next rung on the corporate ladder was product unit manager, and at that point in Microsoft's history, I didn't know of any testers who became PUMs. Those roles usually went to GPMs and some dev managers.

So I decided not to be concerned with moving up to PUM yet. I was a test manager now, and I wanted to be the best one I could be. Besides, I could still move up in pay grade and get great reviews if I did a great job. That became my new goal.

I started with a good team in Publisher, but I knew that if I wanted to make a real difference, I was going to have to build a great team. I had built some great relationships with people over my career, and I maintained both a personal and professional relationship with them. People like Chris, Anil, Juan, and Quentin not only worked for me, but they were friends. People asked me, "How can you be friends with your employees and still get the best out of them?" I pointed out that I didn't become friends with people who didn't give me their best. I'd learned that lesson at Burger Chef.

One of the first things I did after joining Publisher was get to know the team. Not only did I meet with my direct reports one on one, but I also met with all of *their* direct reports one on one. These meetings became known as "skip level one-on-ones."

I wanted to know what everyone thought about the team and the way things were going. I also wanted to learn what their goals and aspirations were, what motivated them as individuals. In my years as a manager, I'd learned that everyone is different, and while there were some generic management tools you could use to motivate a team, it was best to learn what your people truly cared about.

I used to say that a team of people is like an orchestra. Sure, there are some beautiful elegant instruments in the string section, but there are also some strange ones like the oboes. They all get played differently, but they can each make beautiful music in their own right. Your job as a manager is to learn how to get the best out of each one, as well as to pull them together as a team and get them all playing together. A well-organized and managed orchestra can always make beautiful music together.

When I worked with people, I always tried to understand where they were coming from, and I wanted them to understand where I was coming from. (Ironically, that was the advice from my professor that had led to me dropping out of college years and years before.) When I assigned someone a task, I not only told them what needed to be done, but why we had to do it. That way, they understood the end goal, and if there was a better way, they were free to come up with it. Sometimes they didn't agree with the goal, and I allowed them to voice their concerns, but in the end I was the boss: If they didn't convince me, we did it my way. In the end, we each reserved the right to say "I told you so."

I also made sure to give honest feedback. If someone did a great job, I told them so, and when they did a bad job, I told them that as well. But I also told them how they could have done better, so that it turned into a learning experience.

Once I'd met all my leads at Publisher and their people, I knew what was working well and what wasn't. One area where I thought we could do better was automation, so I called Chris to see if he was interested in joining the team. I also called Juan, Quentin, and another person I'd met while working in Word. Her name was Tammarrian.

Tammarrian worked for Dan Hoffman. She was a very smart, athletic woman who really cared about quality. She wasn't a lead, but I knew that she would make a good one.

One day, while we were both in Word, she mentioned that she wasn't very technical. I was surprised.

"I'm not," she said. "I even wrote in my review that technical skill was an area I needed to work on."

Later, when I learned that she had a master's degree in electrical engineering from Stanford, I went back to talk to her.

"Do you think that I'm technical?" I asked her.

She said, "Of course. You're managing the automation team and a development team."

"What do you think I took my degree in, then, to get so technical?" I asked.

"Probably computer science," she said.

"I only have a high school diploma," I told her. "But you thought I was technical, and so did everyone else, because I told you that I was technical. In the same way, people believe that you aren't technical because that's what you tell them. When I take on a job, I learn all I can about what everyone's working on and the language they use to describe it, and then I use the same language. And when I know what the technical challenges are, I hire people who can overcome those challenges.

"Now I want you to figure out what you don't know and learn it. Learn the language of the project you're working on. When you become a manager, hire people who know more than you do. Most importantly, *stop saying you aren't technical*."

She took the advice. Over the years, Tammarrian would work her way up from individual contributor to test lead, to test manager, and then to test director, managing several strong technical teams throughout her career. For now, though, I just wanted her on my team at Publisher.

Unfortunately, of the people I'd asked, only Chris was available to join the team. I brought him in as one of my leads. He would head a team that would test a subset of the features in Publisher, but more importantly, he would be my technical lead who would work on tools and automation.

As I mentioned before, sometimes development and test can have an adversarial relationship. ("Unless we send *you* in the box, you'll fix the damn bug!") But that was not the case with my development manager in Publisher, Vikram Nagaraj. Vikram was new to the team, as was I, and we both realized pretty quickly that we could do things better.

For one, the test team had a habit of spending too much time planning for testing instead of doing it. They were basically taking on some of the work of Jerry's program management team: working with the program managers, whose job it was to create the program specifications, to help them create those specifications and to make detailed test plans, rather than just writing and running their tests. This made the work easier for Jerry's team, but while my team was making their test plans, the developers were busy writing code that no one was testing. The idea of planning for tests while the dev team coded made some sense on its face. But in practice, it caused a complete lack of testing as the program code was being written, which meant that when the dev team finished coding, they had nothing to do until the test team finally started to enter their bugs, very late in development. In the end, it made the project take much longer than I thought it should.

Vikram and I knew this had to change. We came up with the idea of acceptance testing. Acceptance testing meant that a tester would start testing features much sooner in development, until they found a bug that blocked them from testing that feature. Once that happened, a developer would have to stop coding to fix that bug.

At first, neither my team nor Vikram's team liked this. The developers in particular didn't like it because they thought it would take longer to code a feature if they had to stop and fix bugs. But in practice, if the developers were fixing bugs along the way, the testing phase at the end of the project was much shorter, which gave the developers plenty of time to finish their features. It was the right thing to do, but a change in workplace culture is always painful, and again I had to shoulder the burden of making that change.

But it worked. In fact, it worked so well that we finished the product early. Publisher was one of the products that shipped with Office, and we were the first ones done. At the daily meeting where all the products discussed their readiness to ship, I even got a bow from the VP when he heard what we had done.

The Office product with Publisher in it was a success, and at one point someone decided that there should be a new version of Office called the Small Business Edition. It would include Word, Excel, PowerPoint, and Publisher, along with some productivity apps.

After we'd shipped Publisher, a new product unit manager came in to run the Office Small Business Edition project, as well as Publisher. He hired a new dev manager and a GPM for the new product, as well as a new PUM for Publisher. Finally, he asked me what I preferred: Did I want to be the test manager on the new Small Business Edition or on Publisher?

"Both," I told him. He was surprised, but happy to save the headcount, and he agreed.

In spite of the fact that the last version of Publisher was done early, the Office product shipped late. Microsoft decided to bring in a new VP.

This guy's goal was to ship the next version on time. He thought that the reason Office had shipped late was that it had too many bugs, and in his mind, too many bugs came from too many features. He decided that the solution was to have fewer features.

I tried to point out that the acceptance testing method we'd used in Publisher allowed us to code plenty of features while still shipping on time. I told him that I thought acceptance testing would work in Office as well. But he wasn't interested, and he said—in a meeting that included test managers, program managers, and development managers across all Office products, most of which were bigger than mine—that we would do it *his* way.

"That's not the way we're going to do it in Publisher," I told him. I didn't see why we had to slash features just because he said we had to.

The VP wasn't very happy. "If you do that and you aren't ready in time, you won't ship in the Office box," he told me. Since that was where most of our revenue was from, my boss was very concerned. Vikram and I told him not to worry, and in the end we were right. We did more features than everyone else, yet once again we were done first.

My friends in Word and Excel would claim that the reason we could do this—twice—is that our product lacked the interdependencies that theirs had, and therefore it was easier to code and test. Maybe they were right. To me, that was just another reason why we shouldn't have had the same restrictions placed on us.

In spite of our being right, this VP was never a big fan of mine for the rest of my career. I wasn't too worried about that, however, because soon after this, it started to look as if my career was coming to an end anyway.

Twenty

BUBBLE WRAP

It was the summer of 2000, we had just finished another version of Publisher, and I was thinking about what to do next. We'd made a lot of changes in the way we developed and tested Publisher, and I was happy with the status quo.

But of course, that wasn't enough. As a manager, I'd learned that the thing I enjoyed most was fixing things, whether that meant turning around an underperforming employee or putting new processes in place to make a business unit more efficient and successful. Once things were working well, I got bored and started to think about the next opportunity. I used to say, "I don't want to fly a plane on autopilot. I have to be engaged." And even though I was challenging myself by working as a test manager on two products at once, I knew that Publisher was on autopilot.

Another thing that was going on in my life outside of Microsoft was angel investing. An angel investor is a person who invests in a new company before venture capitalists invest, and well before a company goes public.

Dan Hoffman had left Microsoft, and early in 1999 he started a new Internet company. This was around the time of the Internet boom. Companies were being formed and going public, making people rich. These companies usually had no earnings at all, but at that time, according to pundits, earnings didn't seem to matter. It was all about users—or *eyeballs*, as the pundits would say.

Dan started a company that would allow people to have their own websites with their own domain names and emails for free. He was looking to raise money from angel investors, and he called me. I was excited about his idea, as well as excited by the idea of getting in early on an Internet investment. So I told Dan I would take the whole round—that is, he wouldn't need any other investors than me.

With my investment, Dan had enough money to get the company off the ground. Soon he had a lot of users—nothing like giving something away for free to get those eyeballs—and he needed to hire more employees.

It was time to expand, so Dan decided to present to venture capital firms, and a few decided to invest in the company. They paid much more for their stock than I did, and it seemed that Dan and I were on our way to hitting it big.

It was beginning to look like I was going to make a lot of money on this investment, so I decided to invest in some other start-ups. I was much wiser now than I had been during my real estate days, when issues with debt and leverage had caused the entire shoe store enterprise to topple. So I made a simple rule for myself. I picked a number which represented the absolute most money I'd be willing to lose through investing. If at any time I lost more than that, I decided, I was done.

That settled, I started to attend angel investor conferences. At one of them, I met Dr. Roger Muller. Roger was my age and an emergency room physician. He had invested in a few companies and made some early money, and he was looking for more places to invest. After talking for a while, Roger and I decided that we would pool our knowledge in order to find companies to invest in.

Working together, Roger and I began to invest. Our habit was to choose companies that had *real* products or tech behind them—the kind of tech that other companies would want and would be willing to pay for—as opposed to companies that just had a lot of eyeballs without any innovative tech to back them up. For example, one of the companies we'd invested in was Cantametrix, which was developing a technology for taking in sound, determining whether or not that sound was a known song, and matching it to other songs. We didn't think our companies would have to go public for us to make money. They could be bought by one of the larger tech companies—maybe even Microsoft. So Roger and I not only invested our money in these companies, but we found other people to invest along with us. We even became members of the board in some of these companies.

In the winter of 1999 and early 2000, each round of fundraising was done at higher and higher valuations, which meant that the value of our companies continued to go up. Roger and I thought we were onto something, but then, in the spring of 2000, the market crashed. People started to talk about the "Internet bubble" bursting. Initially, Roger and I weren't too worried about the bubble because of our strategy of investing primarily in companies that had what we considered real tech value.

But something did change. Usually, because angel investors were necessarily taking more risks in working to build a company

from the ground up, we got better terms, and the venture capitalists, who came later, had to take what they could get. But now,
as tech stocks fell and companies needed to raise funds more and
more frequently to stay open, the venture capitalists started to
ask for lower prices and better terms than the angel investors got.
And because they could afford to take entire investment rounds
single-handedly and provided companies with a whole network
of people for support and advice, they got what they asked for. In
many ways, it was an offer the companies couldn't refuse.

We started calling these deals *the haircut*, because the VCs
always wanted to take something off the top. We started calling
the VCs themselves *vulture capitalists*.

Just when it looked as though the markets would fall forever,
things seemed as if they were turning around. In the summer of
2000, the NASDAQ started to move up. We thought we'd dodged
a bullet.

Around this time, a major company started talking to Dan
about acquiring his company. Dan negotiated a deal that would
have made us millions, but as we were about to close on it, the
major company got cold feet. Instead of buying Dan's company
outright, they announced that they would pay the early investors,
which included Dan and me, twice the amount of money we'd
put in, while reserving the option to buy the entire company at a
later date. We certainly would have liked to sell out completely,
but we were happy to double our money.

I was beginning to think I was a genius. But back in the dot-
com days, everyone thought they were a genius.

Roger wasn't in this deal with me, but he saw the same potential in our other companies. The problem was that the VCs were able to get better and better terms due to the overall market nervousness. Roger and I started talking about how we could counter this.

The simple solution, we finally realized, was this: If we can't beat 'em, let's join 'em. Roger and I were good at raising money for these companies, and we thought that rather than bringing all of these people in as angel investors, we should start our own VC fund and compete for these deals at the same level as other VCs.

At Microsoft, we were starting to plan for the next version of Publisher, but I had no real interest in that program anymore. I had been with Microsoft long enough to earn a one-time three-month sabbatical. I decided that I would take that time off and use it to start educating myself on what it would take to form a VC fund. In the back of my mind, I was thinking that if I made enough serious money in the VC firm, it might be worth not coming back to a job where I still felt I was on autopilot.

But when my boss, Don, asked me about my plans for after the sabbatical, I made the mistake of saying that I didn't know what my plans were going to be. I should have said that I would come back and focus on the next version of Publisher—at least until I was sure that wasn't going to be the case.

This concerned Don very much even though I didn't know how much at the time. He knew that a very large percentage of the people who went on sabbatical ended up retiring, and he assumed I was going to do so as well. So he started thinking about what any good manager would do: how he would fill the hole my leaving would create.

Over the summer he did just that, but in a much more drastic way than I would have done. He made Chris Burroughs the test manager—in other words, he gave him my job.

Chris called me right away. I called Don. He said, "I have to take care of the living. Chris is the living. You're the dead." To him, the decision seemed obvious.

"I never said I wasn't coming back," I argued.

"You never said you *were* coming back."

I tried to keep my composure during the rest of the phone call with my boss. As far as I knew, I was still alive. Even Chris thought so, enough to call me right away when he got the news. I'd been knocked around all kinds of ways in my life and my career, but never quite like this.

One thing, though, was clear: If I decided to stay with Micro-soft, I was going to have to find another job.

As the summer ended, I thought about what to do next. In the almost ten years I had been with the company, I was promoted many times and reached my goal of becoming a test manager. I got many great reviews, and with them bonuses, raises, and much more stock. Over the past few years the stock had also split five times, which meant that every thousand shares I'd received when I was hired was now about 16,000 shares. I also had all of the additional stock they gave me, some of which had also gone through some of those splits.

At the same time, I was also invested in ten different start-ups, and I had a lot of money tied up in those companies. I could start the VC fund with Roger, continue to raise money for those companies, and sit on their boards to help them become a success, or I could stay with Microsoft and continue to make good money— money I might need if the market crash returned and these companies didn't make it.

We didn't kid ourselves about our chances. I was thrilled with the money I'd made on Dan's deal, but it wasn't clear that we would repeat that kind of success with these other companies. My co-investor Roger also had concerns. After all, he was a doctor making good money as well, and neither of us was certain that this was the best time to start a new VC fund.

I also didn't kid myself about there being an emotional element to this as well as a financial one. At Microsoft, I'd risen as high as a tester had conventionally been able to go. If I stayed, would I just be a test manager on autopilot for the rest of my career? But against that, Suzie and I had four little kids at home, and we were both concerned about losing the steady income from Microsoft.

I had to talk to Suzie. After discussing everything, we came to a compromise. I would continue to work with the tech companies, but I wouldn't announce my retirement from Microsoft, and I'd tell them I was returning to them after my sabbatical. If the companies worked out, I would leave Microsoft. If I lost this money, however, I would stay with Microsoft until I'd earned back every penny I'd lost.

When I told Don that I planned to come back, he said, "The job belongs to Chris now, but I will give you plenty of time to find something else."

That time was just what I needed to see what would happen with my VC work. So Roger and I agreed that we'd start working on putting together a fund, but that neither of us would leave our jobs.

That turned out to be the right choice, because in the fall of 2000 the market started falling again, and this time it didn't stop.

In the VC world, the money dried up. You couldn't even get a VC to give you a haircut. They just wouldn't invest at all. Because our companies couldn't raise money, they had to start laying people off. This truly was a bad winter as one company after the other had to start cutting back.

Roger and I still thought we could pull this off. After all, our companies had great tech, and some major corporation would want to buy it from us. And they did—but they wanted it at fire sale prices. We weren't quite ready yet to start selling things for pennies on the dollar.

But then the market crash continued into the New Year. The dot-com bubble had truly burst. Times weren't as different as we'd thought: For a while, all that had mattered were "eyeballs," but in the end it came back to revenue, and if your company didn't have revenue, your company failed. Even our companies with their great tech were done, and soon we had to start accepting those pennies-on-the-dollar deals.

Remember Cantametrix? The company was later bought by Gracenote, which was later bought by Sony, who sell the technology today—which they bought from us in one of those fire sales.

Roger and I still see each other to this day, but neither of us has ever been tempted to invest in anything again. Toward the end of the bubble, I looked at the amount of money I'd written down that I was willing to lose. I'd lost more than that. When we were done, we were done.

I like to look back on those times and think about how smart we were to find all these great companies with their useful innovative tech. I like to think that had we been a year or two earlier, we would have made millions of dollars. I also like to remember that only one of the ten companies I invested in actually went out of business. The rest were bought out, and some of the technologies we worked on are still being used today.

But while that's nice to think about, the fact is that I lost a small fortune, and in order to earn it back, I needed to find a new job at Microsoft fast. But doing what?

Twenty-One

ENTERPRISING

In February 2001, Chris Burroughs had been the test manager of Publisher for six months. I still had my office, but Chris had my job. He wasn't happy about the way he'd gotten it and was quick to tell me that he thought our boss, Don, had screwed me. While I agreed with him, it was in the past, and now I needed to decide what I was going to do next. Based on the stock market and the way my start-up investments were going, it was clear I needed to stay with Microsoft.

I hadn't really been looking for another role at the company, but I knew the situation was urgent when Don said that I'd had more than enough time to find something, and he would give me until the end of the *month* to do it. I either had to have another job soon, or I would be retired. So I started looking.

I knew a lot of people at Microsoft, and I'd maintained a good relationship with all of them. I started calling the people I knew, and within a short period of time I found a couple of test manager roles and a director of test role. The director of test position would have given me the chance to manage other test managers, but all of the jobs I'd found were still in test. I knew that if I was going to stay at Microsoft, I needed to make it interesting for myself, which meant that I needed to keep moving up. I wanted to be a product unit manager, and as far as I knew, no one in testing had ever done that at Microsoft. In order to get that title, I figured I'd have to apply for it directly.

But as the days turned into weeks and the end of February was fast approaching without any likely PUM positions available, I knew I would have to take one of these test jobs I'd been offered, even if none of them was ideal. If I did take one of these jobs, I knew that I would make a commitment to that group, and I certainly wouldn't leave until whatever product they were working on was done. I would have to put my search for a product unit manager position on hold.

Then I got a callback from one of my friends who told me about a role she thought I was perfect for. It was apparently a lab management role, and while I agreed that it was something I could do in my sleep, it felt like it might be too easy. Lab management again: It was almost as though I was going back to the beginning. Since time was running short, though, I thought I'd better at least give the hiring manager a call.

The hiring manager was named Darren Muir. He was a general manager in the Windows division, a friendly and direct man who was about five years younger than I was. I liked his directness, being direct myself, and Darren and I got along from the start.

Darren asked what I was looking for in a position, and I said I would only take a job if I could add real value to the company. "I have to feel as if I am making a difference," I told him. "That it matters that I'm showing up every day."

Darren described the available role. If I took the job, I would be the manager of a lab that did integration testing: That is, the lab took Microsoft server products—like Windows Server, SQL Server, which was our database product, and Exchange Server, which handled email—and installed them all on a set of machines similar to the ones that a customer might use to run a business. These weren't ordinary customers—these were what we called Enterprise customers, big businesses like Boeing or Safeway. The goal was to make sure that all of these products worked together for Enterprise customers, as well as to find any issues that a business might run into and report them to the team to get them fixed.

But I noticed one thing: Currently, the lab was only testing the compatibility of Microsoft products.

I told Darren that while it certainly was important to make sure our products worked together, the fact was that most Enterprise-level businesses didn't just use Microsoft products. They also used our competitors' products, as well as built their own applications. We had to work with those products also. If a computer that was running a competitor's product crashed whenever its user opened Word, it would mean that customers couldn't use our products.

Microsoft was great at shipping desktop products like Word or Excel that people used one at a time, but Enterprise products were a different story. While we'd been taking over the desktop market, companies like IBM, Sun, and Oracle had been going after the Enterprise market. Now Microsoft was trying to compete with them, but we were very much still playing catchup.

But beyond that, one of the major problems that our Enterprise customers had was that the sheer size of their businesses usually meant that their users would operate the products in ways that, although we tried, we couldn't completely predict. Inevitably, they would find bugs in our Enterprise products that we hadn't found, and some of these bugs had to be fixed before the business could install and use our software.

The usual workaround for this issue was to issue a service pack that contained these fixes (in the lingo, an "SP"). The service pack would always come out some time after the initial release. Over time, however, customers began to recognize that any early bugs would get fixed in a service pack. Thus they would wait to buy the product until the service pack came out, which meant lower sales for the release.

We talked about ways to solve that problem. Soon, I thought I might have an answer. The Enterprise customers had their own internal tests that they would run to evaluate our software on a set of machines specific to their own setup before they installed that software throughout their business. It was these tests that uncovered most of the bugs we would have to fix in the service pack.

"Wouldn't it be great," I told Darren, "if we could get ahold of those tests before we rolled out our server releases and perform them here in the lab? What if we took our lab and installed not just our stuff, but whatever products the customer was using at their business? That'd be true real world testing—sort of like a cheat sheet for the final exam. And right now, quite frankly, if this is a final exam, we're failing it."

Darren agreed that it would be nice. But how the heck could we get these Enterprise customers to give us their "cheat sheets" and really change this integration lab into a lab that would make a difference? "How can we find out exactly what they're using?" he asked.

"That's the beauty of the plan. We invite them here to help us build it."

The plan was simple. We would build a lab that was filled with hardware, but we wouldn't install anything on the machines. We would invite the Enterprise customer to the lab and build a replica of their environment with whatever software they were using. Our stuff, our competitors' stuff—it didn't matter. Our lab would contain whatever they were using to run their business.

We would of course find problems. But since we'd be inviting the Enterprise customers in early, while our products were still under development, we could fix those problems before we shipped, and by the time we shipped, we already knew that they would work for the customer because we'd tested them *with* the customer. In other words, when the products shipped, they would be deployable by the customer on Day One. No more waiting for service packs.

"There's another part to this," I told him. "We'll have to build a new lab for this, and it'll have to be under glass. A very large, tourable facility. We have to show the world that we're doing this. We have to invite the press in to see it and to write about it."

Darren recognized that building this wasn't going to be cheap, but he agreed it was something that we should do. He said that we would have to take it to his boss.

I didn't have a problem with that. I thought it was a very exciting opportunity, and I was sure I could sell it.

That first afternoon, Darren told me to put together a PowerPoint presentation that we would take to his boss in a couple of days. I was happy to do it, and I had the time, since I was still working in Publisher where the only job I had from Don was to find another job and get out.

A couple of days later, Darren and I met with Darren's boss. We handed him our presentation. Like most of the VPs at Microsoft, he immediately jumped to the back of the whole thing where the costs were, and before we could make the case, he said, "What is all this? I thought you were being hired to run the integration lab."

I said, "We are. We're just doing it in a way that's never been done before."

It took us about an hour, but soon Darren's boss was sold on the basic concept. Still, he also saw that this would cost a lot of money. He reminded us that a lot of companies were cutting back. The economy wasn't doing great, and the stock market was still tanking.

I argued that the best time to do this was while other companies were cutting back. "We should make this a free service for our customers," I said. "After all, even though we would be helping them with their deployment, something they've always done on their own, they would be helping us ship better products."

The VP agreed, but he said we would have to take it to the senior VP.

I remember thinking, *When did Microsoft become so bureaucratic?* But then again, I was asking for millions of dollars—all as part of trying to get my new job.

A few days later, we were off to the senior VP, and a few days after that the president of the Windows division. Things were moving fast, which was a good thing because I was running out of time to find a new position. Darren, the senior VP, and I all met with the president of the Windows division in the senior VP's private conference room. The room was decorated with framed, signed hockey jerseys and had the latest and greatest audio-video setup I had ever seen. It also had a large flat-screen TV on the wall long before we all had them in our houses.

It was here that we finally met some serious resistance. Once again, we were told that times were tough and that companies, even Microsoft, were cutting back (though there was no evidence of that in this room). I was told that the buildout of the lab itself would cost a small fortune, and the hardware would be even more.

It was at that point I remembered my days at Ashton-Tate and the device lab. I blurted, "The hardware will be free."

I got looks of disbelief from upper management. How would the hardware be free?

"When we build this, and the press comes in and starts writing stories and taking pictures of Microsoft working with a major Enterprise customer, whose company's hardware is going to be in the picture?" I asked. "The answer is the one who gives us their hardware for product placement for free."

I was given the approval to move forward right then and there.

It was now the end of February. I was only a couple of days away from handing in my badge and being retired by Don, who'd said I was "dead," when Darren made the formal offer for me to join his team. I remember getting the email. I wasn't surprised that I'd received the offer. After all, we'd spent the last couple of weeks getting this approved. But then I saw the title he was offering me: product unit manager.

I looked again to be sure. Yep. I was now a PUM.

When Darren and I had begun to talk, we were talking about an integration lab, but what we ended up talking about was so much more. This endeavor would also require a team not only of testers but of program managers to work on the plans, marketing people to sell the plan to our customers and the press, and developers to drill down on the issues we found so that they could be assigned to the proper teams to resolve. All of these teams would require managers, and those managers would report to me.

So was born the Microsoft Enterprise Engineering Center, and I was its PUM. I now had my new challenge and my new title. I'd achieved another one of my goals, and once again I was in a position where I felt the need to prove myself to people who'd put their trust in me. But first, I needed to build a team.

One of the positions I needed to fill was test manager, and of course the first person I thought of was Chris Burroughs. Chris had only been the test manager of Publisher for six months, but I knew he wasn't happy there and was already looking for another job. Chris was a very nice and loyal guy. He never got over feeling as if I had been forced out, and he never trusted his boss because of it.

When I'd heard that Chris was looking for a new job, I gave him a call. I told him what we were doing, and he was immediately interested. I asked him if he could leave Publisher so soon, and he told me that he had hired a test lead who could easily move into his role, and that the project would continue without issue. When he told me that my old friend Tammarrian was the person he had in mind, I knew he was right, but I also knew that Don would be pissed when Chris told him that he was coming to work for me.

I underestimated how pissed Don would be. Don outright told Chris he couldn't go and accused him of stabbing him in the back, even though he'd basically created this position for Chris in the first place by stabbing me in the back. Chris would have none of it. He told HR that he was leaving, even if he had to leave the company to do so. Thankfully, it didn't come to that, and soon Chris was on my new team as the test manager. I was glad to see that Tammarrian also got the test manager job in Publisher without any issues from Don.

Another person that I knew I would need was someone who was a real talker, someone who could call these businesses and get them to put their IT people on a plane and work with us. Again, I had the exact person in mind: my old friend Mark Johnson.

Since leaving the army, Johnson had gone on to college and studied computers. He was working as a software developer at the phone company in Florida, which was in the process of laying people off. Sadly for Johnson but perfectly for me, Johnson was on their list.

I called and told him about what we were doing and how he could help. Johnson wasn't a big fan of leaving the great weather of Florida and moving to Seattle. "Why would anyone live in a place that's cold when they don't have to?" he asked. I told him that Chris and I had both had the same concerns before we moved here, and it worked out fine for us.

Johnson decided to fly out and check the place out. Luckily, we had Chamber of Commerce weather when he visited, and he was sold. He would join us a few weeks later.

(To skip ahead: Johnson's retired now. "Why don't you go back to Florida?" I always ask him. "Why would you live in a place that's cold when you don't have to?" But he doesn't listen to me; he loves it here now.)

We were all making great progress on the lab. I was putting in a ton of hours, but I was having a great time. It was now time to approach the hardware manufacturers, and I decided to start with one of the biggest in the world: IBM.

I made the call, and soon I was connected with a VP at the company. He was very intrigued and asked if he could come out and see what we were doing. I agreed and set up a meeting at our lab the very next week.

Seven people showed up. We were supposed to meet for two hours, but instead we met for six. I'll never forget what they said at the end of the meeting. "We knew it was just a matter of time before Microsoft really came after the Enterprise business. Now that you have, we want to partner with you." They agreed to send me servers, desktops, and laptops, all for free. And once their competitors got wind of this, they started signing up to give us hardware as well.

Johnson was busy signing up customers to come to the lab. Even before the lab was finished, the computing press started coming in for tours and writing articles. And soon Johnson had our new lab booked with customers months in advance.

The plan for the lab was to have one main data center right in the middle of the floor with glass all around. There would also be meeting rooms and conference rooms, as well as three ECLs, or Enterprise Customer Labs. Before we were even finished building the lab, we realized that based on the business we were already getting, we would have to expand that to five ECLs.

Soon the big day was upon us. I had planned a big grand opening celebration. All of my employees and of course my boss, Darren, would be there. We would invite the vendors who'd loaned us all the hardware, as well as our early and future customers.

I mentioned that I had been putting in a lot of hours. In fact, my entire team had been putting in a ton of hours, but they didn't have my bad back. I don't know if it was just the excitement of what we were doing or if it was the adrenaline, but I had forgotten all about my back over the past few months. Sure, it was tight now and then, and it would zing me from time to time, but I ignored it.

I shouldn't have.

It was the day of the grand opening. Everyone, including me, was running around with last-minute touches. That night at seven, we would throw a hell of a party. Everyone began to arrive around six, and by seven the data center was packed. We had tables filled with great food and plenty of soda, beer, and wine. People were coming up to congratulate me and my team. Darren was thrilled and came up to shake my hand. I was so proud.

But then, after we'd shaken hands and as Darren turned away, I felt a pain I hadn't felt in a long time. Straight across my back, it felt like someone had stabbed me with a dozen knives. The pain shot down my right leg, and suddenly my legs just went limp. I had no legs.

I reached out and grabbed Darren. Darren turned to me and said, "The handshake was enough; I don't need a hug." But when he saw my face, he knew something was wrong.

I would have gone straight to the floor, but he held me up and got me to a chair. Johnson looked over, saw that something was wrong, and came over. I was in serious agony, but I didn't want to ruin the party. I told Johnson to get me into a chair that had wheels and get me out of there.

Johnson thought that if he rolled me out of the lab, it would draw attention, and there was no way around that. So he decided to draw a different kind of attention. He quickly pushed me though the party, yelling, "Make room for the king of the lab! He's too important to walk!" And he pushed me down the hall to an empty office.

As soon as we got there, I asked them to move me onto the floor and to get some ice. I put the ice on my back and asked them to call Suzie. Darren wanted to call an ambulance, but I said that would draw too much attention.

"This has happened to him enough times that I'm sure he knows what he's doing," Johnson said. "Let's just do what he says."

So they did, and once Suzie arrived in the parking garage, they wheeled me down to the car and helped me in. Suzie took me straight to the emergency room.

Twenty-Two

THE BEST THERAPY

The first thing they did at the hospital was give me pain killers. I told them about my previous surgeries, and they ordered an MRI. After the MRI, a doctor came to talk to me. "You really have a messed-up back," he said.

"Tell me something I don't know. What are you going to do about it?"

"There really isn't anything I can do. My goal is to just get you back on your feet and out of the hospital."

I was staying in Evergreen Hospital, which was just down the street from our house in Woodinville. Suzie was worried, as was I. I'd always known that someday my back would give out for good. But was this it?

Suzie had to get home to the kids, but she said that she would return in the morning. After she left, I lay there and thought about what I would do if I really couldn't get back on my feet.

What if I couldn't return to Microsoft and finish what I'd started? I began to feel sorry for myself.

And then I thought, *This is why I don't take narcotics. They mess with your head.*

The next day, a different doctor came to my room. He told me he'd talked to the emergency room physician and reviewed my films. He went on to say that I'd be discharged when I could get out of bed and walk to the bathroom.

"While your back has a number of issues, there really isn't anything we can do," he said. "There are just too many things wrong with it, and another surgery would only make things worse. You really shouldn't be working."

I said, "I've heard that before. What does my working have to do with anything?"

The doctor asked how many hours I had been putting in. When I told him, he said, "That's a lot of hours for someone with a good back." He went on to say that the discs above my fusion were starting to tear, and I just shouldn't be on my feet as much as I was.

I told him I understood. "Just get me on my feet," I said, "and then we'll worry about how long I stay on them."

I was in the hospital for a week before I could make that twenty-foot walk to the bathroom. After I was discharged I would be at home, but still mostly bedridden. The hospital said they would send a physical therapist to my house to continue to work with me.

The next day the physical therapist arrived. She was a very large woman with really big hands. I remember that the last time I was in physical therapy, it always started with a pleasant massage. If this woman gave me a message with those hands, she could really hurt me.

She started by asking me to walk as far as I could. I could only walk a few feet with a walker and with a lot of agony. She said that she would be coming by three times a week, and she predicted that it would be at least three months before I would be well enough to return to work.

I told her, "Three weeks."

She looked at me like I was nuts. "Take it slow so that you don't do any more damage or cause yourself too much pain."

"Let me worry about the pain. Just tell me what exercises you want me to do."

While I was home trying to recover, Chris stepped in to run the lab. I was always able to count on Chris from our days back on PowerPoint, and now was no exception. Johnson was always there for me too, and he became my eyes and ears. He would swing by my house and give me updates almost every night, and I was able to check and respond to email using my laptop from bed.

The news he brought was generally good. More and more customers were signing up to use the lab, and we were already talking about expanding the place. The only thing that could have been better was if I could have been there.

The physical therapist with the big hands came to my house and kept me on track with the exercises. I was also supposed to be taking narcotics, but I didn't want to trade the pain for my brain, and I was trying to work from home. That's not to say I didn't fill the prescriptions—I just didn't take them every day. I must admit, however, that there were days when the pain was so bad that I had no choice. I had to break the cycle of pain. There weren't many of those days, but they did come. My hope was that they would come less and less over time.

The kids had seen me in the hospital for my back before plenty of times, so my being upstairs in bed for so long was surprisingly normal. Right after school ended, they would come up to the bedroom to show me the things they'd learned that day, and we ate dinner together in the bedroom as well. They knew I loved pudding, so sometimes they'd make it for me and bring it up. It was all surprisingly normal.

And with each day that went by, I was able to walk a little farther and stand a little longer. The physical therapist was amazed at how quickly I was recovering. At the end of the second week, I was able to walk up and down my upstairs hallway with the help of a walker. By the end of the third week, I could do that ten times with a cane, and I could get downstairs.

By the end of the fourth week I was able to work from the office again. Not quite the three weeks I'd wanted, but not the three months she'd predicted. I couldn't walk very far and stand very long, but I could be there.

Of course when I got to my office, my back was killing me, but at least it felt good to be back in my lab. I set up my chair so that it reclined as far as it could with me still able to use my computer. At one point, Johnson said, "You're as close to lying down as you can be while still sitting at a desk." But that was the only way to keep the pressure off my back and the pain to a minimum.

I drove myself to work every day. It was only about a fifteen minute drive, but by the time I got there, my right leg was almost completely numb. It was very difficult for me to walk from the parking lot to the building, even with the help of a cane. I went to see my regular back doctor, and I wasn't surprised when he said there wasn't anything he could do. He told me that I had degenerative disc disease, and that my back would just continue to get worse. He once again suggested that I stop working. When I refused, he said he would give me a disabled parking placard that would allow me to park closer to my office.

"I'm not disabled, though," I told him.

He said, "If you want to keep working, you'd better reduce the amount of time you're on your feet." He thought the disabled placard was a place to start.

I wasn't happy about this, but the shorter walk from the car to my office helped.

The press continued to give our lab good coverage, and we were doing daily tours. One day, the president of the Windows division came for a tour to check out *his* lab. He said something during that tour that I will never forget and that made me very proud. At the end of the tour, he turned to me and said, "George, you convinced me that we needed this lab to go after the Enterprise business. But now that it's here, I don't know how we ever hoped to go after that business without it."

I smile even now as I write this.

This isn't to say that the EEC was all smooth sailing.

Every team has an administrative assistant. This person usually reports to the product unit manager and handles his calendar, meetings, and travel. They also support the team, handling things like ordering and budgets.

When I first started the EEC, I didn't have an admin, but Darren said that he had someone whom he could transfer to my team. This person had had a serious problem with his previous manager. It seemed that this admin really wasn't very competent, and this was very frustrating to his boss. I have to think that it was just as frustrating for the admin. No one wants a job they're not doing well.

At one point, the admin's previous manager lost his patience and yelled and cursed at the admin. This was very upsetting to the admin, and he went to HR to complain and quit. No one wanted the situation to end like that, but these two people couldn't work together anymore. So Darren asked if I wanted the problem, or should I say, *challenge*.

I said, "Sure, as long as I get to talk to the admin first."

When I sat down and talked to the admin, the first thing he did was vent for a while about the way he had been treated. I allowed him to do so. Then I asked if he thought his boss was justified at all. Did he have reason to be frustrated? The admin agreed that his boss did have reason to be frustrated, but that he still shouldn't have yelled. I told him that he certainly could have handled it better, but that was water under the bridge. I was interested in talking about how we could move forward.

I asked him about the skills that he thought a successful admin should have. As he listed them, I asked him if he had those skills. He told me that he knew he lacked most of them, but it was because no one taught them to him.

While I'm a big fan of taking control of your own career and learning what you need to be successful, I told him that I was willing to work with him in order to help him acquire the skills he lacked. I also told him that Microsoft had internal training classes he could sign up for. "But we have a finite time to get this done," I went on to say. "In two months, you're either going to be good at your job, or you're going to recognize that it isn't something you can do. In that case, you'll have to resign."

He agreed to try. Over the next weeks we worked very closely together, and in some areas he did improve, but in most he did not. He just didn't have the attention to detail this job required. There were days when he was frustrated, and I would just tell him to continue to try. I told him that I would not lose patience with him, and that he shouldn't lose patience with himself, but that he would have to decide if or when it was time to give up.

After about six weeks, he came to me and said, "This just isn't the job for me." He told me that he appreciated the time I had taken with him and the fact that I never gave up. He sent a letter of resignation to me, Darren, and HR. He was very appreciative and said nothing but kind things about me and the company.

Darren and HR were thrilled with how this had turned out, and the EEC went on with a new admin in place.

Over the next couple of years, we built and ran a facility that added a lot of value to Microsoft, its customers, and its partners. Darren allowed us a tremendous amount of freedom, and it really felt as if we were running our own business. We found lots of bugs that would have impacted the deployment of our products, and we were able to get them fixed before we shipped.

Of course, we encountered some resistance from other teams. We weren't just testing Windows, but all of our server products, including Exchange and SQL. And while our own Windows teams were receptive to our issues, to other teams we were just some Windows guys telling them that their software had bugs.

I would go to meetings where they discussed their product's readiness to ship. These meetings were attended by all of their managers and their VP. I would tell them that they had a bug that would stop a certain company from being able to use their product. In response, they would ask, "Who on your team installed our product? Do they know what they're doing?"

I was amazed at how quickly they went on the defensive. It was like I was telling them that their kid was ugly.

I had to find a way to be seen as a resource and ally instead of as some critic from another team. After thinking about it, I realized that these teams had the same problems Windows did before we built the lab. Their customers got the product and installed it on a few machines first in a testing lab to see if it would work in their environment. When they found bugs, they would let the team know, and of course these bugs would be fixed in a service pack.

It took time to get past their initial attitude that we weren't one of *them* and that we couldn't possibly understand *their* complicated products as well as they did. But I met with their management teams to work it out. I asked them about their issues with their customers, and I asked who their important customers were. Most importantly, I made sure they knew our lab was a resource for them as well, not just Windows. Our lab was a company-wide resource.

Soon, it paid off. We were doing customer engagements that were not only being attended by other Microsoft teams, but in some cases led by those teams, and all of our Enterprise-level products—not just Windows—were getting better and better on release as a result. The lab was making a real difference for our company—we truly had built the *Microsoft* Enterprise Engineering Center.

After the EEC had been in operation for two years, we were finally at the point where things were running like clockwork. In other words, we were approaching that "autopilot" stage that I was never a fan of.

It was important to me in my career that I either had to be fixing something or building something. It had to matter that I was showing up every day. If I went home at the end of the day and truly believed that things would have been the same whether I was there or not, it was time to do something else. Sadly, it was starting to feel that way again.

So I decided to have that conversation with my boss, Darren. I told him that it was time for my next challenge. We both agreed that Chris could run the lab as well as I could. But what should I do next?

Darren asked me, "What's the biggest issue our customers have to deal with?"

I considered before answering. "We know that we can use the lab to find the issues that result when our customers deploy our products," I began. "But the trick is that we can *fix* our own products. The real compatibility issues come when our customers try to integrate our products with applications from other companies. Since we have no control over *those* applications, that's the real challenge."

And even before he asked me whether solving that problem was what I wanted to work on next, I was intrigued.

Twenty-Three

COMPATIBILITY

The App Compat team was very large, with almost 200 employees, and a lot of them were contractors. They had a team of testers to find the bugs and a team of developers who had to figure out whether the bug was caused by something in Windows or something in the outside application. They also had a team of program managers who worked with our Enterprise customers and the companies that created the applications they used. There was definitely some overlap with the EEC lab, but while the lab mostly worked with Enterprise customers and how they used our server products, the App Compat team focused only on the third-party applications they used. They also worked with the companies who developed these apps.

There were far too many people on this team for me to follow my normal course of meeting one-on-one with everybody. Instead, I met with all of the managers and leads to learn about the ways they did things and why.

Here's how it worked. If the tester found a problem, they or a developer on the team would have to determine whether the problem was with the new version of Windows or with the third-party application. When the bug was with the application, a program manager would have to call the third-party company and let them know. This could lead to some interesting conversations, as the company could say that their app had worked with the previous version of Windows but not with the new one. To them, that always meant that we had broken their program. To us, it might have meant instead that we had just exposed a flaw that was always there.

The other thing I found out was that all the testing was done manually. That is, the team had no automation.

Imagine a library filled with all of the software applications that run on the Windows platform—some widely used, some not. A tester comes into this library, takes the application back to his office, and runs some rudimentary tests on it. Does it install on Windows on his desktop machine? Does it work? Does it print? Can he uninstall it?

There. The product is tested. He's done, at least with this application. But he gets to do this again with the next application and the one after that. Over and over again.

Does this process seem boring and inefficient, almost painfully backward to you? It did to me. It reminded me of my time at Ashton-Tate back in 1989, when I had to manually test all those printers, plotters, and cameras. But it was now 2003, and when I went to work on the Application Compatibility, or "App Compat" Team, they were testing these applications in the exact same way.

When I talked to the members of my new team about that, I was told that App Compat testing couldn't be automated. There were just too many applications in too many languages, and it was quicker to do it manually. When I heard this, I understood why they had so many contractors. These tasks were just too repetitive and boring to give to a full-time Microsoft employee.

I also learned that in part due to the number of contractors involved, an App Compat test pass took weeks. This was a problem for the Windows team, because if they wanted to make a last-minute change to the Windows product just before they shipped, the App Compat team would say that they would need a lot of time to retest the apps—time that the Windows team didn't want to give them.

On top of that, there were six full labs in App Compat. No one could tell me what some of them were used for. In those cases, I went into the lab and disconnected the servers to see who, if anyone, would complain. Only one person ever did, who'd been using one of the mostly abandoned labs to run some tests, and who'd ignored my email announcing that I was going to be disconnecting the lab.

"I didn't take it seriously," he told me. But he—and I hoped the rest of the team—knew to take the changes I was bringing seriously after that.

My gut told me that we could get the same App Compat work done with fewer people and in less time, but I would need an automation expert to help me.

I called Juan Beaufrand. Juan was still working in Office, but his career had started to stagnate. He did very well under me when we were both in Word, and I told him that we had some interesting challenges here that could get his career moving again. Juan agreed to come on board and help me. I also needed someone to deal with our customers, both in resolving their issues and helping to show them that a lot of them could have benefitted from using the EEC lab. Johnson was the perfect guy for that, so I called Chris and asked him if we could move him to my team, and he agreed.

Once my team was ready, I talked to Darren about my plans. I told him that I could reduce the number of labs, reduce the amount of time it took to do a test pass, and reduce the number of people we needed to do it, starting with all of the contractors.

Darren cautioned me that reducing headcount might require a lay off. It wouldn't be as simple as losing one person, he told me, reminding me of the incident with the admin early in the EEC. "We might end up in a situation where we're going to have to lose a lot of people at once, and the one-on-one approach you took there won't work," he said.

I didn't agree. I pointed out that the reason we had so many people, most of whom were contractors, was because we had no automation. With Juan Beaufrand, we were already starting to change that, but with so many applications to automate, we needed everyone to work on automation.

The contractors weren't the problem; as temps, they expected their employment to end at some point, and they knew that the vendor company would find them a new assignment. The problem was that a lot of our full-time employees didn't have the necessary skills to work on automation. Sure, we could have let them go as well and hired people who did have the skills, but any idiot manager could do that. Instead, I wanted to see if they could acquire the skills. I wanted to see if we could turn around every one of our full-time employees.

I talked to HR and the training people at Microsoft, and we put together a three-month training program. I also called a meeting of all the testers, and I told them that after this training program, they would either have the automation skills necessary to work in this new team, or I would help them find employment elsewhere.

Some people were excited, but most were very nervous. I didn't blame them. They knew that their jobs were on the line. But they also knew it was entirely within their control whether they continued with us or not.

I am happy to say that at the end of the training program, a large percentage of the people made it through successfully. A subset of the ones who didn't just needed a little more individual training, and a subset of those ultimately had to move on.

In the first four months of this new role, by introducing the team to automation, we substantially reduced the time it took to do a test pass. We also cut the size of the team in half, mostly by reducing the number of temps, and we reduced the number of labs from six to two by partnering with Chris and the EEC.

My first review within this new role was one of my best, and I received another promotion. I now was one level below partner—a long way up from that first lab job twelve years ago.

A partner at Microsoft is a person who not only gets rewarded for their individual performance, but for the performance of the division they are in. This would mean a lot more money and stock. But just as few testers became product unit managers, even fewer became partners.

It looked like I'd found my next goal.

Twenty-Four

ADJUSTMENTS

I was with the App Compat team for nine months when word of a reorganization came down. Reorgs were something that Microsoft did a lot. Usually they were simple, like a new vice president and new management team. Sometimes they were bigger, like "Now the product is one whole product called Office, and not separate smaller products called Word, Excel, and PowerPoint."

But this reorg was different. This would change the way Microsoft's management structure had worked from the beginning. The new model, which I liked to call the "trio" model, was simple. Initially, most Microsoft products had been run by a single product unit manager. Under the PUM, as I've described, was a trio: a test manager, a development manager, and a group program manager. The PUM usually came from one of these disciplines. While I was that rare product unit manager who came from test, most product unit managers, as I've said, came from development or program management.

But the powers that be at Microsoft had now decided that if a PUM came through development, he might be a very good PUM for his development team, but not so much for the test or program management teams. Since I had come through test, the theory was that I might be a good PUM for the test team, but not development or program management.

To solve this problem, Microsoft expanded the trio concept upward. Instead of having one product unit manager, there was now a trio of directors, each one running their discipline's team and together running the business. That trio would also report to a trio above them, each of whom would also represent their discipline. Above that trio was usually a senior vice president.

Now that trios had come to Windows, I officially became the director of test for the Windows Core Fundamentals team. I would be working with a much bigger team, but my level and pay would be the same. Together with the director of development and the director of program management, we ran this business. We reported to a trio that had a vice president of development, a vice president of program management, and my boss, Darren Muir, who was the general manager of test.

Just as few testers became PUMs, few became vice presidents, and though Darren was peered with two vice presidents, he was still a general manager. He didn't receive a promotion through the reorganization. It's not that Darren expected to be made a vice president the second the reorg was announced, but he did think that his shot at making vice president had increased under this new system.

I thought he was right about his upward mobility. That was the main reason I liked this new structure. Not only did this concept play to my strengths as a tester, it also created opportunities for testers to move up in management, as every product unit manager position was now a trio and had to have a test person there. The opportunity for testers to become vice presidents also existed now where it hadn't before.

Other people didn't like the idea. One of those people was my friend Chris Burroughs. He was now the product unit manager of the EEC, and he wasn't a fan of suddenly having to run the business in partnership with two other people. So Chris decided to leave the group and go to the part of the business where they still had product unit managers. In this case, he went to MSN—a subject that we'll come back to later.

As part of the reorg, my App Compat team was rolled into the new Windows Fundamentals team. This team was very large, with almost 700 people. Our trio would have a lot of separate teams, and I would need a test manager for each. But first, I would need one for my App Compat team.

That role was currently taken by Juan, but while Juan did a great job managing his test leads, management wasn't his passion. Still reserved, he preferred working on automation and tools, and as test manager, he felt that he spent more time managing people than getting his hands dirty with the technical work. I supported Juan's desire, and the fact was that I could use his help in the technical area. So while his level stayed the same, he moved from managing the entire test team—including managing managers—to managing a team of individual contributors who worked in a technical area that he loved. Being closer to the day-to-day work, Juan could now get back into the trenches.

It's strange to think now about the fact that when I'd first met Juan—or Chris, or Tammarrian—they'd all been individual contributors, with no desire to move into management. I'd been partly responsible for moving them in that direction during my career, explaining to them how management would bring them closer to their own goals, as well as being better for the company. Since then, Chris and Tammarrian had both become excellent builders of teams in their own right.

Mentoring in this unofficial way was something that I really enjoyed. Microsoft had an official mentorship program, but I thought it had a little too much overhead for me to "formally" sign up. But I'd started informally mentoring people when, as I moved from one group to another, some people would ask if they could continue to meet with me to discuss their careers and ask for advice. I was happy to do so, as I thought that it was a great way to give back.

One of these people was Tammarrian Rogers. Tammarrian had never worked for me directly, but she was one of the first to ask me to be her mentor. Now, like Chris, she'd gone on to unofficially mentor a number of people herself.

I know this is somewhat egotistical, but sometimes, when I think about the people I mentored going on to become excellent managers in their own right, I like to think about the movie *It's a Wonderful Life*. How would some of these people's lives be different if we'd never met? I'd like to think I made a real difference in their lives—just as people like Johnson, Bob, and Chris himself, on that first day in the Ashton-Tate lab when I'd never tested a device in my life, had made a real difference in mine.

With Juan doing more of the technical work, I asked one of the people I'd been mentoring, Meir Shmouely, if he wanted a job as test manager of the App Compat team. Meir was very interested in what it would take to move up in the company, but at the time, he was a test manager working in a small product unit based in Israel, and he really didn't have much opportunity to move up. It was the same problem that I had faced in PowerPoint. The best move for me back then had been to leave San Jose for Redmond, and I felt that it was the best move for him as well. Meir agreed, and soon he would move to the States to take the App Compat job I'd offered.

The timing couldn't have been better for him or me, because soon after he arrived, he would have the chance to demonstrate that he could not only run App Compat, but fill my shoes as well.

My back had never fully recovered after the EEC episode. I wasn't able to stand very long or walk very far. I used a cane a lot and parked close to the office, thanks to my disabled parking tag.

In particular, flying was very difficult for me. Between standing in the security line and sitting on the plane, I was in serious pain. I had to take plenty of pills—even narcotics—just to get through the flight, and I always needed a few days in bed after a flight to recover.

As a result of the injury, Suzie, the kids, and I had stopped going places or doing things that required a lot of walking. We still made sure to have a few big vacations, but we had to stop going to the street fairs that Suzie loved, which only worked if there was a bench that I could sit on while Suzie and the kids walked around. And trips to Seaside, Oregon, where we loved to go to the beach and walk the prom, were now too painful. I tried to make things easier on the kids by buying a boat and a lake house, which

I furnished with a pool table, pinball machine, video games, darts, a hot tub, a basketball hoop, and plenty of other things to amuse them. I think they made some great memories there. But still, a lot of the outdoor activities we'd come to love had largely come to a stop—or at least my participation in them had.

That's when it was time for my back to remind me that it could knock me down whenever it wanted to. This next attack was so simple that I feared my days of walking at all were over.

I arrived at work like I had for so many days before. I parked in the handicap spot and started to walk the twenty feet to my office. But when I stepped up to the curb, the pain shot across my back, and I went to the ground as if I'd been punched by a heavyweight fighter.

One of my employees was walking by and thought that I had turned my ankle. I asked him to help me to my office. I remembered that the office right across from mine had a couch, and he helped me to it. With that, I thanked him for his help and told him that I'd be okay. But I knew I wasn't okay.

I had a meeting with HR later that day to go over the review model for my people, and I wanted to get that done. So I called Suzie and asked her to come and pick me up, and I called my HR person and asked if she could come early so that we could finish before I went to the emergency room.

When she heard that, she came rushing over. She said that we could postpone the review until another time so that I could get out of there right away, but I told her that I wanted to get this done, since I had no idea how long it would be before I could return to work.

When she arrived, I was still on the couch in the office across from my own.

"Do you need help to get to your office?" she asked.

"No," I said, although I should've said yes, because as I stood up a pain shot across my back and my legs gave out. I fell forward, slamming my head hard into the whiteboard on the wall. The HR person let out a gasp and ran toward me.

"Would you help me to my desk?" I finally asked.

As I sat down, I felt something warm running down my head.

The HR person said, "Your head is bleeding."

I said, "I know. Let's just get this done. We have about twenty minutes before I told Suzie to come and get me."

The review model usually takes a couple of hours, as HR often wants to question the raises and promotions you want to do. But for some reason, this time I got very little pushback on my decisions. Maybe it was the blood running down my face, or the light moans and grunts every time I had a back spasm. Whatever the reason, we got through the whole thing just before Suzie arrived to take me to the hospital.

For the first two days at Evergreen Hospital, after the MRI and all of the usual discussions, I stayed in bed, taking pain medicine and muscle relaxers. On the third day, they had a physical therapist come to my room, and we started doing some stretches and back exercises. Once again, they told me that I would be in the hospital until I could walk the few feet to the bathroom, and once again, that took about a week.

When I was discharged, they said that they could send a physical therapist to my house again, but I declined. After the last physical therapist, I had the exercises memorized.

My back slowly got better, but I was tired of this happening every year or two, and decided that I was going to find a doctor who could fix my back once and for all. Over the next few weeks, I visited five different doctors. Each one did a quick physical evaluation and looked at my films, and each one said that there was nothing they could do. My back had too much damage.

The last doctor I saw was much more thorough and informative. He was an Asian man who spoke with a slight accent. He spoke forcefully and in such a direct way that I had immediate confidence in him. I told him all of the issues I was dealing with—the chronic pain, the time away from work, the reduction in the time I spent walking or doing things with my family—and he listened.

Most back doctors have one or two backlit screens that they can put an x-ray on. This guy had a whole wall of these screens, and once I was done telling him my issues, he put up all of my films. He then pointed to them one by one and told me what he saw.

"This one shows a lot of scar tissue along the bottom of your back. This scar tissue can touch the nerves and cause pain. This one shows that you have arthritis in your back, and that can also cause pain. You can see here that your fusion goes to the fourth vertebra on the right side, but it has become separated from that level on the left, and the fusion itself has some cracks in it. You can also see that the two discs above your fusion are torn."

This was a long list, and so I asked what we could do it about. I was very disappointed when he said, "Nothing. If your only problem was the scar tissue, we could remove it. If your only problem was the cracks in your fusion or a tear in a disc, we could fix that. But trying to fix all of these things in your back would be like taking a machete to it. It would only weaken it more and accelerate the deterioration of the discs above the fusion."

He went on to say, "I do have some advice for you. The first is to stop trying to find a doctor who will try to fix your back using modern techniques. Let me explain what's happening: If you take your modern car in to fix it, they'll plug it into a computer that tells them what to fix. If you bring in a '57 Chevy, they can't do that; there's no place to plug in. Your back is that '57 Chevy. We can't take a back that had three surgeries twenty years ago with a fusion made out of bone chipped from your pelvis, remove all of that, and start over with today's techniques. It just won't work."

"So you won't try," I said.

"No," he said. "But if you go to enough doctors, you will find someone who is willing to try, and trust me, you will be the worse for it."

I took this in.

"The second bit of advice," he said, "is to stop letting your back stop you from doing things with your family. Do them. Just don't stand or walk. Use a wheelchair."

"How disabled do you think I am?" I asked. "I'm still working."

"I know you are," he said. "And the rest of the time, you're lying around. You're not getting out and enjoying your life. You're stopping your family from doing so. I know you don't need a wheelchair now, but if you keep going the way you are, you will need one all the time. So instead, use one part of the time."

I told him I'd consider the wheelchair idea, but that I wasn't a big fan of it. I also told him that I'd stop trying to find someone to fix my back for good. The doctor looked at me and then reached out his hand. As I shook it, he said, "You have a very good attitude. I know with everything that is wrong with your back, you must be in a lot of pain all the time. I'm surprised you're not sitting in a corner crying somewhere."

I said, "Do you think that would help?"

"No."

"Then what would be the point?"

I went home. While I wasn't thrilled with what I had heard, at least I felt I really knew what was going on. I told Suzie everything the doctor had told me, including the wheelchair part. I was surprised when Suzie didn't dismiss the idea as easily as I did. She said, "If you were in a wheelchair and didn't have to stand in the security line or walk through the airport, we could take more trips."

"I guess."

"Would you be willing to start going to street fairs again if one of the kids or I pushed you in the chair?"

Before I could answer, the kids starting calling dibs on who would get to push the chair.

Finally, she said, "If you used a wheelchair, we could start going to Seaside again."

That was the selling point to me, as that was one thing I truly missed. The next day, I ordered a wheelchair.

I returned to work after about a month. While I used a cane at work, I used a wheelchair everywhere else. Not necessarily around the house, but on our family outings. A few weeks after I got the wheelchair, we went to a street fair. While I was a little self-conscious at first, it was fun to go. And a few weeks after that, the entire family and I went to Seaside.

It was fun walking the prom with everyone. The kids even had fun taking turns pushing the wheelchair, and they had a place to put all of their bags of candy from the candy store on Main Street.

A few months after that, we took a trip to Florida. I was amazed at how fast a person in a wheelchair can get through security to the gate. And while the plane ride itself wasn't great for my back, the entire trip was a lot less painful. I didn't like that I had to use this chair, but I did like that we were doing things as a family again.

Windows, which my trio peers and I were working on now, was a massive product unit with thousands of people. I felt like I'd made a real difference for the company in my last few roles, but as one of many directors of test on Windows, I was starting to feel like a cog in a very big machine.

I've said that I didn't do autopilot, and now I was learning that I didn't like being a cog either. Sure, we had made a real difference with our changes in App Compat, but that was done, and the team was now running smoothly. There were some opportunities to make some effective changes in Windows, and I took them, but it wasn't enough to really move the needle.

I had told Suzie that I wouldn't think about retiring again until I'd made back the money I lost in my start-up investment days. I had earned that money back and then some. And since I'd returned from my second serious injury at Microsoft, a lot of people were asking me why I didn't retire rather than come in to work every day. "Why would you put up with this level of pain?" they asked.

I explained: "Because even if I retired, the pain wouldn't. I could be here in pain, or I could be at home in pain."

What was worse than the pain, though, was feeling like I was a cog. I'd told myself that I would keep working for as long as it mattered that I was showing up every day. But in a product unit as big as Windows, my leaving would be a small hiccup. No matter what, I would finish the job I started, and I would stay until we shipped. The question was, would I finally retire after that?

Twenty-Five

CROSSING THE FINISH LINE

Around the time we finished up Windows Vista in 2006, I was having lunch with John Nicol. John was now running MSN. MSN was an online information and email service, sort of like a newspaper. It had a number of pages, or sections, such as Money, Autos, Health, and others. As you'll remember, Chris had gone to work on MSN, where he now worked for John as the PUM of the dial-up service. Coincidentally, our friend Anil Mehra, who was still in San Jose, was running the MSN TV business.

At the time he'd left the EEC, Chris had asked why I didn't think about going to MSN as well, especially since I'd been so excited to be a product unit manager, a job which I now had to share with two other people. I told him that I thought the trio model made sense and that it was my best chance to make partner. Unfortunately, that hadn't yet panned out.

Now, at lunch with John, I told him that I was thinking of retiring from the company. He asked me why, and I told him that I had to be in a position where I felt I was adding value every day.

John said, "I thought you were going to stick around until you made partner."

"That would be great. But I realize that not a lot of testers get to partner."

John considered this. "What if I had a job for you where you could continue to have an impact and a shot at getting to partner? Would you be interested?"

I said yes.

Each page on MSN had its own product unit manager, and under the PUM was a test manager, development manager, and group program manager. Each of these product unit managers managed their page as if it were its own business, but no one was really looking across all of MSN as one customer experience.

It reminded me of the early days of Office, when the product unit managers of Word, Excel, and PowerPoint treated their product as if it were independent rather than an integrated part of Office. Microsoft had fixed that issue with Office years ago. What John was offering me now, if I accepted a position working under him as a director of test, was to help MSN do the same thing.

Building the Microsoft Enterprise Engineering Center had been a major accomplishment, and the changes we'd made in App Compat made a huge difference. Thinking about John's offer and the potential impact it might have, I decided that I still had more to give. Like an old boxing champion, I thought I had one more fight in me, and I decided that I wanted to go out on top.

The only question had been who or what would be my next opponent—and now, with John's offer, I had my answer. After five years in Windows, I was off to the online world.

First, I would have to hire a team.

After I'd left the Windows Fundamentals team, Meir had replaced me as the director of test. This gave Juan the opportunity to become the test manager of App Compat, but Juan still liked writing code and working on tools and automation. He asked me if there was any opening for him to work with me at MSN. I really wasn't aware yet of the needs in that area, but I knew that whatever they were, Juan could handle them. I always thought that if someone good was available, you snapped them up and worried about their exact role later. It's the same as running a sports team. If a great player becomes available, you go out and get them. Juan was a great player, and he was my first hire.

As Juan and I joined MSN, I learned that the online world wasn't very different from the shrink-wrapped software world. That is, when you worked on software, the going wisdom was that you took just as long to test it as you did to develop it. That's because if you missed a big bug, you might have to re-release the product, and that cost a lot of money when you thought about the manufacturing costs of CDs and boxes. But in the online world, people were getting the software—or in the case of MSN, the *information*—in the form of webpages, which cost a lot less to update than boxes did.

In spite of this, these pages were developed like regular software. That meant that if a developer coded a page for six weeks, a tester tested it for six weeks, even though the impact of a bug was much smaller. It was a slow process.

I started to talk to the test managers about the turnaround. I told them that I thought we could get the product out faster by testing less, but being very quick to react with product updates if our users found a bug we missed. But the test managers didn't want to listen at first. They had their process, and since they reported directly to the PUMs rather than me, they didn't have to listen to what I had to say.

Until they saw the results, nobody was going to implement the changes I wanted to see. So I needed to demonstrate the benefit of reacting to customer feedback rather than doing exhaustive testing in advance.

Another thing I noticed was that every team had different ways of doing things and different tools to help them get things done. I asked Juan to take an inventory of the tools and automation to see if we could combine some of these tools and reduce duplication of effort. In the process, we learned that some teams had nobody working on tools and automation at all.

Once Juan knew what some teams had and what others lacked, I decided to hire my own team to start working on solving the problem. I also asked the test managers to suggest who on their teams would be available to join this cross-team effort. Most test managers assigned someone to the team.

I also knew that I would need a strong program manager to write the specifications for these tools and to work on communicating our efforts to the product unit managers. So I asked Mark Johnson if he wanted to join my team. He did.

Over the next two years, my team continued to grow. Chris, John, Anil, and I were back working together again, and I even had Johnson and Juan on the team. It started to feel like a reunion, and my working relationship with the test managers naturally grew stronger as we started testing across all of MSN as if it were one product.

In addition to automation and tools, we also worked on metrics for home page uptime and performance, such as how long it took a page to load. We also started measuring things like the impact to a page's load time based on the ads that were on the page.

Still, despite our efforts, for the most part the pages that made up MSN were still being developed and tested like Word and Excel. There was a lot more I knew we could do, but as I started to figure out how I could bring about these changes, another reorg was announced.

As part of the reorg, a new senior vice president was taking over, which meant that John Nicol would have a new boss. This VP wanted MSN to be organized more like Office and Windows. Even though he didn't specifically say trios, I guessed—correctly—that this was what he meant.

John didn't see it at first, and he made a first proposal for the new organization that didn't involve trios. The new VP decided to get specific and told John that he wanted him to go to the trio model. He went on to tell John that he only had to hire directors of development and program management, because he thought that I should remain as the director of test.

Once again, I was happy with the trio model, but my friends Chris and John were not. In fact, the second Chris knew trios were coming, he left and became a product unit manager in the server division. John stuck around and made the changes the new senior vice president wanted, but as soon as they were done, John made it clear that he was moving on to something else as well.

It didn't feel like so much of a reunion anymore without them.

As I said, I always liked the trio model, and I was thrilled that it had come to MSN because now I could really focus on improving the way we tested.

One thing I noticed, however, is that while John had been a general manager at MSN, the boss who was coming in to replace him was a vice president. John joked that it took a VP to replace him, but I'm sure he wondered why he wasn't also a vice president if this was a VP-level job.

I also noticed that the two directors of development and program management that the new VP brought with him to MSN were partners, while I was not. But to me, that meant my chance of making partner had just increased.

It was the summer of 2008, and it was review time. Though John was moving to another group, he would be doing the reviews before he left. As his parting gift to me, he met with the new vice president and told him that he was putting me in for a promotion to partner.

The new vice president was hesitant at first. After all, he didn't know me, and this was a big promotion. He was nice enough to talk to me about it.

"Before I can support this move, I'd like to see you in action,"

he said. "Maybe for about six months, or until the next review."
The next review, I knew, would be a year away.

"I've been with the company for seventeen years," I told him.
"I've been at my current level for the last four. I am who I am,
and I'm not going to change. If I haven't demonstrated by now
that I'm ready to be a partner, then the next six months won't
change that.

The new vice president said, "But I haven't actually *seen* you
demonstrate it."

I said, "Is it my fault that you just got here?"

He smiled and said, "No."

I said, "Then look at my review history. Talk to John and to
the senior VP. Then make me a partner. Hell, in six months, if
you decide that was a mistake, let me know, and I'll be happy
to resign."

I know that John really went to bat for me, and I think the new
vice president was impressed with my directness and confidence.
I also knew that the senior vice president would support this, and
so while I was excited when I was made a partner during this
review cycle, I wasn't really surprised.

I'd started seventeen years before as a lab engineer, after being
turned down four times, and now I was a partner. Microsoft truly
was a place that rewarded hard work and results. I gave them
both. In fact, I gave this place my life, and they changed my life.

Of course, I now had a new job and a new boss, and I still
had plenty to prove. For each team we now had to form a new
test, dev, and program manager trio to run the business that had

previously been run by the product unit managers alone. As the new partner engineering manager in charge of test, I had to fill the test roles for the new trios. Some of the current test managers would move into these roles, but for some of the others, I would need to find more senior level people.

Anil Mehra was still with MSN in California. We decided to leave that team down there and form a trio. Anil would report to me running the test team. I also needed a test person for the MSN home page. Though Tammarrian and I had known each other since my days in Word, and though I had been her mentor for years, she'd never actually worked for me. Finally, I hired her. I also went after Meir, who came over to run the performance and infrastructure team.

We now had our trios in place, and it was time to really bring about some change.

I still felt that we were developing these web pages like shrink-wrapped software, with one day of testing for each day of development. I talked to my trio peers and said that I thought we could use more time in development and less time in test. Of course my dev counterpart was thrilled, since this meant more time for his people to code. My testers were less supportive, and they thought that as a lifetime tester, I was going to the dark side. But I truly believed that we could deliver content a lot faster and that quality would not suffer if we put a system in place that allowed us to test faster and to release faster.

The solution we came up with was simple. First we needed great automation and tools, and I still had Juan for that. We also needed to test our products on a live site with little impact to users if something went wrong. We decided that one way we could reduce the risks was to "flight" our releases—that is, release an updated page to a subset of our users. If they ran into a problem, we could roll back the change. If they didn't, we could increase the number of users who had the updated page. We tried it, and it worked well.

Another area we wanted to work on was performance, or how long it took for a page to load. We've all seen how long some pages take to show up on your computer screen after you click a link. We didn't want our pages to take that long. We knew that ads had a big impact on the page load time, so Meir and his team got started on a tool called the "ad impact" tool. We even got a patent for it—including me.

I was having a great time at work implementing these changes, and I was having more fun at home as well, in spite of my bad back. Suzie and I and the kids were going on a lot more vacations, and I was still using the wheelchair. I was amazed at how comfortable I was using the chair. In fact, I started to feel too comfortable. I wasn't able to stand very long or walk very far. Before I'd started using the chair, at least I had spent some time walking. What little exercise I was getting was now nonexistent, and my waistline was showing the effects.

I still wasn't using the wheelchair at work. I was also one of the few managers who'd never taken a business trip. This was about to change.

MSN had a group in California that Anil worked with, and my vice president thought that it would be a good idea if we went down there and met with the team face-to-face. I knew I could do the trip, but I also knew that I couldn't take pain pills on the trip down, as my brain had to work once we got there. So when the day came for us to go, I showed up in a wheelchair. My coworkers wanted to know what had happened to me. "Were you in an accident since we saw you yesterday?" one asked. I had to explain that I was in a wheelchair a lot outside of work.

I used an airport wheelchair, but when we got to our offices in California, I only had the cane. We had a lot of meetings that day, and there was a lot of walking. I had only one chance to lie down on a couch, and I took it, but by the end of the day I was in serious pain. My coworkers could see that, and by the time we were back to the airport I really needed that wheelchair.

When we got back to Seattle, I had a car service take me home. It would be three days before the pain let up and I could return to work. I wasn't asked to take a business trip again.

As is usually the case in Microsoft, the second you get comfortable, a reorg happens. This time, now that MSN was really working, was no different.

Mobile was growing very fast, and MSN was playing a part. The team was not only making sure MSN worked well on cell phones, but they were also working on maps and other applications for mobile devices. This was going so well that the senior VP decided that we should have a dedicated team working on mobile. So the Bing Mobile team was formed, and my boss was asked to run it. A new vice president was hired to run MSN.

This meant that we would now need two trios: one for MSN,

and one for Bing Mobile. My boss moved his development partner to Bing Mobile, and the group program manager partner would stay with MSN and work for the new vice president. I was asked which job I wanted: Bing Mobile or MSN.

I said that I would do both.

I don't know why I said that. I was already a partner. It certainly wouldn't make me a vice president. I guess it was just out of habit. But fortunately, my boss told me that I couldn't do both and that I would have to pick.

I had been in MSN for a few years now, and now that I had made a difference, I knew that the feeling of autopilot might set in soon. Plus, I knew that mobile was truly the future, so I decided to go with the mobile job. Anil took over the MSN job, on my recommendation. I had tried to get Anil to move up to Redmond for years, and he would never agree to move out of California. But now we had a much larger carrot. This was a partner-level job, and partner was a major deal—major enough to get Anil to take the job and move up.

Anil and I worked closely and made sure that our teams shared all of the best practices we could. The one thing I felt that I still wanted to work on was how we tested online products. This wasn't something that Anil completely supported, as he cared about quality above all else. I cared about quality, too, but one of the things I'd learned along the way is that it isn't hard to find bugs. The hard part is figuring out which ones would impact your customers the most. I thought that with the online and mobile worlds, the quicker you got the product to your customers, the sooner you would know that. I wouldn't advocate doing less testing in Word or Excel—bugs missed in those products could have a major impact on a user. But for free mobile apps, I thought that we could take more risks.

I also thought that we could get our developers to do more testing of their own code. For a lot of teams, the way it worked was that a developer would write the code, and when he thought he was done, he would hand it to a tester to find bugs. But back in my Publisher days, when I was trying to implement acceptance testing, I'd learned that if we got developers to fix the bugs the testers found while they coded, rather than letting them pile up and fixing everything at the end, we would have a higher quality product. This had worked well in Publisher, and we'd finished testing earlier than the other products.

Now I wanted more. I didn't just want the developers to look at bugs sooner; I wanted them to find the bugs themselves. I wanted them to write the code, and when they were done, I wanted them to test their code. Why should a developer write code and then hand it to a tester just to hear that it doesn't work? Couldn't the developer figure that out?

That's not to say that we still didn't need professional testers. We did, but professional testers should be writing new test cases, tools, and automation, and they should be doing testing of the overall product, not individual modules of code. A developer shouldn't release code that didn't work, and they should be able to use the testing tools to make sure that it did.

So I came up with the concept of "combined engineering." Other than an integration test team—that is, a team to test across the entire product, much as a person would use the product— there would be no testers for the developers to hand their code to. They had to make sure their code was basically functional before they handed it off. If the integration test team was handed code that didn't pass basic functionality testing, the developer would get the code back.

In the online world, the higher-ups loved this idea. In the application world, they hated it. Even I wouldn't have been a fan of it if I were still in applications, though I thought more testing on the part of the developer would be useful on every product. Still, I was asked to put together a proposal, and I started working with my counterparts across the online services division to flesh out the idea and implement it.

Another reorg was coming. Reorgs were always a good time to think about what was next. The last few in MSN and Bing Mobile had really helped get me to partner, but I had no idea where this one would take me. But this time, I was thinking about something else: I had just turned fifty-five a few months earlier.

As I've said, employees didn't get their stock options from performance reviews all at once. Instead, they vested over five years. For example, you might be granted an amount of stock during the August review, but you would actually get one fifth the next August, and another fifth the August after that, until you got it all in five years. After you had been with the company five years, assuming your results were good enough to earn a stock grant every year, you would be vesting one fifth of five grants every year. People who thought about quitting or retiring always had this concern, since they'd be walking away from that next vesting a year out. This became known as "golden handcuffs": There was always this big chunk of money waiting for you if you stayed one more year.

But Microsoft had a retirement benefit that few people were aware of. If you retired at age fifty-five, and if you had been with the company for fifteen years or longer, you could continue to vest your stock, even though you didn't work there anymore. The handcuffs were removed.

I had turned fifty-five that year, and in October I would have been with the company twenty years. I'd wanted another top moment to go out on, and I felt that the changes I'd started by introducing combined engineering had been that top moment. It was a moment worth going out on.

I had a hell of a career at Microsoft. I started at the bottom and pretty much made it to the top. I was touched by a lot of people, and I like to think that I helped a lot of people in return. I developed friendships that would last a lifetime, and I made enough money to raise a family in a way I could only dream about as a kid in the projects. Retirement had seemed like a dream many years ago, but now I knew that it was finally here.

So my decision was made, but first I had to tell my boss that I was retiring. We were coming up on the August reviews, and I'd learned a long time ago that just before the review was not the time to say you were leaving the group, or in this case, the whole company. Depending on your boss, you could easily get screwed as they decided to take care of the living.

I trusted my current boss to do the right thing, but I also knew that he had a finite amount of budget and rewards to give out. It would be easy to give that money to the people who were staying. Frankly, I wanted the rewards I'd earned. Besides, I wasn't going to leave right after the review. I wanted to stay until October 31 to hit my twenty-year anniversary, but I knew I'd also stick around for as long as they needed me.

Review time came and went, and I did okay. For the next couple of months, I continued to do my job as well as I could. I knew that I was retiring, and I could have easily coasted. I've seen many people in my career do just that. They knew they were leaving, so they stopped caring. They didn't think twice about alienating the people they worked with—after all, they were never going to see those people or this place again.

I knew that this was shortsighted. When I joined MSN, I'd been reunited with people whom I'd worked with at Ashton-Tate twenty years ago. Long ago, I'd had that conversation with John Nicol about the adversarial relationship my test team had with development. If I hadn't listened to him back then, if I'd kept feeling like I was at odds with developers and alienating them in the process, would I have gotten the job working for John in MSN twenty years later?

But for me, it was even simpler than just not burning bridges or damaging relationships in a way that could come back to haunt me. No, for me it was as simple as this: This company took care of me, and they deserved my best until my last day.

Toward the end of September, I told my boss that I was going to retire. I thought that he would push back and ask me to stay. In fact, I was hoping to hear that, if for no other reason than the ego stroke.

But to my surprise, my boss said that he had kind of expected that I would retire—after all, he knew I had just turned fifty-five.

He went on to say that he was moving to another job, something I kind of knew too. I would have to tell the new vice president that I was on my way out the door.

I hadn't even met the new vice president yet, but I'd heard that he was coming by to talk to people before he took a couple weeks of vacation prior to taking over the role. I made sure to get on his calendar.

We met the next day. He seemed like a nice guy who really knew his stuff. He had heard about what I was doing with the new combined engineering model, and he was a big fan. I almost didn't have the heart to tell him that I was retiring, but I did. He wasn't happy to hear that, and he was even less happy to hear that I wanted to leave the end of the month. He asked if I wouldn't mind staying a little longer and helping him with his reorg. I agreed.

When they heard that I was retiring, almost everyone at Microsoft—except Johnson—told me that I wouldn't know what to do with myself in retirement. They were used to getting emails from me at 3:00 a.m. and on weekends. "We'll give you a year and you'll be back," some would say.

Even Suzie told me that I was going to miss directing all of these people. I told her that I could put all of my energy into directing *her* now. She didn't see the humor in that.

But it was very strange to keep working at Microsoft, knowing that I was going to leave. I'd hear people talk about planning the next big thing on our project, and I'd know that I wasn't going to be involved. What was more, I'd made a lot of friends at

Microsoft, but I knew that for many of them, the only thing we had in common was Microsoft. On some level, I knew that once they were still working here and I wasn't, we'd drift apart, and that made me sad.

Still, it came down to this. For years, I'd been focused on achieving my goals in the company. Now, the goals I wanted to achieve were things outside the world of Microsoft altogether. I wanted to learn to play the piano. I wanted to learn Italian. Most of all, I wanted Suzie and me to see the world. The people who were closest to me understood that, and they knew that I was making the right decision at the right time.

A "little longer" ended up being until the end of the year, but it came pretty fast. Finally, on December 31, 2011, I turned in my badge. My time at Microsoft was over, and I was retired.

Or was I?

Twenty-Six

FINE, DON'T TELL ME

was usually off work between Christmas and New Year's, and I'd return to work on the second. But for the first time in over twenty years, January 2 came around, and I had no place to go.

I knew that it would be easy to sleep late and watch TV, but I wanted to get a lot done. So I decided to treat my retirement like the next stage of my career. There were so many things I'd put off while I built my career, and now I wanted to make sure that I got to them all. I started by creating a to-do list. I listed the things I wanted to do every day: things like practice the piano, learn Italian, check email, trade stocks, and walk.

While the wheelchair did help me to get around more, it didn't help my overall health. What little walking I had done was now gone, and my weight shot up to 247 pounds. That was heavier than I had ever been, and that extra weight didn't help my back. So I decided that if Suzie and I wanted to get serious about seeing the world, it was time to get in shape and lose weight. Most importantly, I wanted to ditch the wheelchair.

I bought a treadmill, and though I could only walk for five minutes at a time, that's exactly what I did. I also bought a weight machine so that I could work out without lifting free weights off the floor.

A lot of career-minded people neglect their health, and I suppose I wasn't that different, but the stakes were higher for me. What if I lifted too much or walked too far, blew out my back, and missed work? In fact, there were many times when I blew my back out and missed work without working out. At the time, I felt like I couldn't take the risk, but now that work was no longer a worry, I could. In fact, on the first day I worked out, I did actually tweak my back a little and spent the next day in bed.

I didn't let this stop me. Instead, I made sure that I did all of the stretching exercises the physical therapist had taught me every day before and after I worked out. Soon I was walking for six minutes a day instead of five. Then I was doing six minutes twice a day, and after a few weeks of that I was able to bump it up to seven. By the end of the year, I was walking thirty minutes a day, and I had lost thirty pounds.

Once I stopped worrying about missing work if I started exercising, not only did I *not* hurt my back—I made it stronger. Avoiding exercise for fear of hurting my back had actually been hurting my back even more. I wish I would have learned that sooner.

As I write these last few pages, I look over at my exercise equipment. Next to it is my cane, and next to that is my walker. In the garage gathering dust sits my wheelchair, and I hope it will be there a long time.

While keeping fit was something on my daily list of things to do, I also had long-term projects that I wanted to accomplish. One of them was writing this book. Another was recording a music CD.

Singing was something I've really enjoyed since way back in the projects, when my father used to take me around and get me to sing everywhere in hopes of getting me discovered. Shopping centers, hospital lobbies—anywhere there was someone playing a piano. Heck, even places where there wasn't a piano, like the corner, or even walking down the street. You never knew who might hear you.

I was never discovered, and although in my youth I'd wanted to be a professional singer, I knew that it was a very difficult way to make a living. So I took the entrepreneurial path. It was a path that almost destroyed me, though I learned something from it. But singing was something that I had always hoped to get back to, and now that I was in a position where I didn't have to earn a living at it, I thought now was the time to give it a try.

During my last few months at Microsoft, I mentioned my musical plans to a coworker, and he told me about a producer he knew. Erich Benedict at With an H Studios. I decided to meet Erich.

Erich turned out to be an extremely talented man who could play almost any instrument. He ran a recording studio where he helped a number of people release CDs. I went to his studio, which was actually in his house, walked in the front door, and was greeted by a tall man with long black hair and a deep voice. Erich led me down the stairs to a room at the back of the house that had a keyboard in the back and guitars hanging on the wall. On a desk was a computer, and to its left was a mixer with tons of dials and knobs. There was also a video monitor displaying another room. I asked Erich what that room was, and he told me, "That's where you sing."

So I sang for him. Erich didn't tell me that I was great and ask how much money I could give him. Instead, he told me that I was rusty and that I didn't really know how to breathe like a real singer.

I was impressed that he wasn't just looking to make a quick buck, but that he wanted to make a great product. He gave me the name of a vocal coach I could work with, and he asked me to come back to see him in a couple of months. I decided to take his advice.

I also learned that Erich played in a number of bands. Since I was planning my retirement party, I asked if he and his band would like to perform. Of course he agreed. After all, that was the way he made his living.

"One more thing," I told him. "Would you mind learning a couple of Sinatra songs?"

As the date for my retirement party approached, people kept asking me what I was going to do after I retired. I told them that I hoped to write a book and do some motivational speaking. Most people thought that sounded good. But when I also told them that I wanted to sing, they usually laughed. No one had ever heard me sing. There wasn't a lot of that going on at Microsoft.

Over a hundred people came to my retirement party. Of course there was Suzie, the kids, and Suzie's sister and her parents. There was my brother Dennis, who played a very important role in my life in the projects and in Florida, and there was my sister Madelyn. There was Mark Johnson, my friend since 1969, who taught me so much about life and the way things worked. John Nicol and Chris Burroughs, who I met at Ashton-Tate and who both joined me at Microsoft. Vikram, my co-conspirator from my Publisher days, and my friends Anil, Quentin, Juan, Tammarrian, and Meir. There was Roger, the guy I'd lost so much money with during our venture capitalist days, who became a lifelong friend that made the whole thing worth it. There were all of the friends from our neighborhood who'd helped us so much when the twins were born. There were also the bosses who'd taught me so much, including Darren and Jeanne and all the new friends I'd met in MSN and Bing Mobile.

Of course they all asked what I was going to do next. "Sing," I said.

They would laugh and say, "No really, what are you going to do?"

When I repeated, "Sing," they just said, "Fine, don't tell me."

Soon Erich and his band the Poptarts were playing, and it was my turn.

I stood there in front of all the people who came to my party, and I started to tell them the story about how I'd gotten to where I was—basically what you've just read (shorter, though). When I'd finished, I turned and put on a fedora, just like Sinatra would wear. People smiled and cheered, maybe thinking that I was done.

Instead, I started to sing the song "My Way."

When I started singing, everyone was quiet at first, and then, as I kept singing, they began to smile. When I sang the words *so amusing*, I stopped and laughed, and the crowd laughed with me. I still remember the looks on their faces—both at the moment when they realized I was about to sing, and then when I was done and they burst into applause.

It was the most fun I'd had in a long time.

Epilogue

MOVING AHEAD

It has now been almost three years since I retired. I have continued to work with Erich on my music. We have released three
CDs, and we continue to perform live.

My first CD was a collection of Sinatra covers, which we titled
Come Fly With Me. Of course I did the singing, and Erich played
almost all the instruments. It was a lot of fun to do, and soon Erich
and I were even doing live performances. Our second CD was all
Christmas music, and it included a new song I wrote with my vocal
coach, Larry Bridges, called "The Magic of Christmas." Erich and
I even made a couple of music videos that we put on YouTube.

My third CD is called *Get Back Up*, just like this book, and it
has six original songs on it. The title song is also called "Get Back
Up." Again, I wrote the words, and Erich wrote the music. It is
filled with the kinds of clichés that Mary Jane, my co-writer on
this book, hates, but I hope it illustrates all of the lessons I plan to
teach as I get out there and do some motivational speaking.

It would have been easy just to tell myself that I'd missed my
chance to be a singer. I should have gone for it when I was young.
But the fact is that sometimes life gets in the way and you have to

postpone your dreams. That doesn't mean you have to let them go completely. It just means that you have to find a way to get that chance again. And when you do, give it all you've got.

I still have degenerative disc disease, and it's not going to go away. Just the other day I was putting on my socks when a pain shot across my back and sent me to the floor. Suzie was outside and couldn't hear me calling for her, so I just lay there a while before managing to crawl back into bed. When Suzie came back in, I told her I'd be in bed for a while, and I was for a couple of days before I was able to get up and around again.

This has happened before, and usually it only takes a couple of days. Sometimes it takes a couple of weeks. Every time, I wonder whether this was the last time, whether after this, I won't be able to stand up again.

But despite my back, I've continued to exercise and even joined a gym. I am walking forty minutes now, and though I'm still kind of slow, I can do a little over a mile and a half at my rate. The other day, Suzie and I took a walk, and I went two miles. I've lost fifty pounds since I retired, and we've even taken a few vacations. The last one was a cruise to northwestern Europe, and even on the ship, we went to the gym every day.

I don't let the pain I feel every day interfere with my life. Life is too short, and there are too many things that I want to do. And I know that it's just a matter of time before I'm back in that wheelchair, but until that happens, there's no stopping me. Hell, even after it happens, I won't stop traveling, speaking, and singing.

And the kids, well, they're all grown up. Nick graduated from college and is actually working at a company that works with Microsoft—specifically, with my old friend Chris Burroughs. Steven, Joey, and Maddie are all in college now. Joey prefers to be called *Joe* now. We still prefer to call him our "miracle baby." Steven and Joe are studying computer science, and Maddie is studying game design. All of them are hoping to work for Microsoft.

All of my brothers and sisters are doing well, too. They all escaped the projects for good, and all of them are successful in their own right. My brother Dennis went into construction as a carpenter's apprentice and moved up the organization into management. He recently retired and still lives in Florida, where we visit him as often as we can. He is still a great friend. I like that he builds things, including houses, and I still remember how we looked at the good ones and dreamed about them when we first moved to Florida when we were kids.

I continue to stay in touch with the other friends I've made over my life. Johnson has also retired from Microsoft, as has John Nicol. John's traveling a lot, and I see him every few months. Johnson lives twenty minutes away from me, and we see each other often. Chris and I own lake houses on the same lake, and Juan's wife, Mary Jane, helped me write this book.

Chris, Juan, John, Anil, and I have lunch together as often as we can, though not often enough. Friends like Meir and Tammar-rian, as well as some others, have asked me to continue to mentor them, and I meet with them either in person or over Skype whenever we can. These guys and some others have made a real difference in my life, and I am better for having met them.

Over the years, I learned that hard work and perseverance can get you anywhere. I started in the projects of South Philly eating government cheese. I made my first money selling tomatoes door to door and collecting soda bottles. I learned that sometimes taking a risk pays off, and sometimes it doesn't, but there is always a lesson to be learned.

I also learned that there's nothing wrong with getting help when you need it, but that getting help should be a short-term thing. Soon, you have to depend on yourself.

Life is full of challenges and opportunities. You will get knocked down probably more than you like, but that's life. Learn from it—but most importantly, get back up!

ABOUT THE AUTHORS

George A. Santino has been a fast food restaurant manager, life insurance salesman, realtor, sports bar owner, liquor salesman, shoe repair owner, real estate investor, software tester, software engineering manager, and Microsoft partner. Since his retirement, George has embarked upon a new career as a professional speaker and author. When George isn't writing or speaking, he is singing or composing the lyrics to his next song. He has released three CDs, all of which spent some time at the top of the Amazon Hot New Releases list. *Get Back Up* is his first book.

M. J. Beaufrand lives in Seattle with her husband and two children. She is the author of the young adult novels *Primavera*, *The Rise and Fall of the Gallivanters*, and *Dark River*, the latter of which was a finalist for the Edgar Award.